A Tormented Life Freed

A Woman's Fight to Overcome Adversity

Laurie Smyth

Laurie Smyth

ISBN: 978-0-9871-8661-4 *(sc)*

Printed in the United States of America

Contents

Part 2 The Awakening

Acknowledgments

To the many people, who helped and supported me through this long journey. Your input into my life has been uplifting and inspiring. I am more grateful than you will ever know, thank you. Betty, my dear friend, I wouldn't be the person I am today if our paths had not crossed. Thank you, you helped save me from the darkness that loomed and threatened to overwhelm me. For those who stood courageously by my side, supporting and praying for me I am eternally grateful. To my family, who have travelled this life with me, I love you, now and always. I am indebted to you for your loyal support and encouragement. You are the pillars around my life that constantly sustain me. I dedicate this book to two men who have fought valiantly beside me, who meticulously picked up the pieces of my brokenness and repeatedly made me whole again. Men who enthusiastically and wholehearted supported the writing of this story, cheering me on from the sidelines and encouraging me when I lost my momentum.

This book is for you

Thank you and I love you both.

To my father and my husband we have all endured a long and arduous journey yet we stand victorious. .

A Tormented Life—freed

'It is the fire of suffering that brings forth the gold of Godliness'.

Madame Guyon

'It is not the critic who counts, nor the man who points out how the strong man stumbled, or where the doer of deeds could have done them better. The credit belongs to the man who is actually in the arena, whose face is marred by dust and sweat and blood; who strives valiantly; who errs and comes short again and again; who knows great enthusiasms, great devotions; who spends himself in a worthy cause; who, at the best, knows in the end the triumph of high achievement, and who, at the worst, if he fails, at least fails while daring greatly, so that his place shall never be with those timid souls who know neither victory nor defeat'.

Theodore Roosevelt

Authors note

This book is a personal expedition, a very individual voyage. It is a true portrayal and illustration of my life and the choices I made up until the time of writing its content. I have had people tell me the story was too graphic and real making it hard to read whilst others have told me they just couldn't put it down. As you read through the pages you will yourself make judgement in relevance to where you are on your own life's continuum. The point to note is we are all trying to navigate through the same tumultuous and sometimes peaceful oceans of life; the difference is how we ride the waves.

At times during my journey of 48 years, I didn't ride with much finesse, other times I rode like a professional and sometimes I fell off smothered in a blanket of water. Life to this day has tested me on so many levels; it has presented complex challenges, gruelling problems, senseless tragedies and unanswered prayers. I suppose it is not unlike your own journey.

I anticipate as you read this book you may embark on your own journey, a path of personal awakening and self-discovery. I entered this world, like you, naked with an undefined life. I later defined it by the choices I made. For me, life flitted between being a circus, a minefield, a marathon and a dance.

Laurie Smyth

If I could impart some wisdom to you, it would be to live your life with authentic passion and purpose. All your worldly tributes and accolades are easily forgotten, the real legacy you leave behind is the creation of genuine relationships, true relationships that last the test of time. These relationships will be what carry you through the hard times of your life.

The words written on the pages of this book are a piece of me and my world. As you read them my history will merge with yours, what you do with that part is totally up to you. I hope you will remember this story far beyond the reach of the words, but the messages written may stir something deep inside you.

May you be blessed on every level.

Chapter 1

It is 1972. William McMahon was prime Minister of Australia and petrol was 10 cents at the pump, a far cry from the prices of today. The average Australian house price was $27,000. Eleven Israeli Athletes were killed on their way to the Munich Olympics where Shane Gould won 3 gold medals. The Watergate scandal struck America and 'Number 96' debuted on Australian Television and caused a huge controversy over its explicit content which by today's standards would be classified as 'normal'.

I was born in 1963 immigrating to Australia in 1966. I was the firstborn of two Scottish professional parents, growing up in a suburb in eastern Sydney—Sutherland. As the trees and their leaves changed colour ready to embrace the new season so I embraced the new country in which I grew. I was like a bud ready to bloom in this carefree, perfect playing field. Australia was full of features yet to be unearthed and explored. To me it was a world bursting with sincerity, flooded with warmth and sunshine and free from concerns or danger.

As an adult writing this book, I look back and recognise children see life in all its innocence and beauty, they see it completely through untainted eyes coloured by their limited experiences. All they see is potential and dreams. As adults, I believe we forget how to see the world without our sunglasses on. We become so overcome with life's hardships, circumstances, hurts and fears that we forget how to dream. Imagine if as adults we could dream as we did as children.

At 8 years old, I knew how to dream, and dream I did. I knew without a doubt I wanted to be a lawyer. I would be rich, living somewhere in a nice big house on the beach, close to my parents. On a daily basis I created play scenarios and imaginary situations that stimulated my mind and at times challenged me physically. I saw the world as a true gift of discovery. Forest Gump said it perfectly when he described life as a box of chocolates. My life was just like that a delicious piece of delicately wrapped chocolate waiting to be explored and enjoyed. Back then I had a real inquisitive nature. I was eager to learn and investigate everything, I was fearless.

In the early '70s, the world was vastly different to the one we live in today. It was the age of hippies, freedom, experimentation, self expression and my baby boomer parents along with millions of others like them explored varying ways of having fun. Television had become the new past time. Broadcasted programs were not infected by evil and horrid visions of disaster and doom, like 9/11. The space race was on and men landed on the moon for the first time.

We thought we lived in exciting and changing times.

Everything was cheaper back then, much, much cheaper. I used to buy crispy, crunchy, big potato scallops—double the size of the ones you buy today for just two cents, you could also buy a ten cent bag of lollies and chew on them all day. It was a time, where adventurous and energetic kids, like me, preferred to roam the streets and play outside in the sun rather than being trapped inside the house captivated by an oversized talking box. In my youth, I despised rainy days—not that we had too many—as they trapped me like a prisoner—in my own home.

My favourite days were the ones where my friends and I terrorised the neighbourhoods with our re-enactments of fantasy cowboy and Indian battles. Each of us ran and hid behind large trees, rolled in thickly flowered garden beds all to give us the best vantage points to shoot our weapons for our territorial wars. We would split into groups some of us would be Indians some Cowboys, I always like to be in the Indian's team simply because I thought they were better fighters. We fired our imaginary Winchester long-barrelled rifles at each other. As the bullets penetrated our young flesh we would fall to the ground and pretend we were dead or dying, for the count of ten then we could get up and re-join the group, ready to fight again. As an Indian, I loaded my large intricately patterned wooden bow with long-feathered arrows and fired at will. It was an awesome game.

At times, we actually had what we considered the real deal. We wore heavy, intricately patterned steel toy guns, which dangled from cow skin leather gun holsters which slung low on our narrow hips—when we had these toys I preferred the Cowboy side. On other days we spent hours building four-wheeled go carts. We hunted and found broken discarded pram wheels and old pieces of discarded wood left strewn next to the roadside. Our makeshift carts were held together with whatever we could find—usually off-cuts of rope or string and often during our downhill adventures a wheel fell off, or the wood broke and I scraped my butt or knees on the gravel, boy did that hurt.

Treacherous and risky by today's standards, but, it was so much fun. Not even the painful bouts of gravel rash or having to scrub my open wounds with a steel brush to remove the gravel lodged deep in my skin deterred me from perilously pitching my body uncontrollably down the sealed roads and steep hills. On the days when the neighbourhood was devoid of kids I would play in the park located at the end of my street. I loved to roll in the grass, climb the magnificent old trees and splash through the swirling pools of water. However, my mother held a very different and I believed misunderstood perception of the park as she didn't like me to play or walk through it at all. She regularly argued with me over my choice to continue to hang out there, but, it was the shortest and simplest route home. Plus, I thought it was the coolest place to play.

I never thought this carefree contented life I had created could be shattered as quick as it was. At the time I was completely unaware of the fragility of life, or, the profound effect just one tragic event could make on a person psychologically, emotionally and physically. I didn't know one event could radically change the course of a life—my life, it simply wasn't something I ever thought possible especially when I felt happy and safe. I was about to enter into a vile, horrifying nightmare which would shatter everything real in my life. It would destroy my familiar sanctuary, devastate my wellbeing and change me forever.

Chapter 2

I was struck by a large meteorite. An event so devastating that it would leave huge craters and turbulent storms in my life for a long time to come.

School was over for the day and I started the slow trek home. The winter's afternoon sun touched my skin with warm yellow rays; its soft smooth fingers caressed my face and revitalized my spirits after a long tedious day at school. To me, school was a laborious task, unstimulating and uninteresting, my teachers boring and domineering. I preferred to amuse myself with more recreational activities, such as the development of daring acts on the steel monkey bars, rather than cultivating the concepts of Math's or English and the gaining of wisdom. I was not a brainless kid as I had won school awards in math's and state awards for my art work, I was just not stimulated by the lessons or teaching methods used and had lost interest.

Every afternoon after school had finished for the day, I would walk the short distance home. My usual route took me past a small fish-and-chip shop located on the corner. The heavy sweet aroma of homemade thick frying chips would drift towards me tempting me to come in and buy some. The owner, a middle aged stout and very friendly Italian man, would sing as he cooked and served me my standard order of five crispy, golden brown, potato scallops. At that time they were two cents each and easily affordable. I would watch as he sliced the potato into thick slices, dip them in a large bowl of thick creamy batter then tossed them effortlessly into the hot vats of oil. I loved to watch as the fat bubbled around them turning them a golden brown. My stomach would churn in anticipation of the delicious flavour knowing it would meet my tongue soon. After I received my prize, my five steaming hot scalps wrapped tightly in newspaper, I would tear off one corner and smother them in a lather of salt and brown vinegar. Then I would slowly walk home, through the old trees and fragrant flowers in my much-loved playground the local park and I would savour every mouthful with every step.

I always timed it perfectly. I would finish the last mouthful of my afternoon tea, just as I left the park and rounded the final corner near my house. I did not want to leave any visible evidence of my snack anywhere on me. I had just enough time to quickly rub my face on my navy blue school jumper and wipe my hands on my skirt before I reached my front door.

On this particular as I drew near to the house, I could hear my new young brother screaming; his shrill voice spoiled my buoyant frame of mind. I was sure that he knew exactly when I was near and timed his ear-piercing cries just for my approach. I drew a deep breath, sighed, and stealthily entered the house. My aim was to quietly creep past him and reach the tranquillity of my room unnoticed.

I remember seeing my frazzled mother, who was temporarily

house-bound from her professional career sitting directly in my path. I watched as she tried everything to soothe and calm him, but nothing would stop the screaming. I empathised with her. I understood the strain she felt, as the constant noise wore me down, and I wasn't with him 24 hours a day like she was. He was a difficult child, who limited her ability to complete even the most menial of tasks.

I realised there was no way I could slip past her unnoticed. So I entered the room and her desperate eyes met mine. Unspoken, yet unmistakable words passed between us "help me, can you give me a break PLEASE".

I dropped my bag on the floor and offered to assist her, reaching out to take my tiny brother from her willing arms. However in reality I really just wanted ear muffs and a gag, but, I smiled at him instead, not that it made much difference he screamed on regardless of what anyone did.

She quickly moved to the kitchen, to get her purse and asked if I would go to the shop for her. She needed potatoes for dinner and had no other way to get them. I jumped at the opportunity, happy to once again be away from the household commotion and the constant bombardment of sounds. I gathered her small string bag from the kitchen counter, placed the coins she handed me in my pocket, and walked happily out the door. Behind me, I heard her apprehensive, rapidly fading voice, her instructions clear and precise: "do not go through the park". Over my shoulder, I yelled back "I won't" and cheerfully skipped off down the road. I was relieved to be released from the constant volley of noise which my home life had become. I cheerfully walked to my destination with her coins jingling in my pocket.

As I stood at the counter to exchange the coins for my chosen potatoes, I noticed the large heavily-laden multi coloured lolly jars strategically placed right in front of my craving eyes and of course I wanted one maybe three. I silently wished I had some spare money for a couple of those deliciously chewy chocolate-covered cobbers, but, it was not to be. I turned away from the counter and my temptation and left the store. Instead, five boring brown dirty potatoes sat snugly in the coloured string bag as I carried them thoughtlessly homeward.

For the second time on that day, I found myself sauntering through the thickly wooded gardens of the forbidden park. This time I carried an essential part of the evening meal instead of my usual school pack. I can remember playfully swinging my package back and forth as I enjoyed the luxuriant fragrance of the flowers that surrounded me.

The difference between this visit and my previous one was that long shadows moved into the park, menacing patterns darkened my familiar garden, as the clouds played hide and seek with the sun. I noticed the large, leafy branches of the weeping willows spilled over onto the footpath like a cascading waterfall and I imagined running my fingers through the leaves like I would if it was water.

I sauntered slowly down the path, my mind not focussed on anything specific. I heard the low vibration of the crisp browning leaves of the majestic fully cloaked trees as they rustled in the gentle breeze. In the distance I could see the big exposed circular concrete water pipes where my friends and I regularly played. The water slowly trickled like tears gracefully flowing down the cheeks of an upset child. They fed the large circular pipes that quickly sucked the water away from the park to some unknown location. I recalled the feel of the icy water as it had previously caressed my bare feet. The recollection sent a shiver up my spine. The sound of the water echoed as it scurried away through the pipes. It sounded like hundreds of tiny feet disappearing in the distance.

Visual pictures flowed easily across my awareness. Colourful and vivid memories of my friends and me, as we talked and laughed, pushed each other and joyfully played in the water. We became predators stalking tiny tadpoles, ensnaring them with the secret hope of fostering a pet frog. I was a great predator but I was a hopeless nurturer, the catching part was easy, it was the survival part that was the hardest. As you probably guessed I never had a pet frog.

In the distance I saw my friend's house as it emerged through the last of the big trees and I knew I was only minutes away from returning to my home and the turmoil it held. For a short-lived moment I considered a brief delay and a visit with my friend, but then I remembered the potatoes in my hand and their purpose, the evening meal, I sighed and knew there would be no intermittent pause in my journey, not on this day.

I was fifty metres from the low single wire fence which

bordered the park and the busy road. Oakwood St and my home where my mother and brother waited lay another hundred metres away. I was minutes from home, only a few overhanging trees hampered my journey and obstructed the mental visions of the commotion left behind twenty minutes before.

As the road drew closer I recalled my mother's words' don't got though the park', they taunted me from within. A pang of guilt rose and I quickened my pace. I knew if I was going to get caught, it would be in the most vulnerable spot, near the fence. As I entered it I was just about running. She hated me being in that park but I couldn't comprehend why. I loved being in its presence. To me it was full of beauty, wonders and secrets, it held such delight and charm and I wanted to spend all my time there.

Guilt made me switch on my over active imagination. So into my picturesque mind's eye I ventured. I walked in an open field, colourful fragrant flowers on long thin stems dotted the landscape as far as I could see, my hands reached out beside me and touched the tops of them as I slowly walked through the wind swept open plain. The sun stood directly overhead and its bright rays illuminated the path before me. A gentle wind brushed my face like a soft feather, tickling my cheeks. The breeze toyed with my long black hair, it blew lingering strands around my face, blocking my view. Beside me a shiny black horse gently nudged my hand, as he sought affection . . . .

I was wrenched from this fantasy, momentarily startled, by a young man in his early 20's. He stopped me in my tracks, as he suddenly sprung from behind the last of the large weeping willows, twenty meters from the road. He stood directly in front of me, deliberately blocking my path. What did he want? I knew behind him lay the safety of my home, I saw the steady stream of traffic as commuters returned home after a long busy day at work. His presence confused me and I was unable to think rationally. I silently wondered what he wanted as I stood still trying to comprehend the situation I was in.

Chapter 3

It wasn't long before, I realised this was not a normal situation and I was in serious trouble. I think what I alerted me to danger was the man's dishevelled appearance and his expression. Even though I knew deep in my gut this situation was not right, my innocent mind was unable to process the actual details of the imminent threat. I couldn't identify the situation; simply because I had no resources to draw from, no knowledge to comprehend or identify any options. I simply couldn't think of what to do. What I did feel was real earth shattering fear.

A fear very different than riding the 'big dipper' at the Sydney show, this was immobilising fear. It froze both my mind and my body. What I do remember about that moment was my whole body began to shake with uncontrollable tremors. Water welled in my eyes and cascaded down my cheeks. I remember he stepped closer to me, his eyes were wild and alert, and they searched both me and the surrounding area. As he slowly lifted his hand, I noticed his fingers were tightly wrapped around a wooden handle and a large, shiny blade was thrust in front of my face. The knife was long and smooth on one side and jagged on the other, a bit like a bread cutting knife my mother used. Seeing it took my breath away. My mother's warning echoed around the cave that my mind had run away and hidden in. Why had I not heeded her voice? Why didn't I listen to her, if I had, I would be home. Internal questions echoed in the distance as answers ricocheted in my mind questioning the facts …was I going to die, the pointy steel knife certainly made me think so. I feared the pain it would bring and I felt like I would simply collapse on the ground in front of him if I didn't do something quickly.

Somewhere, deep within me, a tiny voice rose up. Sounds tumbled from my lips. My alert ears heard the softly spoken words. A question. I initially wondered where it came from, then realised I had spoken; I said "please don't hurt me, my mother is waiting for me, and she needs these potatoes for dinner". I lifted the string bag up for him to see I was telling the truth. They felt like they had trebled in size, their weight made my arm shudder. A smile levitated around his mouth, but didn't really touch his face. He looked deep into my wet timid eyes and assessed me like the school doctor sizing me up for my next physical check-up. A anxious moment passed, our eyes locked in a secret one sided dance. My mind trapped in the cave went completely blank, yet my body trapped in the real world was fully alert, as it waited for any response.

My response came in the guise of the harsh forceful capture of my arm. The clutch so sever it indented and marked the skin just below my shoulder. The pressure increased as his tightly coiled fingers bit deep into the flesh, turning the skin a dark shade of pink. Using this pressure he unexpectedly forced me to turn backwards to face the way I had just travelled. This unforseen movement twisted my torso in an unnatural adjustment, the vertebrae in my neck snapped against each other which caused my head to jerk backwards. This momentarily disorientated and temporarily stunned me. Pain shot through my jaw as my teeth snapped sharply together. My vision blurred, my legs became somewhat unsteady and I stumbled slightly. I remember at this point he heaved me upwards and pulled me close to his side. My body fleetingly touched his lightly clad mass and I shuddered and wrenched myself away as far as my surrendered arm would allow.

My heart galloped like a wild horse in my chest, irrepressible and uncontrollable sobs escaped from deep within me. My body's natural impulses were forced into submission by his harsh tone and coarse statements, as he told me to shut up and move, or something really bad was going to happen. My childish body succumbed to his oversized powerful directing hands and my mind surrendered and I physically moved in an unwanted direction. My unstable, quivering legs moved forward. They carried me further from the safety I saw in the distance, as I looked regretfully over my shoulder.

I remember his annoyance as I couldn't move my pint sized limbs—half the size of his—fast enough to accommodate his desired pace. To motivate me to go fasted he dug his fingers further into my flesh and I recall crying out in protest as the hot, searing pain shot like a bullet up my arm. His facial expression scared me as I didn't know what to make of it, I saw an expression that resembled a ravenous lion with relentless hunger and it was one I didn't understand. What I understood was I was the obvious prey.

He stepped closer towards me, his body only inches from me. He quickly leant down towards me and brought his mouth close to my ear. I felt his hot inconsistent breath as it swept over face. I smelt a heavy stench of alcohol. I hated the rancid odour alcohol left behind, I had smelt it numerous times on my parents breath after they had drunk too much and wanted to kiss my good night. It stunk. Through the overwhelming aroma I heard the words, "move faster, or, I will hurt you right here." His expression, his dialogue and the cold steel blade placed on my tear-stained cheek compelled me to move quicker, my legs began to run.

From the sanctuary of its cave, my mind frantically tried to catalogue and pigeonhole the situation. Unfortunately there were no explicit cave drawings or factual artefacts to provide me with the details I needed to help me. In the 70's we were taught to respect the older generation. In actuality to me he was the older generation, but this just felt wrong. In the new millennium children are cautioned to be careful, taught how to prevent a situation like the one I was in. They are educated on how to seek help. Back then, there was no such thing as 'stranger danger', or campaigns about child safety, it wasn't seen as an issue in the '70s. At the time all I knew was the situation I was in was wrong. He felt wrong. Physically I wanted to run, but for some reason I couldn't. I was trapped like a tethered horse in a wild storm.

The constant tethering of my arm resulted in a pulsating throb.

Pain ricocheted from my shoulder all the way down to my clenched fist and up again. To distract myself from the ongoing ache I internally tried to rationalise our destination. We had walked, he walked I scurried, to the backend of the park, an area I had never been to before, but had seen in the distance from the safety of my bike many months before. I knew a tall wire fence with a diamond mesh pattern separated the park from the local cemetery.

Voiceless questions like whispers in a crowded room rattled around my head. Terror and fear did not silence them. The nightmare would unfold whether I liked it or not, I was after all a part of the story, a voiceless victim swept away in the words on a page. I was at the mercy of the writer and his personal vision, how graphic and vicious the story would become was totally up to him and his imagination. My own imagination returned to the safety and familiarity of what I knew and understood my family. I wanted to see them again, I didn't care that my brother continually cried. I would have welcomed his cry if I had heard it in that moment. The faces of my family hovered in my imagination but were quietly washed away with the tears that continued to silently fall.

My hand clung tightly to the string bag full of potatoes. Their weight provided a form of comfort and solace in those dark moments. I recall lifting them up and drawing them close to my body, hugging them tightly. Through the darkness I welcomed the visual memory of my mother as she nursed my crying brother and another flurry of quiet tears toppled to the ground leaving a mixture or water and dirt in the wake of my footprints. In front of me stood nothing familiar, I had entered into unfamiliar territory, nothing in the place I trod could offer me a sense of hope, there was none to be found.

Before me stood a landscape full of thick, dense trees with light rustling foliage underneath. A tall wire fence dissected the trees, separating two very different areas. Seconds passed before I realised where I was. I stood at the border between my favourite park and the gloomy cemetery.

The sturdy wire fence towered over me, an impossible mountain to climb with the unsteady legs I possessed at that time. As I looked down, I saw a portion of the wire fence folded back upon itself, lifted slightly. I realised this would allow limited access to the cemetery beyond. Horror filled me as I was physically dragged to this entry point. I was then flung to the ground, and forced onto my uncovered knees.

A rough, distant voice provided specific instructions as to how I was to go under the fence, and wait on the other side. Time froze. I could not move a muscle. It was like I was anesthetised, yet still wide awake; able to hear, feel and see everything, but nothing really registered with my brain. My mind went to the darkest recess in its protective cave and buried itself under a warm blanket of dirt. The awake part of me wanted to scream and scream, but I knew no-one would hear me out here in the middle of nowhere.

Physically I kept moving, I don't know how but I did. Automatic pilot most likely. The next task was to get under the fence so I carefully threw the string bag full of potatoes under the fence, then nudged my body head first, my face rubbing in the dirt, under the lifted wire and into the grounds of a place I was terrified of being in, the cemetery. As I dragged myself through the small gap using my hands and elbows like pulleys, the stiff wire scrapped at my back. Luckily a soft scattering of leaves and foliage softened the ground as my belly passed over it.

I remember I was nearly through; only one leg remained on the park side, the rest of my body lay face down in the dirt in the cemetery, only a fence separated me from him. However his hand lay firmly on my calf and I felt the coldness of the steel blade as he placed it on the back of my leg. His action made me freeze, it prevented me from standing up or going any further, so, I lay face down in the dirt and waited. My hands searched and found the comfort of the bag of potatoes.

I didn't lie in that position long, maybe a few seconds before I was roughly pulled to my feet. He had joined me. As I stood up, it dawned on me where I was. I started to freak out as I now stood in the creepy, ominous cemetery, the one I had always feared. My over active imagination fired up and tales of horror quickly overrode any positive memories. Horror stories now taunted me. I always thought the place creepy, eerie, especially the open and damaged grave sites and I imagined rotting people slowly rising from their broken resting places to come and see me. This place really scared me, and being here completely frightened me.

Fear and panic overrode every other emotion and thought I

had; fear of being left here, to die a horrible unknown death, and panic of never being found or seeing my family again.

I was pulled deeper into the ominous grave yard. Terror and dread grew more with each step I took in to this ancient burial ground. Suddenly, taking my surprise my captor's demeanour changed. Enthusiasm radiated from him, his tone mischievous, amused, his eyes intense, hungry and determined. This change in him not only confused me, it scared me. I couldn't understand what this meant but somewhere I realized whatever was going to happen was going to happen now. I could feel it.

I tried to back away from him, but I was too slow, he grabbed me and tossed me like a rag doll to the ground. The light foliage and hard clay ground dug into my back and scratched my legs as I landed. My skirt lifted and displayed my underwear, and my uncovered legs slightly splayed open. For a split second, I felt completely disorientated.

Adrenalin surged through my veins, enabling me to hastily try and get up. I knew I had to run, had to get as far away from this place as possible. I fought to bring my legs together and stand, but my reactions were not skilful or practiced enough for the strength and experience of a 20 year old man. He was fast and determined. He pushed me backwards, and grabbed both of my legs with his hands, and yanked them fully open. I shrieked in disagreement as I tried to scramble backwards away from him, but my movements were fruitless.

He overpowered me, and threw me on my back. His sizeable

body, advantageously pinned me to the ground, beneath him, whilst he positioned himself purposefully between my legs, locking them in a compromising and open position. He victoriously smiled, as his eyes met mine. He knew he had won. I felt hopeless and overpowered. My peripheral vision enabled me to see that he had placed the knife within reach, near my face, but I was too scared to move, frozen, unable to think rationally.

His hand slowly reached between my legs. I felt his fingers as they explored my body, then abruptly he ripped off my underpants. I was completely exposed, vulnerable in every way. I just wanted my daddy. Where was he? Why couldn't he save me? He had protected me before, why not now? Why was this happening to me? What had I ever done to this man? Why did he want to hurt me like this?

He knelt between my legs and stared at me, thoughtfully reflecting on the picture he had created. At that moment the hour glass stopped flowing, time stood waiting. I couldn't look at him, I felt like I was hovering on the edge of a steep cliff. I wanted to fall but I couldn't as I was held in place by an imaginary rope. I tightly closed my eyes, not wanting to see anything anymore. I remember thinking my first thought of death as I lay in the dirt broken. I wondered if he would be the one to forcible push me over the cliffs edge. I think I might have welcomed it at the time. I was ready. I knew that it would all be over then, no pain, no hurt, all of this one, finished.

I heard him as he unbuckled his jeans. I felt his body heat

merge with mine as he came closer to his target. I heard a disgusting sound of spitting, and I felt the wetness as it struck me between the thighs. An unidentified scream rose from the depths of my being. It passed my lips as an immense, hot searing pain struck me, and I was unceremoniously and unsympathetically ripped open and left bleeding.

My physical attack was over in minutes, the mental pain would last a lot longer, and the scars would run very deep, not only for me, but for him also. He was done. It was over, but I was too shocked to move. Every muscle in my body ached. Light traces of blood pooled beneath me. I was suspended in time, caught between each second as the hammer steadily pounded the lower half of my body. I opened my eyes to see him towering over me, standing tall. His eyes pierced mine, searching intently for some thing unknown to me. I wasn't aware of it at the time, but I suppose he used this time to consider and review his options. He had a major decision to make. Endless and immeasurable seconds ticked by, our eyes locked in a silent struggle.

I noticed his shoulders slump slightly, the tension in his body released, as if a profound burden that had once weighed heavy upon him was decisively and completely removed. Hastily, he retreated from me and quickly dressed himself, unable to look at me any longer. Fully clothed, he leant towards me, grabbed my and and pulled me to my feet. Offhandedly, he instructed me to tidy myself up. We silently walked side by side towards the hole in the fence.

My legs quivered beneath me, they screamed out in pain with every step. My stomach tossed, every muscle trembled. My whole focus was on the distant hole in the fence and what lay beyond it—my home and my family. I knew my freedom lay on the other side of the steel wall that held me captive, and every step I took brought me closer to my escape from this nightmare, from this evil vile man and what he had done.

I clearly saw the hole in the fence line and my pace quickened, as did my heart beat. I visualized my release. I could feel it, I could see it and I craved it. A sharp tug, and the searing pain it caused interrupted my focused escape. Again, I was forced to look at him. He glared at me with what appeared to me to be hatred. I felt his dark eyes as they penetrated deep into my inner being. Tiny rivulets of cool water ran slowly down my cheeks, as fear threatened to overtake me again. He finally spoke. I heard a calm voice this time, and words which told me to "go", and as a passing comment, he told me to not forget to tell my mother.

I searched his face, scanning for the truth. Was this a trick? I didn't have to think about it for too long, something on his face confirmed his words. I believed him, and I ran. I ran like a wind that swept through a corn field, flattening everything in its path. My bruised and battered legs cramped and screamed in pain, but still I did not stop. I was ecstatic. My shackles had been removed, broken, and my unencumbered feet moved swiftly, taking me away from that decaying place. I was on my way home, alive.

I felt euphoric when I reached my house. I didn't care that my brother was still screaming, I embraced the comfort that this familiarity brought. When I reached my frantically pacing mother, I was dirty, covered in dried mud and spots of blood, leaves bonded to my unruly messy hair. My dirt-covered face was smeared with deep tear stained rivulets, resembling roads on a map.

She looked at me perceptively. I didn't have to speak; she somehow knew. I presented all the potatoes to her, for I had lost none. Anxious tears flowed from her eyes, as I allowed her warm safe arms to engulf and comfort me. She held me close for a long extended moment. I couldn't believe I was home, alive.

Chapter 4

I was taken to the hospital and the formalities began. I was poked and prodded, then sent to the police station so I could formalise a statement. I wasn't sure if I had the strength to talk about it all over again. All I really wanted to do was curl up and go to sleep and forget the day ever happened.

A few hours after the assault, my mother and I were notified that the police had located a suspect, and we were again summoned to the police station. This time, to identify the man who attacked me. My father had been called shortly after I returned home, but was stuck in the long traffic jams with thousands of other noisy, impatient Sydney commuters as they all tried to exit the city to return home. I wanted him, needed him there to support me, to hold my hand as I went back to the police station. But I didn't know whether his presence would have been a blessing or would have caused more of a crisis for me.

The never-ending event just seemed to go on and on. All I really wanted to do put the incident away somewhere in my mind, but as I constantly retold the story to strangers, as well as, being shunted and forced to do things I didn't really want to do, the vivid pictures repeatedly flooded through my mind, reinforcing a mental picture I wanted to forget.

I arrived later that fateful afternoon, with my mother, at the bustling Sutherland police station where I was escorted down a long narrow hallway with rooms attached on either side. That was when I spotted him and my heart missed a beat. He quietly stood apart from the other casually dressed men, against a wall, in a small room. None of the other men held my focus; in fact I barely saw them. My eyes were instantly drawn to him, the man I knew to be my assailant. Fear surged within me like a fast flowing tide as it pounded the rocky shore. I drew close to my mother, seeking her protection.

My mother and I were met by a woman in a blue uniform who quickly ushered us into an adjacent, small, undecorated plain room, where I could no longer see any of the men. Pangs of anxiety rose in waves. Terror and panic blazed through my body. Sweat glistened on my upper lip and exploded across my palms. My stomach stirred, like I had swallowed hundreds of fluttering butterflies. I didn't want to do this; I just wanted to run and run and run.

The calm, unpretentious police officer who had been assigned to be my escort dutifully informed me of what I needed to do to complete the process. I was told I had to enter that unfurnished, formal room where five men stood, and pick out the man. Simple in theory. However, her words chilled me, every cell turned to ice, I was frozen in time, unable to function, listen or comprehend and my body certainly didn't want to go into that room. No way, my mind screamed at me. My mind and body were in total harmony, they had one goal, to get me away from this God-forsaken place.

In the '70s, there was no one-way glass, or, sheltered hidden rooms for victims to stand in, to conceal them and protect them from the glares of the suspects in this kind of line up. The process was conducted all out in the open, the victim, me this time, had to walk amongst the suspects, confront each person individually and point out the person.

I doubted that my mind could make my body move anywhere near that room. I questioned why these people wanted me to walk in there. Didn't they understand what I had been through, even though I had told them the story repeatedly they must not have understood. Maybe they didn't believe me. Maybe that was why I had to do this, to prove I was not lying.

I felt like I was having an out of body experience, my body was doing things I had never felt it do before. My legs trembled uncontrollably. Their vibrations caused my whole body to shudder wildly.

I wondered if I may collapse at any moment, and I thought that might be a blessing if I did. The rational side of my brain told me I had to go in there, but, my emotional side was completely unwilling to even slightly react to this fact. Through my mental torment I heard words of encouragement as they were whispered gently in my ear.

I asked myself if I could embrace them. Could I step into that room, and do what was required of me? I searched my mother's face for support, but she was unable to assist me, all I saw was her sadness and regret. I was lost in my own private dream, a horror story and I was the main character. I felt totally abandoned, alone and scared.

I became aware of the slight weight of a hand as it softly rested on my shoulder and gently guided me out of my sanctuary, into the awaiting arena. A blue-clad gladiator stood by my side, a stranger who offered protection, and directed my every move. The weight on my shoulder was like my guardian angel, it encouraged and helped me see reason when all else had failed. What it couldn't do was ease the turmoil that raged within my physical body.

I was manoeuvred into the centre of the room. I stood there unsteadily for a few moments as I tried to rationalise this situation I was in. I couldn't believe I was there in that same room with the man who had raped me. Fear and anxiety struck me in waves, threatening to drown me.

I felt a slight pressure on my shoulder and I looked up into the calm, perceptive and discerning eyes of my guide as they reached and held mine. They offered understanding and support as well as the knowledge that I was not on my own. My challenger stripped of any weapons stood in a row before me flanked by other non descript men. I was unable to meet his or any of the others eyes.

The rules of engagement had been clearly explained to me before I entered the room and they were once again spoken clearly to me. I knew and understood my task. I was required to pick my offender out from the line up in front of me. A simple task for some, but I battled to actually do it. The faces of the men floated before me, my eyes drawn to their complex and varying features, each held a gamete of emotions and gestures but only one really caught my attention. I knew exactly where he stood. I smelt him. Sensed him. His presence overpowered the room. My hand lifted automatically, a finger shot out. It fired a fatal blow that would condemn this man. Relief washed over me, bathing me in a soothing embrace like a hot bath on a cold winter's night. I turned to leave, as I knew it was over. But not quite . . . .

My new trusted guardian became a traitor. A new demand was made of me. Internally I wondered if this day would ever end. What did they want now? The request came quickly and was tough; I had to touch him, to ensure that I had chosen the right person. I was horrified, sickened and disgusted at this request. I didn't want to touch him or feel him on my skin. I stared at my one-time ally, dumbstruck. A strong, sharp, bitter taste flowed evenly into my mouth. It made me hyper-salivate and forced me to swallow rapidly. My stomach revisited my afternoon snack. The taste of my favourite snack had turned sour and it was a taste I would never enjoy again.

The quiet stillness of the room was shattered by my father's ear-piercing cries. A sea of uniforms swarmed around him, preventing him from approaching me. Angry words raged from my anxious father's lips and were thrown like daggers directly at my attacker.

The whole scene was surreal, very dreamlike to my young mind and I fought hard not to fall into the dark abyss which beckoned me. I knew I would need to move soon if I was to put this all behind me, or, my body would fall to the ground and not get up, beaten by the ongoing and never ending requests of the adults around me.

The arena had become confining and I felt trapped in an iron cage, one I desperately wanted to be free from. I had done everything required of me so far. Why did I need to touch him? I wanted my dad to take me far away from this place, but he was trapped in a sea of bodies with no possibility of escape. My father's disturbance was only a temporarily interruption to the task I still needed to complete. I still had to touch the man. I wondered what would happen if he grabbed me again.

This thought triggered an out-of-body sensation, the thin line that held my mind in control of my body let go and my mind drifted carelessly into the clouds above. I would wake up and this day would start over. A gentle nudge in the small of my back brought me sharply back to the reality of where I was . . . . the line up of young men in front of me.

My mind temporarily reengaged and forced my body to move in a very robotic fashion. Somewhere from within me, I felt the tip of my pointed finger touch the soft part of his belly. I was still too small to reach his chest or shoulder, as I would have preferred. My hand swiftly and unexpectedly recoiled. I hastily retreated to the safety of the officer. As soon as I stepped back, I was wordlessly steered from the room, and the rest of that night became a blur in my memory.

Chapter 5

Hours flowed mindlessly into days, weeks passed into months. Life did not hold the same flavour as it did before; it had been soured, tainted forever. My previous, carefree, relaxed approach to life became a behaviour of the past. I grew nervous and anxious. I stayed at home and hardly ventured out, refusing to play with my friends or play in areas that I previously enjoyed. My view of the world changed, it narrowed somehow. I played imaginary games in the safety of my room instead of partaking in my usual activities. The back yard replaced my favourite park and my dark empty thoughts consumed me, they swallowed all the optimism I once felt.

Everyone said the situation me and my family were in would change when the judgment day arrived, as it promised justice. People all around me truly thought that this would be the end of the 'Laurie' saga. I was expected to snap out of it and return to my previously happy and contented self. However, I could not operate like a robot, one that could switch their emotions and feeling on and off at will. The feelings I felt were like destructive forces that wanted to crush me. I tried hard to forget like everyone expected me to, but I just couldn't understand or deal with any of it. The situation was far too extreme and complex for me to cope with or sort out. I knew the way I felt and the thoughts I regularly entertained would not change just because the man was caught and we were in court, seeking a conviction.

The courtroom was large, cold and crowded with unknown faceless people. My name was called and it was my turn to give evidence. I sat nervously in the wooden witness box, my legs dangled in the air as they were unable to reach the floor. A man wearing a suit looked expectantly at me from his high desk beside me. My clammy, moist fingers squeezed and pinched the skin on my forearm. My heart beat fast and loud as questions were fired at me like bullets. My young mind frantically tried to keep up with the proceedings and provide answers to the people asking them. My voice was quiet and reluctant as the explicit details of the event were bantered around the room.

I tried desperately to hold onto the last bit of strength I could summon, but my resolve shattered when I lifted my eyes and peeked through my hair at the man who hurt me. I had purposefully let the darkness fall in front of my face to form a physical barrier between myself and the man seated before me. Yet, his smile struck me, it stung my cheeks like I had just received a back handed slap. Tears welled in my eyes and flowed silently from the corners they streamed down my cheeks.

I searched the room for my mother, my eyes found her solemn face. She sat stoically in the large deserted room. Our gazes met, we held each other in a full embrace and for an undetermined time the room became silent, stilled; it was just her and me. Our voiceless conversation gave me strength. I knew I had to finish this. I would find the courage to go on.

I looked down to the floor of the box that encased me, its simple grains of wood helped focus my attention. I composed myself and answered the final uncomfortable questions. My humiliation was fully exposed, everyone heard my story and judgment was now just a formality. I hung my head in shame and walked disgraced from the court room. My life dishonoured. I had now become an Australian statistic, a victim of crime, with no more relevance or significance to the court, or these people.

I was expected to get on with my life, unmarked or disfigured by the incident. On the outside, I was able to portray a picture to others that I was coping okay, but on the inside, a wound festered and grew with purpose. My deeply buried shame was locked securely away. My sorrow manifested only in hidden, silent words that would never be expressed, and tears shed nightly into my pillow. I mentally built stone walls that rose from the ashes of my life, and allowed it to fully encase me. It would eventually become an inflexible fortress. Painful memories hung like pictures on every one of my newly built walls and a complete loss of trust in all of humanity became cemented deep within the concrete footings.

My family believed life would return to some sort of normalcy. What is normal? Normalcy to one person, is not always the same for another. My life would never be the same I knew that, I didn't know why the rest of my family couldn't see that. My destiny had been changed, my path forever altered.

To cope, I turned inwards. I vowed that the world or anyone in it would not touch me. I imprisoned myself, locking myself away as I tried to confront the dark passenger that loomed in the shadows of my world. I tried to banish my feelings by suppressing them, putting them in what I considered to be well-sealed containers, hiding them in niches on my carefully constructed wall of emotions. However, my feeling of revulsion, self-loathing, disgust, disempowerment and shock only matured over time and spilled out of their containers. A long tormented war was initiated, a battle of mind and emotions against youthful rationality as I tried to understand: why?

An abyss of silent mental questioning surrounded me. The daily reflection I saw in the mirror showed unfocused eyes and an icy void that offered no tangible answers to any of my questions. Simply because there were no answers and there was no one to discuss any of my feelings with. I was unable to process what had occurred, none of it made any sense. What happened as a result of this was my former, carefree, respectable behaviour transformed and disorder and chaos, reined in their place. This left both my parents bewildered.

Our family fragmented. I felt my once loving close and happy family couldn't look at me anymore. My father would leave the room and my mother would look away when I entered. This made me feel unwanted, dirty and rejected. To me it was as if I had no relevance in their lives anymore.

An unspoken, mutually agreed pact had formed between us.

One of withdrawal, distractions and isolation. Long, silent months passed. Our lives torn a part, forever changed. Our loving family bond broken, replaced by false pretences and rituals. We were once three family members who were strongly bonded. Now, we were just three people, living under the same roof. In the days and months that followed, I tried the best I could to cope with my feelings but I found it hard to be happy. What I remembered the prevailing, persistent silences.

Chapter 6

I have come to realise that major struggles are built into the nature of everyone's life, not just mine. I believe we experience them to teach us significant and fundamental lessons. They help us to grow and mature but I couldn't understand why, and quite often, I would silently scream into my pillow and shout, why? What was the purpose of it all?

During my life, especially in those early years, I found the greatest of my battles were not between me and another, but the conflict inside me. The war between my emotions and my rational side was sometimes intense. I would cry, I would get angry, I would punch and break things but none of it took away the internal pain.

A few short weeks after my rape I found myself having to deal with another very difficult situation. I don't know why, but, my school was notified of what had happened. It was supposed to have been discussed in confidence. However, Chinese whispers swept through the school like a fierce cyclone and brought with them destructive, hurtful rumours and innuendos. I became the brunt of off-handed jokes, used by gossip-mongers to make them selves look good for cheap, insensitive humour. The sole outcome was obviously to belittle me in the face of my adversity.

I fought and wrestled both internally and externally with these hurtful, underhandedly slung pieces of clay. People say "sticks and stones may break my bones but names will never hurt me," I never found this statement to be true. Words hurt people and they do have the capability to penetrate even the strongest of physical and emotional amours, especially when it has been weakened by something like I had been through. Some of their vicious words cut me deeply, their barbed comments pierced right into my heart and stayed for a long time.

I had already withdrawn and isolated myself, but, this situation made me withdraw even further. As a self-preservation tactic, I discarded most of my old behaviours. The simple routine ones I still hung on to but I no longer went to school early or played and socialised with the kids. I found it easier and I drew less attention to myself if I just went through the motions of what was expected of me. My life became a series of daily rituals.

At such a young age, I became good at shutting myself away within the safety of my newly created castle walls, as I tried to work out what I did and didn't feel comfortable with. As the months slowly slipped by, I taught myself to be more self-reliant and tough. I did this by simply practising different techniques and assessing the best process to use to get what I wanted and needed. Basically trial and error.

After school, instead of playing like I used to, I would fool around with a homemade Ouija board, as well as a pendulum which my mother had bought for me. She dabbled a lot in the dark arts and her passion fuelled my desire to learn. During this time I recognise that I was quite intuitive, I had an aptitude and skill which I had never identified before. This made me feel good about myself knowing I was good at something. So for me, using these tools to communicate with the dead was not unnatural or scary as some would imagine. It was quite normal and my mother often nurtured and promoted my obsession with these toys.

I believed I could actually communicate with the dead using these apparatuses and I did. At times, the room would become icy cold, and I would often see hazy figures conjured up from the floor or walls, so I knew I was not alone. However none of it healed me or offered me solace from the dark passenger. Over time, I taught myself to read cards, and soon after, progressed to reading tarot cards. Later in life, I would use these skills, to provide readings for people and earn some money.

Chapter 7

A few years passed. I was eleven and it was 1974. My family life had changed, my family relationship had changed. We all knew nothing could take us back to the innocence of the past. Living in Sydney made me feel exposed and I guess it also affected my parents, as my father accepted a long-term posting to Madang in Papua New Guinea. I thought where the hell was Madang.

I was initially traumatised and outraged at the thought of having to give up my life and all that Sydney offered. It was the only life I really knew. However, it didn't take me long to realise that there was a possibility that I could have a chance at some sort of a normal life, away from the prying, knowing eyes of those aware of what had occurred.

So off we all went to a tiny place in Papua New Guinea called Madang. Madang was everything Sydney wasn't. It was small, beautiful, unaffected by the world's boundaries or limitations. It was untamed, un-regimented and it liberated me. I swam in the beautiful clear, clean oceans teeming with colourful fish. I watched the sun set over magnificent mountain ranges covered with oversized luscious coconut palms and dense tropical jungle foliage. Over time I regained some of my courage, I learnt to step out and trust this new world. The experience altered my life in such constructive and positive ways. The move was a welcome distraction for all of us. I noticed that the whole family started to laugh again. My brother four years old when we left Sydney initially hated the country. But not long after we arrived and settled into the new culture, even he began to have fun. I was optimistic that this foreign country would offer a better life for me.

My first year in Madang gave me both comfort and contentment. I felt free, enlightened, satisfied with what this new life potentially offered. I shared my life with new, diverse, confident friends who knew nothing of my past. These were people who didn't judge or ridicule me. A brand new start was on offer, and I accepted it with open arms. I felt free to live again. Madang offered a landscape full of intrigue, glorious sun-kissed seascapes surrounded by exotic, unexplored jungle, and it beckoned me to venture in to it and I did.

Our first home was a three bedroom house in a suburb called Yomba, on the outskirts of the small yet welcoming town. Later that first year, we moved into a larger home in the middle of town which provided easier access to local schools and services. Nothing could have been better for me. I had found happiness and freedom from the bonds of Sydney. I felt alive.

Living in the middle of town was wonderful. I roamed freely. I rode my push bike through the narrow, unsealed streets, galloped my horse on the local greenery and swam in the large, under-utilised resort swimming pools. Those days were happy, carefree and fun-filled.

Madang was a very social place. Drinking and partying were the common recreational activity for the adults, and my parents were no exception. They embraced this culture wholeheartedly as did most of the other white people that lived there. As time passed, the bouts of heavy drinking and partying increased, as did the physical altercations between my parents. During some of these inebriated, aggressive fights, I would either retreat to my bedroom, or scamper down the stairs to grab my bike. I would sprint off and ride unnoticed through the dark unlit deserted night streets, the moon my only guiding light.

As an adult, looking back through the eyes and experience of my forty-eight years, I now understand that the torment my parents felt and the frustration over the past events held them prisoners in their own self-conflict. Conflict they had no skill to resolve. Me, I was a living, breathing, constant reminder of what happened in Sydney. Alcohol, and a move, was only a temporary band-aid for a much deeper wound that festered in different ways in each of us.

I believe my mother felt guilt and responsibility for sending me to the shop; guilt she would never discuss or even openly acknowledge. It was, however, a guilt she would wear daily, and one that would stay with her and settle in her heart. My dad outwardly displayed himself as an unemotional man, yet, in reality he was governed by his emotions, his passion, his anger and his concern for others, unfortunately anger dominated his life during this time. Both my parents were affected just in different ways.

I have heard philosophers say, the keys to happiness include a short memory, as well as, living so that our memories will be part of our happiness. The lifestyle in Madang helped me learn this principle. It taught me how to focus on the good things and not dwell on all the bad, especially past mistakes. I knew I was succeeding, because the dark passenger within me didn't rise up and try to consume me as much as it had before.

Madang was like a field of dreams, full of promise and potential. Nothing was to be feared, just explored and understood. In this haven I was able to create new memories. Over time flowers grew out of all of the dark moments I previously experienced. The native sweet fragrance of the Bougainvilleas surrounded me. These beautiful looking flowers randomly attached themselves to my cold concrete castle walls, the ones I had built to protect myself, and the flowers blossomed.

Madang taught me not to fear life or be afraid anymore. It showed me how to embrace life again. It taught me that storms are a part of life, they come and go like the tide. I also learnt all seas whether rough or calm can be navigated by a skilled captain. I also realized that smooth seas do not always make skilful sailors.

The biggest lesson I learnt was that the hardest and most turbulent times in life bring forth skills and abilities that you can draw upon when needed to combat future events.

Unfortunately, the tranquillity and peace that surrounded me during those first years in Madang were not to last, fading into the local sunset. Schooling opportunities for higher grades in PNG were limited to either home schooling, which required parental guidance and input, attending the local high school offering a limited program, or, choice number three, a sound education in boarding school back in Australia.

My parents of twelve years chose option number three. I guess they thought this would provide the best education for me.

So, I was sent back to Australia.

A new path was chosen for me without consultation. A strict boarding school was to be my home, a place where I would spend the next four years of my life alone, without my family and the life that could have fully healed my brokenness and made me whole again.

Chapter 8

In hindsight, if only my parents had chosen to keep their fragile, damaged, teenage daughter together in the family unit, and let the nurturing, healing environment she was thriving in work its magic on her . . . . if only they had disregarded formal education standards and pressures in lieu of my emotional security, then I may not have found myself writing this book.

To say I felt devastated, rejected, mentally flung back onto the ground of that damp cemetery ground would understate my feelings. Being hurt, abandoned by the people I loved the most, left a huge hole in my heart; one I didn't know how to heal. All that Madang had taught me was lost in the chasms of a dark, unending pit. Sydney and all its previously smothered feelings slowly bubbled to the surface and awakened the sleeping volcano within me. Fiery flames licked constantly at the healing scabs Madang had laid over my wounds and they reopened. A cloud of ash settled over me. My visibility obscured, I could no longer see the hope that once lay in my soul and my future felt as bleak as the skies above me.

My limited experience at life had shown me that adversity is a fact of life. I understood that. I had witnessed my fair share of it already. I had no control over it. What I could control was me and how I reacted to it. I also had control over who I would let into my circle and how I would deal with this new school and their rules and regulations.

The hardest thing was I found I was alone in a far-off land. Unfamiliar surroundings, unknown rituals and strangers with their own personal troubles bordered me on every side. There was no escape; I was trapped in a parent funded prison. I yearned for the family, and the short life I had grown to trust. Madang beckoned me from the depths of my dreams; it whispered my name as the wind rustled the surrounding trees it reached out for me as I reached for it. But, I knew I had to let it go. I could not allow myself to listen and get hopeful of a return.

I covered my ears, so I could no longer hear and allowed the shadows to hide the beautiful visions of the picturesque memories stored deep in my memory. I knew I needed to forget the promises Madang may have provided in my life and overcome the new situation that dominated my life.

I didn't want to start a new life. I was not ready for this journey and I didn't want to embark on it either, but, the pride had abandoned me, sent me away, injured and alone. If I could have spoken I would have told them I was really just a terrified, young cub in need of family support. Instead, I found myself in a harsh unemotional environment, about to face a bleak extended winter on the freezing open plains, alone, surrounded by unknown predators.

Boarding school was a large fully fenced concrete enclosure like an arctic base. It was a desolate, ice covered rocky plain, inhospitable, unfriendly, isolated and confining. At first I didn't know how to act or behave. My new home was governed by autocratic foreigners, with absolute power and extensive rules and regulations and expectations were set and demanded.

Expectations I knew I would never fulfil, simply because I didn't want to, however, I would quickly learn how to circumnavigate them and use them to my advantage.

Living under such a stringent regime was hard for me. My personality and nature, as well as, my past experiences made me rebel frequently. Thoughts of freedom dominated my thinking. I knew to survive. I needed to plan my escape, any escape, even if it only lived in my flamboyant and vivid imagination.

I was not the only person who suffered from family rejection on this arctic base in which we all resided. Young girls like me—children, really—surrounded me, dozens of them. All of us initially shocked to find ourselves alone, amongst unfamiliar people. We were all foreigners, aliens who constantly tested the terrain to see just how hospitable it would be.

That first long lonely night will remain forever etched in my mind like the master strokes of an artist as he creates his masterpiece. My second night was just as bleak and emotionally traumatic as the first. I recall lying face up as my head rested on a flat pillow, on my single dormitory allocated cot, girls the same age as myself surrounded me on both sides, the conditions were the same for each of us. My lightly clad body was covered only by a light blanket and the long room was devoid of light except for the reflection of the bathroom lights which slightly illuminated the hall. I could make out the shapes of my 'dorm mates' as they slept in their beds.

I heard whispered cries of emotional pain beside me. Silently, I reached over and grabbed the hand of the girl to offer comfort. I listened to her choking sobs and slow, sorrowful gulps as she mourned the loss of her life. I sympathized as I also felt her pain. I knew I was not alone in my suffering. My own feelings and self-preservation tactics prevented me from sharing my own pain with her or anyone else, for fear of exposing my own vulnerabilities.

Many girls of all ages, shared this arctic base with me, we were the new recruits, the youngest of the group. Most of us were shrouded by our own internal conflicts and unrest. Some of us joined and formed a friendship, whilst others, like me, were left to their own restlessness. My experiences and perception had taught me I could not trust or rely on anyone else and I carried this with me all throughout my time in boarding school.

Boarding school taught me how to wear two faces, one I would show the world, the one that people expected to see and made them feel comfortable, and the other one, the real face only I knew. Like the joker, my painted face adapted to fit into whatever circumstances I found myself in. Only I knew the authentic person being moulded as I grew in this sterile, unaffectionate environment.

During my time at school I did form alliances, but my personal motto stood firm within me. I would do it alone. I refused to allow myself to be broken by anyone and the only way that could happen was if I allowed people to see the real me. The walls of my protective castle became devoid of the formerly planted Madang flowers and bougainvilleas, and were once again entirely erected, fortified this time. I believed my life would be easier if it was bordered and protected from the outside physical hurts of the world.

As monotonous school schedules slowly ticked by, I vowed no one would ever get close enough to me ever again. This included my family who had abandoned me. They had left me to rot in this prison whilst they amused themselves with holidays and excitement in exotic tropical locations. I internally questioned, was this, a decent and fitting punishment for me after the event that happened? My take on it was, I thought it was a bit extreme, but, I was powerless and incapable to change my current situation. I swore that when I was older, I would never feel disempowered ever again, and I would never lose control of any situation I found myself in.

Chapter 9 Reflection on my life

Looking back, I think my life would have been vastly different if someone had taken the time to really get to know me, to understand the hidden pain of that event and the trauma it caused and the self-destruction it brought upon me and my family. But it didn't happen. I was left to fend for myself like a tiny bird with a broken wing. In the seventies there was no counselling, no psychotherapy and no recognition of post-traumatic stress. No one offered me a splint for my broken wing and I was left to heal alone.

During my years in boarding school I could have reached out and touched the lives of the other lost girls. Maybe even had some lifelong friends, but, *I didn't.* Instead, I closed myself off. *I shut down.* I didn't allow anyone to get anywhere near me, let alone know me. I simply lived life in what I called survival mode.

Hindsight and reflection are great tools and I now use them often. Back then they could of helped me a lot however I didn't understand them until much much later.

Over the years, I have come to recognise that whatever struggle lies before me, I had to continue to move forward. The mountain may look too big from my current vantage point but, the summit and all it holds may only be one step away. For most of my life, I had refused to give things a positive go. I refused to look at situations optimistically simply because I would not allow myself to trust in hope. Instead, I chose to shut myself off from situations and relationships. I also gave up far too soon in most of my life situations, regretfully not reaching my full potential or having the opportunity to unravel the secrets life was holding for me.

Chapter 10

Negative, internal self-talk dominated my life. It drowned me with destructive pounding waves of criticism, which dragged me to the bottom and pinned me on the jagged coral below as the negative words tore at my mind and soul. This left me unable to see a positive future. Self-imposed obstacles rose up before me, which prevented me from pursuing any dreams that Madang had once held for me.

I forfeited the development of positive life and social skills and chased a form of happiness which only made me more of a skilled, sole survivor. I may have once had the opportunity to become a jovial woman who understood the boundaries of love and embraced a positive desire to explore the world and make something of herself, but, I would never know. Instead, I focused my life and skills on learning regimented behaviour and learning how to deal with containment, isolation and rejection. I chose to survive and get through the boarding school ride and that became my only interest.

I knew I would be free again one day. I made it my mission to count down the days. My jail term was 1,460 days. Many things changed in that time frame especially when your sentence is imposed when you are only 12. I was allowed periodic release to visit my family during the school holiday, but our relationship was never the same. It was now burnt, seriously scorched by the blistering flames of rejection, loneliness, bitterness and time. They say absence makes the heart grow fonder. I didn't find that at all. To me, my absence from the family unit was destructive like water is to fire.

Being parted from my family for this period of time changed how I felt about my parents. My love for my family changed. I no longer felt the same way about them. I had changed. My heart had hardened and a distinct barrier grew between us. I have heard it said that the love that burns the brightest leaves the deepest scars, how very true. My family's abandonment and rejection of me left unseen deep blemishes that couldn't be easily erased. I had loved them deeply once, but, now I dared not venture into that territory again.

I had grown so independent, so manipulative and intolerant, that I no longer blended with my family values. Our purpose was no longer mutually agreed upon which made it virtually impossible to merge with this group of people during any of my visits. I found myself constantly in trouble. I was unable and unwilling to conform to the family regime, and the laws that applied to their world. I was not a part of their world any longer. They had alienated me, separated me from this unit by choice, and now tried to enforce their laws upon me which only resulted in more frequent angry outbursts and sometimes extreme punishment.

A cycle of fights and disagreements emerged every time I visited home. As the frequency of these cycles increased so did my lack of control and thoughtfulness for their feelings. I simply didn't care how they perceived me. After spending years locked away in boarding school I learnt how to suppress my emotions, I mastered the art of wearing a poker face. I could sit through the roughest of tirades and not bat an eyelid. I usually came home with an attitude and threw caution to the wind doing what I wanted, and this really angered my parents. However, I refused to let my parents anger get to me or allow their feelings to ruin my holiday.

My parents were at times so disgusted in my behaviour and attitude that neither of them made any effort to understand me or bothered to spend any time with me. Neither of them realised that their actions fuelled the fire of rejection. There were times when they both refused to come to the airport to say goodbye as I departed to return to school. I sometimes wondered why they bothered to bring me home at all.

If only they had tried a different tactic, one that demonstrated tenderness, affection or one of friendship and acceptance, maybe the situation could have been very different. Neither of us tried any constructive avenues to reignite the fire of our relationship. We allowed our doubts and uncertainties to rob our family of any potential benefits that we may have discovered if either of us had only attempted to rebuild a relationship.

Chapter 11

Four years passed my parentally-financed and—imposed solitary confinement period finally over, my sentence finalised. I had earned my parole, to be released from my jailors back to the custody of three complete strangers. My release meant the arrival of my estranged family, an imminent reunion with people who I shared a history with, but nothing else.

My father had accepted a new posting this time, a town called Rockhampton and it was to be my home. I was never to see my sanctuary, Madang, ever again. All its hope and prospects floated in the wind, forever lost as they drifted a long way from Rockhampton.

The life I had created, my solitary and autonomous life of the last four years, would be be altered again. I was now entitled, required more like it, to live in a family unit again, with three other people I hardly knew. I believed I had good reason for apprehension and dread, our past turbulent histories firmly and vividly recorded in the back of my mind. I didn't require any reminders of the crystal-clear illustration to recall the colourful words and isolation I felt every holiday.

I felt external pressure and silent expectations on me to be happy. It was anticipated that I would be happy to move to another city, enrolled in another school and take my list of friends back to zero. The truth was, I didn't feel any of that. I felt nervous and frightened rather than happy.

My previous holiday reintegration experiences marred any foreseen positives, including being positively accepted. I perceived I was seen as just the trouble-maker who came home to visit every now and then, and yes, I got into quite a lot of mischief. I smoked my first joint, drunk alcohol, attended all night parties, had my first sexual experience and tried the local beetle nut all whilst on holiday from school.

I wasn't excited. I was scared. I tried to imagine what it would be like sharing a house, not a dorm, having my own private space, and a bathroom only four people used, instead of twenty. It was a foreign concept after living in close proximity in a dormitory that overflowed with girls, yet, I welcomed the concept of freedom it offered from the rules, tyrants and my current captors.

My family terrified me. I knew nothing about them and they knew nothing, really, about me. Years had passed. I left when I was twelve and returned when I was sixteen, my youth stolen in a prison of academia. I emerged transformed, altered by what I had experienced. I embraced new skills not formerly known in my life in Madang.

Physically and mentally, I was tougher, hardened by my sufferings. To survive boarding school, I had locked myself away in a sealed castle of selfishness. I had embraced a hardened spirit and mind. My heart became impenetrable and irredeemable.

Internally I questioned how could I live with these people again? I had lived so long locked away inside myself, I was unsure if it was even possible to share my life with anyone.

My outside facade portrayed a tough exterior, but I was still a child with needs, my hardened exterior was a poor representation of what was really happening on the inside. To the world it must have looked like I would cope ok, but inside anxiety reigned. I didn't recall any positive experiences regarding the whole family situation, and the family concept was unfamiliar, foreign to me. I wondered how I would transition from my safe autonomous bubble to a life that intimately involved three other people.

What were their expectations of me I obviously had not acted the way they had wanted when I visited, so I had absolutely no idea how to please them and I questioned if I really wanted to. I had taken on the characteristic of the chameleon, I could change my colours to fit the environment I was in, and I had learnt how to adjust well over the past few years. It would take me a few weeks before I could change my form to fit into this environment enough to survive.

When we reunited the same feelings I experienced that first week at boarding school revisited me, apprehension and fear.

I walked out of the front gates of that boarding school, the unemotional base that had been my home for four years, into the open door of a car ready to take me away to new base, a new life. Three tense but smiling faces greeted me. We embraced and kissed for a brief time. For me, it was an awkward moment. Small, inconsequential dialogue lapsed between us, as we drove off into a new world. The life I had known since I was 12, the rules and regulations as well as the people I had lived with during those years were left behind with the setting sun.

Chapter 12

I came to realise that during my absence, my parents and my brother had formed a strong three-corded, loving bond. Laughter filled the air as they openly discussed and relived experiences that I had no part in, holidays they shared and friends they encountered and missed.

During those first few weeks of my reuniting with the family, I was really uncomfortable watching the three of them as they demonstrated affection to one another. My brother demanded affection from my parents and he received it regularly. For me affection was an unfamiliar exchange, something I had not felt or given for nearly four years. I had forgotten what it was like to be cuddled or touched by my parents and it was hard for me to watch the three of them trade affection in this manner.

In the early days of my separation from my family, I would crave affection and any sort of attention, but there was no one there to offer a shoulder to cry on, or, an arm that would encase you to offer comfort in those dark and lonely nights, no one to tuck you in, or make you feel safe and warm. Instead, I would live in an unheated, cold dormitory room full of a number of single wire cots lined against the wall and small wooden cupboards.

I remember my first night in that place well. My single

uncomfortable cot was about half way between the end of the room and the door, a small window allowed light to bounce off the cupboards and illuminate the long room. Numerous girls my age or younger filled the other beds around me. Our whole lives and all of our earthly belongings were encased in the small cupboards strategically placed in our allotted space. That first night I quietly cried myself to sleep, mourning the loss of my life and mourning Madang a place that had made me feel whole.

Those lonely long nights changed my character, especially as I listened all around me as soft sobs echoed across the bleak colourless walls of our new home. In the early days, I felt the same pain as everyone else. I would suppress my own tears with my single pillow. Our beds were close enough that when I extended my arm, I could touch the next person, so I often would reach out and gently stroke the back of the girl next to me with the hope of providing some form of comfort and solace. Eventually the sobs ceased and the dormitory fell silent.

During those difficult and demanding first few months I came to realise we all needed to feel some sort of affection. A simple act, like my innocent touch offered us both hope in the unfamiliar world we found ourselves in. It enabled us to cope a little better with our estrangement from the families that had been ripped from us. This act shared between two twelve year old girls was the last real affection I felt or knew.

So I battled emotionally and mentally as I tried to comprehend the demonstration of people openly cuddling each other. I had no idea this display of affection was normal for people who lived together. It certainly was not normal from the experiences that were a part of my life. I struggled daily, not knowing how to merge into this cosy trio's lifestyle. For some reason, I didn't feel comfortable being a part of it, and, I certainly didn't feel welcomed or embraced by it either. I sensed this family unit was quite wary of me as well. I felt they kept me at a distance; they seemed to expose me only to the necessary sections of their lives.

My brother, aged nine, was much more fascinating. He was significantly more interesting than my previous holiday visits, where he just annoyed me. I was drawn to his amusing and extremely comical nature. He was spirited and made me laugh enthusiastically until pains in my stomach overrode everything else in my life. We spent a lot of time together as we resurrected a relationship that should have been naturally present.

On weekends, we would walk the short distance to the local council-owned and operated Olympic sized swimming pool. We swam, for hours, sometimes all day, surrounded by other snotty-nosed, red eyed children. We ate frozen ice blocks until our brain froze and gave us a temporary headache. We played the old style pin ball machines and fought over the Kiss machine and Space Invaders game. We battled and we laughed and taunted each other until it was time to go home. We had fun.

I found my brother was cute and his laugh infectious. He was quite the show man. His goal in life was to be a clown or a magician. I thought this was hilarious. Not that he wasn't talented;

it just didn't seem to me to be a great career choice.

It didn't take long for me to learn to love this kid again. He didn't judge or condemn me, he actually thought I was cool. Even now as I think of him it brings a smile to my lips. At that time, I was important in his life and I liked the fact someone actually enjoyed my company and liked me for me. With him I didn't need to wear my mask. I let my guard down. I wasn't afraid to allow him to see the real me. With him I felt at home with a kindred spirit.

Chapter 13

After a few weeks, I had found a pattern, a routine I could maintain with my parents. Dad had purchased a new house and was established into his new job. Mum seemed to be searching for work and appeared content, my brother was his usual happy self and I was reasonably settled into a new school and had met some 'interesting' people. I thought we had all found a sustainable rhythm that was relatively easy for everyone, not perfect but we were in what I perceived to be a comfortable pattern.

However, a few short weeks after we moved into our new home, my mother chose to return to Sydney for a 'visit', a short holiday on her own. This was not unusual for her as she was a travel agent and travelled extensively with her work. On one occasion, I arrived home from boarding school for one of my short visits to find my mother embarking on a personal holiday to Sydney. She was gone the whole time I was home. Her departure at the time just fuelled my internal fire of rejection.

Looking back I can see how my parent's actions, attitudes and behaviour towards me on all my visits cut deep. Their actions wounded me and left profound scars both mentally and physically. As an adult, I now believe, one of the greatest gifts you can give to someone is the honour of your attention. The problem was, I didn't receive that from my family. My mother's constant spiteful words hurt my feelings, but her silences broke my heart. She made me feel unwelcomed, unloved and very unimportant in her life. So when she informed me she was going to Sydney once again, it meant very little to me, as I had already become accustomed to this sort of rejection.

Being away for so long made me a stranger in their world, even though we had settled into a pattern I was still a stranger. The four year absence prevented me from being able to discern any threatening undercurrents that could potentially de-stabilise the whole family unit. My families, especially my parent's behaviours and routines were unfamiliar to me. This made it impossible for me to detect or read the little signs of unhappiness, bitterness and poor communication that must have been there. From my limited perspective, things looked pretty normal, okay even. On the outside we appeared relatively happy I thought. These parents might have been my blood, but I was blind-folded and handicapped when it came to understanding what was really going on in their world.

Neither my brother nor I detected any hint or any telltale signs of a problem in our newly formed family. Both of us were oblivious to our surroundings. It was like we lived in an allusion, a pleasant and fun allusion focused primarily on making up for lost time. The spotlight for us focussed on building new build memories, sharing dreams and reconnecting.

My mother's extended absence did cross my mind occasionally. However, I didn't have much time or inclination to worry about her whereabouts or intentions as I was dealing with my own teenage struggles. For one I had come from an all-girl strict boarding school to a lax co-ed state school and the opposite sex as well as my awkward teenage hormones made it hard to fit in. During those first few weeks I experience a lot of conflict, both physically and mentally. I was self-conscious and uncomfortable which brought out my worst side and my behaviour became quite challenging to combat these feelings. I had never been miss popularity at any school and this was never my goal. All I really wanted to do was just find a place where I felt some sense of safety and comfort to spend those years. I knew how to be a rebel, the trouble maker or the misfit and that's how I tried to fit into Rocky High.

In my early years, I always stood my ground and chose to come out swinging. I was a bold aggressive fighter who looked challenges in the eye. My combat tactic was to dig in and fight to the end. I often found myself in the trenches down and dirty but I had resilience and I would get up and start the skirmish again and again until it produced an outcome. Rocky High and its pupils in my grade ten classes were just a new challenge to me.

I had come into the class half way through the year from what they all considered to be a snobby upper class boarding school—little did they know. The class cliques had been created, routines had been instituted and intimate relationships had been well established. Both students and teachers had settled into a comfortable predictable pace, they had found the balance that would get them successfully through to the end of the year. The problem was I walked in and disrupted the natural balance of the class.

I was a big disruption. I was new. An unknown entity and people were curious, but, they didn't want me to get too close to interrupt or disturb the sense of balance they had all created. Circles closed, locking me out. I wasn't hurt by their actions; I was more angered and annoyed by their petty behaviour. So I decided to create a scene that would draw attention and entice the rebels of the school to form my own circle. My strategy worked somewhat, it certainly drew a lot of attention, especially from the show pony girls—who were horrified—and the misfit boys—who thought I was cool.

My first act was to blatantly refuse to wear the short, navy blue skirt which was part of the school uniform—I had found a loop hole in the school handbook which didn't specify the length of the navy skirt—so I wore a floor length navy free flowing skirt with the specified white un-ironed blouse. The second act was to demonstrate my rebellious nature. I chewed gum in class, was chronically late, back chatted the teachers and gave cheek to the snobby girls. I just slipped on my old well-worn, familiar coat and waited for everyone's reactions. I didn't have to wait long.

Firstly the teachers were not impressed with my clothing choice but there was nothing they could do about it and I continued to wear it regardless of their comments. Secondly my behaviour was challenged. Detention became my second home and "wagging" school became a weekly occurrence. The upside of all of this was I caught the eye of a very good looking young man. He was someone I considered to be the best looking guy in the school. He was a tall, athletic, blonde-haired, brown-eyed surfer. I will say we were together for some time and then hooked up again a few years after we had all left school, but, no, it didn't work out. That is that's another story.

Uneventful days slipped into weeks, and my mother still hadn't returned from Sydney. This scenario left my father in a state of mild panic, as he tried to care for two children as well as working fulltime. Curiosity got the better of me and I wondered where was she? What was taking her so long? Why had she not made any contact with any of us? It was odd, but really I didn't think much of it.

And soon after I had pondered these questions my reply came.

I remember it came one day as I sat in a quiet classroom with twenty-five other single-minded, distracted sixteen year old teenagers. My pencil drew circles and lines in non-descript patterns on my spiral-bound book as the teacher prattled on about something uninteresting. My concentration was interrupted as I heard my name called by the teacher who demanded my attention. I looked up and saw my dad as he stood outside the classroom door, waiting for me.

Inquisitive prying eyes focused on me from all around the room. I slowly rose from the hard plastic seat, gathered my books into a large pile and placed them in my oversized bag and slowly shuffled to the door. I felt embarrassed as attentive eyes searched me. I tried not to draw any more attention to myself; however, I knew it was too late for that. Questioning eyes tracked my every move, hungry for any ounce of gossip about the 'new' girl. I had worn the brunt of malicious gossip previously in Sydney, and it had left a foul taste in my mouth, and I would not relive that again if I could help it.

I refused to meet any of their eyes and looked at my father instead. He appeared impatient as he stood waiting for me. However, when I drew closer to him, I realized that what I thought was impatience was actually distress. I noticed he had red, puffy eyes which held suppressed tears as they patiently waited for the right moment to be released. I wondered what this meant. He gave me the impression he was really nervous, upset about something. Something serious had happened.

Mentally I questioned what it could be. My mind created scenes of absolute chaos. The worst, a car accident. Vivid pictures of my small brother's body as he lay in a sterile hospital setting, doctors around him tending to his injuries. NO, I couldn't entertain this thought any further. My father's presence couldn't possibly have anything to do with him, he was too precious to me. I didn't allow my mind to go there again. My brother was my ally, he was the only bright shiny star I had at that time and I refused to let him go.

My father thrust a thin rectangular object into my hand. I dragged my eyes away from my father's face and all that it held, to look down at a small white plain envelope, addressed to me. I noticed my mother's handwriting scribbled on the surface. The tattered outer edges of the letter caught my attention. It had been opened, its content already read by my father who stood beside me. The penny dropped and for the first time I perceived my life in its true reality. I realised I was once again a part of a lie. I had covered my eyes and shared an invented happy and carefree yet false time with my brother whilst the world around us shattered. The reality of my family situation became crystal-clear. I awoke from my lucid dream into another nightmare and the sparkle from my eye was extinguished, smothered by the blanket of my true circumstance. Circumstances I knew were written in the ink on the pages before me.

I held the letter and felt its weight between my fingers. Its physical weight was insignificant, trivial, but, I knew the true weight would be substantial, immeasurable. I can remember looking at the dark script, the words were written delicately upon the paper. I can't recall the actual words written; however, their meaning was fully understood and carried a heavy burden for all of us right through to this day. My mother's intentions were straightforward, she would not return, and could not take my brother or myself with her. I do remember she asked me to look after my brother.

The letters burden had been delivered. Unanswered questions chased the words I had read, they perused answers they would never receive. Why me? Why tell *me* this news? In a letter, in this fashion, of all things! Why had she not rung to tell us in person? Why address the letter to me? I believed the letter should have been addressed to my dad, not me. At the time I thought this matter concerned him more than me. I was completely naïve to the flow on affect this letter would have on the family unit. I didn't understand or comprehend my mother's actions at all. I think she had expectations of me that I would never be able to fulfil. I was sixteen, had no experience or skills with understanding or applying appropriate emotions or emotional responses. I was volatile, unpredictable; even I didn't know what I was capable of. I had only just begun to trust and rebuild my feelings for these people again. I had activated a belief and hope in being a part of a family situation again only to find myself traumatised and my dream crushed yet again.

Was this the best I would get in life? Would my life always be filled with tragedy and tests? What was the purpose of it all? To me life was just one big nightmare with small glimmers of hope and faint glimpses of happiness, like fragmented flecks of fluoro colours randomly sprinkled on a dark oil painting.

I wondered if this was what all families were like. It appeared nothing was easy or ran smoothly where families were involved. No wonder kids run away, and for a split second, whilst reading that fateful letter and looking at the expression on my father's face, I considered it. Pictures of me living my own life, successfully working, happy, laughing with friends flashed before my eyes. In my mind, I was a living example of triumph over my situation.

However, the reality of the situation before me and the desperation, pain and suffering I witnessed on my father's face, as well as the newly found love for my brother brought me back and I knew I would never abandon these people.

A succession of question emerged within me. I kept asking why? Was it my fault? Was this happening because I was now home? I wondered if this situation was because of what had happened all those years ago. I speculated it was my previous behaviour and attitude and the problems between my mother and I that had resulted in this reaction.

Chapter 14

I often wondered about life, why we have to go through the things we do. Life seems to be one lesson after another. I have to say I appear to be always on a steep learning curve and am never on holiday or graduate from the school of life. This makes me sometimes think I am a bit unintelligent, a bit slow, as it takes me a long time to learn things. It certainly felt like that for me as I went through those first sixteen years of my life. Everywhere I turned I seemed to encounter a new battle, a new obstacle to overcome, nothing seemed to come easily.

For months I watched as my dad struggled to fight his feelings and fight to keep his family together. The battle at times overpowered him, incapacitated him beyond belief. He had a desire to build an empire that he would one day share with his family and it collapsed around him. The houses and land he owned was stripped from him forcing us to move into a rented small, two bedroom, bottom-floor flat on a main street in Rockhampton.

We were by no means poor, although, after my mother left things got tough not only emotionally but financially. My father held a fulltime position as a flight service operator, similar to an air traffic controller at the Rockhampton airport and was on a good salary. However as he fought to hold on to and rebuild our broken family, he was forced to take on a second job. Between his new role at a carpet store and his rotational roster at the airport he was absent from the house for long periods of time which left only me to care for my brother. I guess my mother's written wish had come true to some extent.

During these long lonely months, my brother and I drew on each other's strength and we became very close. We forged a connection, an uncomplicated bond of need, a need to be accepted and loved. Together we nurtured each other and in a way we started to heal the wounds of rejection that we both felt.

I remember sometimes at night I would lay beside him as he snuggled underneath the covers. My body weight would trap him tightly under the doona as I gently stroked his brown hair offering some sort of comfort for his pain. My fingers would rub along his scalp and gently lure the strands of hair backward and he would purr like a cat, he loved it.

In the early days of his abandonment he would cry himself to sleep, just like I had done those first days at boarding school. His tears broke my heart because I knew I could never take away his pain. A horrid stillness had descended upon his life. The loss of his mother, his feelings of abandonment and the disintegration of his dreams and expectations was not something that could be replaced easily. It was a gap I couldn't possibly fill, yet it was something I completely understood. I had felt it four years ago.

At times when the rains would come, I would walk and walk and walk. I wanted to feel something, anything, but the ongoing pain I constantly lived with. As the drizzling rain, touched and splattered on my face I would allow myself to cry knowing the rain would disguise my many tears. My brother's anguish cut deeper than any other sorrow I had felt.

No human being can *really* understand another's pain and suffering or what they are truly feeling. I knew I could only put bandages on the wounds I saw, his wounds needed to heal internally. I hoped his scars would heal in time and not change the way he viewed life and I certainly hoped his scars would not run as deep as mine. I would spare him that if I could.

The situation my brother and I were in affected us differently, most likely due to our ages and life experience. I was less affected by my mother's abandonment, my feelings not as intense as my brothers as my connection with my mother was not as deep. However, I had a deep connection with my brother and if I could have changed the circumstances for him and spare him the pain of the situation, I would have done just about anything.

As the months passed my internal demons started to surface again, thoughts of responsibility rose. I felt an overwhelming burden of blame for my mother's disappearance. Shadowy voices held liable for the whole bleak scenario. They reminded me that I had just returned to the family, and it was torn apart. It was obvious, it was my fault. Guilt welled up in me and got worse as every day passed, it continued to rise like the forthcoming dawn. Words of torment and blame were internally flaunted at me and each day my self-esteem was destroyed further. I would continue to have these thoughts for a long time to come.

Chapter 15

Our lives slipped into a steady rhythm. Time had taken all our expectations, hopes and dreams with it and placed them behind us in the past. Months had slipped quietly, mostly unnoticed, away from us, but it had brought a development into our new family unit. We had found mutual harmony and a peaceful reality. Happiness was yet to return, but, we were able to reawaken laughter which had lain dormant within each of us. I believed we were about to turn the corner, we could and would rebuild not all of our family but a part of it.

Months had passed with no contact from my mother who was permanently residing in Sydney, then out of the blue she commenced contact. Her contact destabilised everything we had created it caused major unrest and insecurity not only to my father's emotional state but to my brother and I. She continued to converse with my brother and I through letters and phone conversations and this produced feelings of guilt. She promised a better existence to both of us and this made my brother feel very torn and upset as he loved both our parents equally. I knew his hearts desire was to have our parents reunited and not have to make a choice like the one that was offered to him.

Not long after her initial contact with us my mother wanted a divorce, how their relationship got there, I would never know, as I was not privy to any of their conversations. What I did know was that she continually threatened my father with taking custody away from him. This took its toll on him.

Her continued threats and the torment and distress he felt about losing the rest of his family, I believed compelled him to consider his options. The law required a stable secure home and what he thought was a better home for us included another woman. Where she came from I don't know and I still don't know where he met her but she quickly moved in to our small home and she brought with her two kids. This happened virtually over night and the situation took me by surprise. It was like I came home from school one day and our cosy little family of three had doubled. It was very strange and extremely unsettling.

Soon after the turmoil started the mayhem continued with a new move. To accommodate this new family of six, dad had to buy a bigger house, it became our fourth new home in less than a year.

I often wondered why he did this. Why he would choose this path. Why her? What did he hope to achieve from this move? Did he really think he could be happy? My belief at the time was he did this to keep my mother at bay and I think I may have been right.

The whole scenario was torture for me. I despised these people being in my life. I despised sharing a house with foreigners whom I didn't really like. I felt like a stranger in my own home. This situation was not what I had envisioned when I left boarding school. Definite but invisible boundaries were implemented in our once happy home, my brother and I banded together and lines of division were clearly drawn between her children and us.

It was a catastrophic storm in the making. Even I could see the depths of destruction it held, deep icy dark caverns, filled with disastrous outcomes none of us would fully recover from for a long time to come. During this time, I discovered the true meaning of betrayal. My mother had abandoned all of us, but my father had sold us out to a unknown bidder.

What my father did with his choice was annihilate everything we had previously built and I know he would regret it for a long time to come. My brother and I formed a pact of survival against the odds and we fought the fight for our dying family.

During those first few weeks I watched my father closely, he looked lost and sad to me, but on the outside he wore a cheerful, obliging disposition. On the odd occasion I witnessed his unfeigned feelings, tears he shed in private and the displaced anger he placed carefully in a bubble. I also sometimes watched him as he battled his emotions and rationale as he tried to seek unsought answers to his current predicament. At times I wanted to yell at him and tell him he had made a mistake. If he had only noticed what was right in front of him, what he had thrown away; the potential, the possibilities we had before the move. But I didn't and he didn't. Instead he chose to live a lie with a woman and her children forfeiting his own children.

I watched as his agitation, anxiety and his dread grew daily especially as my mother continued to press the issue of custody. He tried hard to bring his dream to life but he lost his grip and his primary goal: to keep our family unit together. With his limited experience, he considered a new family to be the best option. It was a partnership purely based on necessity, and we all knew it and struggled under the weight of the situation.

My mother's calls came thick and fast, once she was aware of our move, and one day my father intercepted a call from her. She informed him she was taking my brother and he totally lost it. She had invested a lot of time coercing my brother to return to her. This was not a hard task under the circumstances we were in. Both of us hated the situation of sharing a house with these people, so my mother's option did tempt him. She did make an offer to me, however at the time; I was attempting to undertake my Year 11 studies with the hope of re-establishing some of my lost dreams.

The phone call had ended and I was in the bathroom brushing my teeth, my father stormed in, and his face red and angry. He looked like he was going to explode. His body shook uncontrollably with rage and he frightened me. His loud, fiery voice hurled accusations of my betrayal and conspiracy: my conspiring to send my brother to live with my mother who had moved to Brisbane to be closer to us.

The sound of his tense expressions rang loudly in my ears. His words swirled around the tiny, enclosed room. I could see he would not be reasoned with, so I refused to answer his allegations. I tried to remain calm, but I had witnessed this behaviour before, and I could feel the hot flashes of panic and dread as they swept over me in waves. I was backed into a corner, I knew it, I had nowhere to go. The bathroom had only one door and he stood in it. I kept quiet and refused to answer, which just added fuel to his fire, and suddenly he reached out and punched me.

I stepped into the bath and hunched into the corner as I tried to get away from him. My screams alerted my brother, who ran bravely to my aid, but he was just a boy unable to physically defend me. He stood in the doorway tears dripping down his cheeks as he cried and pleaded for our father to stop, and he finally did.

I grabbed my bag and ran up out the door and up the long steep hill to my school, wanting only to put distance between my house and me. My heart beat strong and fast in my chest as the adrenalin pumped around my body, beads of sweat dripped down my back even though the day was not hot. My legs didn't feel the hard ascending bitumen as they sprinted towards my haven.

A new school a school I had just entered after my horrible final term at Rocky High. It was a school that offered hope, understanding and made me believe I could do something with my life. The teachers believed in me, talked to me about going to uni and understood my dream of entering law school. It was the only place I thought to go.

I can remember as I reached the large welcoming gates, I slowed my pace to a brisk walk. I didn't stop to speak to anyone, even ignoring the welcoming comments, going instead straight into the cold, dark classroom of my first class—English. I thought I could hide there for a few moments and gather my thoughts before the class started. I assumed I had at least 20 minutes before other girls would arrive and this would give me enough time to prepare myself mentally and physically to face the day.

The problem was I wasn't alone. I didn't notice her at first, as she casually watched me from the back of the dimly lit room. She was my English Teacher and one of my favourites. She had helped me on numerous occasions and I liked her a lot. She was a tall, good looking woman with gentle eyes and she stood holding an armful of books ready to be moved to the oversized wooden bookshelves. I became aware of her presence when I felt her eyes and her stare as it swept over me. I felt awkward and shamed under the intensity of her eyes. I needed time to think.

She briefly turned to place the books on her rather messy desk, which gave me a chance to evaluate my appearance. I was shocked to see that in the scuffle with my father my school shirt had been ripped, the bottom edge of it opened in a jagged piece. I wanted to cover up the embarrassment I felt and my bag offered the cover I needed. I quickly picked it up and hugged it close to my chest. I knew I wasn't quick enough, I could see it in her eyes and I sensed it in her manner. She slowly turned to face me, her composed face showed compassion and comprehension and I could see she understood the indignity I felt. I knew the questions would soon follow.

I hardly heard the words that fell from her pink stained lips. I knew what she wanted to know, but I couldn't and wouldn't find the right words to answer her. For an extended moment our eyes shared a deep veiled conversation. She discerned the truth. I turned and walked out of school, never to return and I would never see my favourite teacher ever again.

I spent the rest of that day wandering through the Botanical Gardens. I fantasised and contemplated a healthier, more positive life. What would it look like if my parents had stayed together? If I had not been sent away? If I had not been raped? What would my life be like without all that tragedy? I wondered what happiness really looked like. What was it like to having a loving, stable family? Were all families like this? Did everyone have the same level of crisis that seemed to plague our family?

I understood sadness, rejection and pain, but what about the tenderness of love, trust and compassion? To feel someone reach out and touch you in love must be a beautiful sensation. I wondered if I would ever feel something like that.

Like most days the sun dipped in the sky and the warmth oozed from the day. I didn't want to but I knew it was time for me to return home. I recall it being close to 4.30 pm when I reached my house. I recollect walking up the driveway, my bag slung over one shoulder, its weight indenting the skin on my neck. I saw my father and his girlfriend as they stood on the large elevated wooden veranda, which surrounded the new house. I could see my father's anger had not abated and when I drew close to the house he started yelling. His unfounded accusations blamed me for his predicament and the pending loss of his son. He was too blind to see that he would lose his son because of the situation he had put us in. My mother was just capitalising in on and using the advantage she had, knowing my brother hated the current living arrangements and she made a better offer.

Before I could respond he lifted a bundle of garments up in his arms and threw them over the balcony. Unmistakably, they were items that belonged to me. I watched the loose multi coloured garments as they slowly fell and sprawled themselves across the driveway. I started to pick them all up and bundle them in my arms as my mind tried to process what had occurred and what this meant. I heard the words I dreaded to hear, but in the back of my mind knew would come one day, yet I wasn't quite ready for them when they fell from my father's lips.

I was sixteen and had been reunited with my family for all of eight months and it was over.

I stood in the driveway with the softness of my clothes bundled in my arms, the yellow sun dipping in the sky and the darkness waiting to take over, absolutely terrified. However mentally I started to examine my options, uncertain about my choices, I challenged all my alternatives. Yet at the same time, I also felt liberated, free from a situation that I couldn't control and didn't want to be a part of.

I looked up and saw my brother standing apart from my father, his eyes red from the tears that poured down his face, his chest heaving with the sobs that wracked his tiny frame. My heart longed to reach out and touch him to wrap him in my arms and take him back to the tiny flat where I lay beside him and stroked his hair, to a time where we were happy and healing. Over the short time I had known him I had grown to love him with all my heart. He had become my friend, my solace and was my only brother and here we were once again being ripped apart.

I looked intensely into his face as I searched for the right words. There was so much I wanted to say to him, but the words would not come. I longed to cry out to him, to tell him I loved him and to tell him life would work out okay, but I remained silent, unable to express what I desperately wanted to say. I realized I didn't know when or if I would ever see him again.

My parting thought was that I wouldn't be there to protect him anymore; it would just be him and dad against the new trespassers. I hoped dad would see what was really happening under this roof and stop it before he lost everything. Even from my limited life experience and family relationships I comprehended my father's new relationship was temporary. I saw the unhappiness, the discontent and the misery written all over his face. I knew it was born out of hardship and purpose only, not based on love or desire.

I searched my brother's eyes and committed his face to memory. I felt his abandonment and his rejection and I conceded my mother had a lot to answer for. She would become an unpredictable ally, someone who I would use over the next few months to restore my life, but someone I would not trust again for quite some time.

I gathered the few articles of clothing that represented my life and turned my back on my dad's life for a very long time.

I chose the best possible option for my situation. I rang my boyfriend and explained my predicament to him and his family took me in. They offered me the use of their large holiday caravan which was parked in their front yard and for the next few months I lived there until I could find a unit and fulltime employment. During this time, I maintained a secret relationship with my brother aided by my current boyfriends transport. We set up times to speak to each other on the phone and he would sneak out to meet me, often walking down to the local café, to share burgers and talk. I really missed his presence and the joy he brought into my life, but this was better than nothing.

The final shot of rejection by my father caused me to become very bitter, cynical and lost. I felt the world owed me and my spirit hardened towards everyone and everything, except my brother. He had the capacity to melt my heart especially with his tears. Often during our meetings when he felt distressed, I would hold him and try to soothe and encourage him. I knew the pain he lived with, and knew that there would be ramifications and changes in his life from this experience and the anguish it caused. My hope for him was that he would recover and live a happy life and not be broken like me.

A few months after moving in with my boyfriends' family, my brother moved to Brisbane to be with my mother, and I lost any association and relationship to a reasonable, loving family connection.

Looking back the whole situation was a complete tragedy. All our lives were devastated and the family unit shattered by one event.

My father's relationship didn't last. Neither did mine. We were both damaged and lost souls without vision or hope.

Chapter 16

After my relationship deteriorated I moved to a small coastal town called Yeppoon just near Rockhampton with one of my workmates. I had secured a fulltime job in the Manchester department at K-Mart and was travelling to Rocky each day to work.

Two months short of my seventeenth birthday I met and moved in with a self-employed, twenty-one-year-old business man. I was infatuated with him. He made me feel whole again, special even. He filled the darkened, icy crevices of my being with his loving words and his caring actions. *I was in love.* I finally felt important to someone. Our lives, I thought would be like this forever a real life Cinderella fantasy. I imagined us intertwined as one being, as we had created a passionate connection, something I had never experienced before.

Two years into our relationship, cracks started to form and I realised I had chosen a person who could never make me feel good about myself. He was as damaged as I was. I just didn't see it at first however as we got further on in our relationship I understood he chose to shroud and block out his problems with excessive drinking and substance misuse. I recognised what I had done; I had traded my previous, unemotional, non-functional life and adopted his, only to find his was more emotionally dysfunctional than mine ever was.

Around the two year mark his appalling temper surfaced and at times he would turn violent. His anger was always followed by intense feelings of remorse, intensified by his long periods of excessive drinking and more drug use. It became a cycle that I couldn't control. I was not innocent in all of this, I had also become quite the drinker, I also had a mouth that could defy and enrage the strongest of characters, my verbal attacks could be brutal and I used them regularly to get what I wanted, a bit like an unruly spoilt child.

I knew this cycle was happening yet I did nothing about it. Identifying this reality made me feel more worthless and more inadequate than ever before. In reality, I believed I deserved everything he dished out. This was my lot. I was of the opinion my life would never amount to anything and his derogative words and hurtful statements only confirmed it. There was no one in my life to tell me otherwise, to show me another way and I didn't have it in me to positively talk myself out of these thoughts or feelings.

At nineteen I felt trapped in my life, trapped in my circumstances, trapped with a man I knew loved me but treated me with indifference. I felt I was unable to change my situation simply not knowing how. So our life continued in the same vein with both of us unwilling to change the destructive behaviours that dominated our life together. We simply allowed ourselves to be governed by drugs and alcohol and we succumbed to the pleasures they offered.

I became bored and depressed with how my life had turned

out, it had developed into something monotonous and pointless. Our daily life focused around bottles of Captain Morgan Rum, a few joints and listening to the harmonious melodies of Dire Straits.

Early into our relationship I learnt he was far more experienced in the drug scene than I was. I had smoked the occasional joint but that was basically it, I was quite naive in comparison. He on the other hand took drugs on a daily basis and had tried just about everything on the market, whereas I had never been exposed to this level of drug use. He became a great teacher and it wasn't long before I was experimenting with other more exciting drugs such as acid, coke, speed and pills. I progressed through them all with gusto and it added some spice to our relationship and took away the boredom I felt.

I didn't really like acid. My first acid experience frightened me, it was full of hallucinations, rising dark demons, moving objects, voices and walls that breathed. Coke was my favourite and often used. Speed just made my insides rattle and my brain accelerate. My thoughts processed so fast I couldn't grasp many of them, and marijuana made me so mellow and eat far too much. At nineteen, drugs were accepted and fully utilised parts of my daily existence.

We were surrounded by drugs, all our friends used them and to me it was normal. However, even in the drug scene there was a taboo culture, a scene most people didn't touch, yet I found myself drawn into it anyway. It was a culture I thought I would never enter but it fascinated me, it somehow beckoned me. Some of the people we socialised with were regular users. They were different from our other friends. Nothing seemed to faze them; they lived a peaceful quite functional life. They worked and some were parents, the problem was they were continually broke. They really interested me.

The whole scene appealed to me. It was a forbidden product, a societal no-no, and heroin users were considered outlaws who lived an unaccepted lifestyle concealed from the law. Their lifestyles full of risk, unknown hazards and danger, yet it fascinated me! My first experience was the best escape I had ever indulged in, better than anything I had tried before. Certainly better than the "mull" we smoked, heroin had substance to it and for a few months I would regularly indulge myself. I allowed them to blanket my turbulent life with its calming affects and I loved it as all my troubles were washed away with every hit.

When I look back, I never would have believed I could actually put the tip of a sharp needle on my own vein and stick it in. But, when the time came and the needle penetrated my arm, I did not consider my life in any positive terms. As a young child, I had so many dreams and aspirations; plans I wanted to achieve when I was finally an adult. Yet none of them occurred to me at that moment.

Shortly into my serious drug taking days I became pregnant. I was happy at the concept of bringing a child into this world. I believed that becoming a mother would alter my entire situation in a positive way. I craved unconditional love, or, my perception of what unconditional love was, being loved no matter what I did or said. I thought I would automatically receive that from this child. I also stupidly believed that my partner and I would become that happy family unit portrayed in magazines and television—rational thinking in my drug-induced haze at the time. However, it was a completely unrealistic expectation.

I thought if this philosophy was to work, I would have to learn some sort of mothering skills. This was a concept way beyond my reach, as my own relationship with the only role model I knew was not terribly good. So I would need to learn as I went. My mother's parenting and teaching classes were well and truly finalised when I was eleven, replaced by rigid boarding school ideals. So I had limited experience in any beneficial hands on mothering relationships. The difference was I knew I would never treat my child like I was treated, I would try a very different approach and I knew I would never abandon it not matter what. I would give it my best shot.

During my pregnancy I gave up all alcohol and hard drugs, however I did smoke marihuana the whole way through and after nine months I gave birth to a beautiful English rose, my daughter Jade. I would never make mother of the year, but, I loved her more than I thought humanly possible. My love grew with every passing day. It filled me and overflowed, and still there was room for more. I realised my bucket would never be full. I discovered the true meaning of unconditional love, but not from her; it came from inside me.

Looking at her and my new role as a mother unearthed something in me. It made me notice the real world I lived in and just how much larger it was. When I peered out the window I saw a vast undiscovered landscape one I had never seen before. My once tiny viewing portal became a large movie screen. Important life messages were waiting to be screened right in front of my eyes. I started to slowly take notice of the messages that were being broadcasted. I was not easily persuaded however I did stop some of my partying ways to be with my daughter. I was not perfect and I was not always good.

My daughter became my world. Her beautiful blue-green eyes filled me with a new found hope. She represented something I desperately wanted, a better life. I started to see my world differently and I started to question my life choices. I wondered if there really could be a better way for me.

My partner didn't like the constraints that parenthood brought with it, so, he continued with his nights out drinking and partying, this left me lost and lonely at home. This fuelled my sense of abandonment and rejection and I found myself self medicating my loneliness in a veil of drugs and alcohol.

Our true relationship was beyond repair. We just couldn't see it as it was hidden from view under a drug-induced coma, obscured from ourselves and the world around us. We lost ourselves and each other in a void that grew daily.

We existed like this for another two years whilst our daughter grew in strength and beauty. At twenty-one I was far from living the dreams of my youth, instead I was a mother who shared a volatile unstable relationship with a man who was incapable of loving me in the manner in which I needed. I used drugs and alcohol to self-medicate, so that I didn't have to really look at the world I had created.

Chapter 17

When Jade was still a baby, I was surprised to find out that I was pregnant again. I had mixed emotions regarding this pregnancy. I loved my daughter and saw how beautiful she was, and this enticed me to have another child. But, my thoughts regularly wandered to my behaviour, my drug use, my drinking, and I realised that I wasn't in what I would have described as the 'right head space' to have another child. I knew my partner would not support me if I did decide to go through with the pregnancy, as we had just separated again. I knew I would have to do it alone. This prospect terrified me. I had no skills or ability to find a job that could support three people let alone be a sole parent. I rationalised that my drug use could have potentially damaged the child, and even if I had stopped using, it would have been too late. So, I chose to have an abortion.

In the early part of the nineteen eighty's it was illegal to have this procedure done in Queensland. So I bundled my daughter up and together we caught the train down to Tweed Heads, New South Wales, where the procedure would be done, booked for me by a helpful and supportive QLD GP.

I arrived on the Gold Coast, left my daughter with a friend, and went to the clinic alone. It was a day I would never forget. I stood in front of the high counter and anxiously waited to be served. I was still unclear, undecided about whether or not to have the procedure. I wondered if I could I really do it. My mind questioned my intentions. Did I really want to go through with it? I started to think about what my life would be like with two kids and no partner? How would I cope? Was it even possible? Before I could mentally summon up any answers to the probing questions, a nurse offered me a valium, which I quickly swallowed. I yearned for the tranquillity and peace it would bring, and I welcomed the effects as they slowly crept over my body and stilled my menacing mind.

After completing all the necessary paperwork I was taken to a sterile, white-walled surgical room. The valium offering nurse casually prepared me for the procedure. I lay face up on the high surgical bed, draped in a light blanket. I was thankful that the room was silent and serene as I waited for the full effects of the medication to take hold of me. I surrendered to it and allowed it to blanket my turmoil in its soothing warmth.

The doctor entered the room, spoke some insignificant words that refused to filter through my haze, and the procedure started. I could hear the machinery as it hummed and pulsated in the background, like a hungry beast ready to devour its prey. I felt the vibrations of the instruments as they were placed inside me. Through my deep haze, I sensed the baby move. Its presence shocked me. I was quickly brought back to the reality of what was going on and what I was actually doing. At that same moment, I thought I heard it cry out, telling me to stop. But before I could get my mind and body back in sync the procedure was over and I was funnelled into a recovery area. Shortly afterwards I was sent home.

I didn't have to wait long before I felt that I had done the wrong thing, but it was too late and there was absolutely nothing I could do about it. The child was gone. Ripped from my body by my own doing, and I was nothing short of a murderer, and I felt like it. Even as I tried to rationalise my choice, knowing the truth that I was unable and unfit to raise another child, I still felt overwhelmed by the feelings of what I had done.

Since then, I have learnt what happens to the child during that process. It is literally torn apart piece by piece by the suction.
Learning this made my heart ache for what I had done. I had murdered an innocent child, my own child, not someone else's, my own flesh and blood, and not by mistake, but intentionally.

It took years for me to come to terms with what I had done. The hardest part was learning to forgive myself.

Shortly after going through this procedure, I returned to my home town, but I was not the same person. I felt traumatised by my actions and I knew I would never do anything like that ever again. A change had begun in me, a subtle change not visible on the outside but slowly building within me. I moved into a unit with another single mother and commenced work in the local night club.

At the same time, my father moved into town and attempted to reach out to me to re-establish a relationship. He called me without warning one day and invited me to meet him in the local hotel. I decided to meet him, more out of curiosity than anything else. I really can't recall what we talked about, but what I did notice was just how different he had become. I witnessed a real change in him. He was more content, happier, and he carried himself differently. At the time I could not put my finger on it, I just knew he was not the angry, confused man that I left all those years ago. He had found something or done something that made him healthier, happier and more content.

I tried to discreetly study him to ascertain the subtle changes I could see. What was it about him? He now possessed an air of self-control and self contentment. One change was blatantly obvious; he had given up drinking, for he sipped a long cold glass of lemonade. But there was more. I was curious. What else had happened in his life? Something had changed and it really intrigued me. He certainly got my attention, not by our conversation, but by what I saw, the subtle changes, his dress, his demeanour, his mannerisms they were all foreign to me. He was nothing like that man I last saw yelling at me from the balcony. We parted and he gave me a hug, even that act was unnatural. I couldn't remember the last time he had embraced me in any fashion. I couldn't believe the changes I saw. I wondered what had happened to him to change him so drastically.

As we parted, he told me he was praying for me. What a statement! *I thought he was joking.* However his face told me differently. *He was serious.* I didn't believe in any of that God stuff. Nothing good had happened in my life to make me believe in any form of God. I laughed at him and told him not to bother, for I was already lost and happy the way I was. In spite of this I internally pondered his statement (*my first real reflective period*).

A few months trickled by. I started to realise nothing in my life made any sense, it held no meaning, no purpose, Jade gave me purpose, but, my life still felt empty. I grew more and more unhappy as every day passed.

I reconnected and disconnected from my yo-yo relationship a few more times, dabbled with other people, but, nothing made me feel whole anymore. I tried to drown my life in alcohol, I took more drugs and I slept around more, and still nothing filled the void that constantly grew within me.

I started to see my father quite regularly, I even worked for him for a short period of time, nonetheless I still grew increasingly restless and nothing seemed to fulfil me or make me feel satisfied. I don't know what changed in my life, but one day as I sat sipping a hot cup of coffee, I looked at my beautiful young daughter as she played in the backyard and decided there must be more to life than what I was currently living.

I started to consider and evaluate my life's choices. I realised that my on-again-off-again partner of five years was never going to change from his drunken path and doing drugs everyday, which would make it impossible for me to become "clean". I started to weigh up where I would be if I stayed with him. I knew I couldn't continue on this path. I could see how completely self-destructive I was. I would kill myself if nothing changed and I could afford that as I had responsibilities, another's life was in my hands, one I would die for.

Chapter 18

Over the course of a few weeks I mentally planned to make a clean break, to leave my life in Yeppoon behind me. I could not see any other way around it. As I looked around me at the people I associated with, I saw visions of myself in days to come. I knew I wanted more from life. I also knew living in the same situation was not going to make change happen so I packed up all my gear (not that I had much left, as I had sold most of it to pay for drugs and alcohol), and I took off for another coastal town in northern Queensland called Townsville.

I spent my final night with my mother and shared our last supper together in her home in Rockhampton. Conversation flowed between us but was full more of casualness and superficiality than seriousness or significant matters. It was a precious moment in time that passed all too soon. As I prepared myself to leave I grabbed my mother and we held each other for a long moment, neither of us cried, but we both felt the weight of the pause between us. I saw the pain my life's choices caused her written on her face and portrayed in her slightly upturned mouth. The fact that I chose to run away from the life I had created to become 'clean' was not something any mother desired for any of her offspring regardless of the circumstances that guided them there in the first place.

And so the long journey began . . . .

I can recall, I sat in my old beat up white ford driving all day as the sun moved from horizon to horizon baking me in my seat and turning the skin on my right arm a shade of dark pink. My small daughter wearing only a pair of blue cotton pants intermittently slept curled up in her favourite blanket on the back hot vinyl seat. Her waking hours were spent quietly playing with her toys as the wind gushed through the windows swirling around her cooling her hot bare skin. I drove to Townsville knowing I was cutting my Yeppoon life off. I had absolutely nowhere to go and no support systems in place in Townsville, I had nothing. It was just Jade and me.

I drove this distance, well over six hundred kilometres, purposefully knowing I had no substances with me. I had no drugs or alcohol at all and no money to buy any. I had put a lot of thought into this journey and the goal I wanted to achieve. I wanted to kick the drug habit I had formed over the last three years of pure indulgence. I wanted to change my life and at the time I believed this was my only option. I knew I didn't have either the strength or courage to achieve this in a place where everything was familiar and comfortable and I was surrounded by temptation.

I remember that day as I drove into Townsville, it had been a really hot day. There was an overwhelming pungent odour of sweat and vomit sitting on the heavy oppressed air even though the windows were down the air hung around us gripping our skin. Jade had been car sick with the mixture of heat and momentum, chunky bits of food clung to her favourite blanket. I had already started the sweats, my body trembled and I had begun to feel really physically ill. Mentally I knew what I had to do, but, physically my body failed me.

I drove into the first caravan park I could find; it was a large park on the outskirts of town. I can't even explain it to you simply because I don't really remember any details about it. After years of working with people using drugs—at a much future point in the story than we are at this point—I know how dishevelled people can appear, how speech can be slurred and the smell that accompanies a person when they are de-toxing, well it is quite extreme. To the manager of the park I must have looked a bit like a train wreck as I pulled up to that office that day to hire one of his vans for a week.

Jade must have won him over with her cute little smile and dark spiky hair, because I doubt it wouldn't have been me in the state I know I would have been in. I paid for the week with the only money I had, a whopping $74.00. I stayed in the van for nearly a week as I "dried out" and fought to get my life back. I can't recall what happened to my daughter during this time. Nonetheless she was taken care of and by all accounts I doubted I would be nominated for mother of the year. I have no recollection of those first few days, or, who fed us, or, showered Jade. Someone was looking out for us. All I know is that we were okay and I had done it.

It wasn't long—days really—after the cleansing of my mind body and spirit that I applied and got a job as a nanny looking after two young boys. Jade and I moved into a nice two storey home near the beach with a pleasant divorced man in his early thirties and his two children. And for the first time since leaving Madang I feel my life started to move in a positive direction. A few months later, I moved into my own house close to the city centre and got a job as a waitress. Jade had turned two and had strongly bonded with her day care mother who freed me up to work in a more full time capacity and life started to look up.

As the days progressed, I felt more secure in my self and I felt more in control of my life however, I couldn't help myself. I folded to peer pressure, and when my hospitality work colleagues whom I partied with regularly shared their drugs with me and I accepted. The allure of them no longer held me captive and I could give or take them and at time refused to participate in the party drug scene.

Six months into my stay in Townsville my boss, who owned the restaurant I was working in, offered me a job as a call girl. I thought, why not? I was sleeping around any way. I thought I may as well get paid for it. So, I did. My new job earned me big dollars but it would be a short lived career change. I didn't really mind the work; yes I considered it to be like a job. The clients I saw were all ok, they treated me respectfully and some even offered me big tips, which offcourse I accepted gratefully. My short tenure in this new industry prevented me from experiencing anything distasteful or offensive. It came to an abrupt end one evening when one of the drivers lost some money in the house. The two fifty dollar notes had fallen out of his pocket and dropped down under the wooden stairs where I found it upon first light.

Offcourse I placed those crisp notes neatly folded in my pocket and denied ever finding them. I think he was a little annoyed with me, as he threatened me with a pending raid. Back in the early eighties prostitution was still illegal and a frowned upon industry. At the time I didn't see the irony of his threat and I panicked and packed up in the middle of the night and drove back to my hometown.

The drive home was fast in my new white ford, previously bought in Townsville and cooler with air conditioning. By the time the sun reached the eastern sky and Jade was waking from her pleasant uneventful night sleep I reached the town of Yeppoon. Everything looked different as I slowly drove up the streets. The shapes and colours were altered, distinctly changed from when I lived there previously. The hazy glasses that once covered my eyes were removed, revealing the true prospects of my future in this place. I noticed the scene hadn't changed, but I had and I didn't fit in anymore. The fact was I didn't really want to.

I tried to settle into the 'old' routine, even reigniting my old relationship with my partner, but nothing worked, the flavour had changed the spiciness had gone and everything was so annoying so monotonous. I didn't enjoy any of it like I used to, the fun was gone. To my Yeppoon friends I probably looked the same. Nothing had really changed physically, I looked healthier, my skin glowed with youth and my mind was sharper but, everything on the inside of me had. Mentally I was very different. Townsville offered me a safe place to grow and change my way of life, it provided me with enough time to modify some deep seated negative behaviours, attitudes and perceptions. Townsville showed me there was a lot more of life to be explored. I had tasted something different, something better, a new spice had entered my world and I didn't want to lose it.

Independence had changed me. My self esteem had flourished and I had learnt to trust myself. I had grown emotionally from my time in Townsville and I didn't think I could go back to the way it was before. So, I made another choice that changed the course of my life.

Chapter 19

Not long after my return, I made the decision to truly end my on again off again relationship. It was destructive and I knew it. At twenty one, I found myself a single mother with no employment prospects, no skills and on the road again with another substance abuse problem. It wasn't drugs this time; alcohol was my poison of choice. However the difference was I was not running away to get 'clean' I was running away to create a future. To make a life for myself away from the temptations and wiles that Yeppoon held.

I knew I couldn't move forward if I stayed in the same small town as my ex-lover, with all our shared friends and acquaintances. So, I made the decision to move away and start again. This was a big decision for me as my life was based in this town. But somehow I got the courage to pack up my life, get in the car and drive in the other direction this time, to the Gold Coast and Main Beach would become my home for the next short instalment of this tale.

This was my first big positive step forward; it was a real leap of faith. It was also the toughest I had known before. I had no friends; no home, nothing and I found it initially hard to settle. I had come down to the Gold Coast as my partner's brother and his family had offered me a place to stay. I accepted their offer, but the situation became quite uncomfortable and did not work out for either of us. So at the end of my first week on the Gold Coast I found myself homeless.

Being homeless was a whole new concept for me. However I landed on my feet, like someone up there was looking out for me. One of the other reasons I chose to move to the Gold Coast was because I had received a place to study in a Diploma of Hospitality being offered at a local trade school. The course was made up of a small diverse group of people each with their own agenda. We met our instructors each day at the Broadbeach Hotel for our practical training where we were placed in teams. I teamed up with a polite generous girl who had also just relocated to complete the course and we hit it off straight away.

During our second lunch break as we discussed our lives I told her of my situation. I was considering going home as I couldn't see another option. I could not afford the rents on the Gold Coast as I didn't have a job, so I was caught trying to live on the single parent pension until I could secure some work to support Jade and I. She was quick to offer me and my daughter her lounge until I could get on my feet. It was an offer I didn't refuse. I didn't want to return to Yeppoon and I genuinely wanted to finish the course I was enrolled in.

So I found myself sharing accommodation with two other people in a small ground floor, one bedroom flat in Main Beach and our room consisted of one three seater lounge and a coffee table that was used by everyone.

It was a very tough time. We had no privacy and Jade had nowhere to play or exercise her three year old limbs. I would take her out as much as I could. Actually we spent nearly all our waking time down on the beautiful sandy beach two hundred metres from our front door. Every day I woke up on that lounge I battled the voices telling me to go home. I questioned what I was doing, what sort of life was I providing for my daughter? In actual fact I wondered what sort of mother I was, especially raising a child in this environment when I knew a warm bed and home waited for us in Yeppoon.

Thankfully I didn't have to battle my thoughts for long as my circumstances changed quite rapidly, and again, it was like someone was looking after me.

A week into my couch surfing experience, a large two bedroom ground floor unit, with a large living area and backyard became vacant in the same block of the flats we shared. We signed the lease and moved in straight away. It was like heaven and things became mentally better for me. The move gave me some personal space and my own room which Jade and I shared. Jade could play and make noise and be a kid again. Around the same time, I found a really remarkable home based child carer to look after Jade, which freed me up to seek work.

All of this secured the deal for me. I decided that I would not turn back, it was obvious things had fallen into place for a reason and I wanted to give it a go. I unquestionable would stay and build a life for myself and my daughter on the Gold Coast. Yes, I had pangs of desire to return to my old life, but I had made a choice and I knew I would stick to it. I knew I was not yet strong enough to go back. I also knew I was still weak and could easily slip back into my old habits, and that was a life I no longer wanted.

Securing employment would be tough for me, or so I perceived. However, I had enough sense to realise even before coming to the Gold Coast that I needed some formal skill behind me to source a fulltime position. I had limited hospitality skills, simple basic bar skills except that I was close to completing my Diploma which would give me the piece of paper that would hopefully help me. I could pour a good beer and mix the odd drink, I had proven that in Yeppoon, but, working on the tourist strip on the Gold Coast was quite different than working in a small town bar.

To say I didn't feel adequate would be an understatement. Nonetheless the Hospitality School had put my name forward for an upcoming position at a five star resort called the Chevron Hotel in Surfers Paradise and I was thrilled and scared at the same time.

I was called for an interview.

As I conducted my recon mission I realised I had never frequented a place like that, it was quite spectacular. It was way above what I was used to. My local beer garden and the bars were squalid in comparison to this place, with its nine bars, three swimming pools, five eating areas, two night clubs, cocktail bar and shopping area as well as the motel and cruise boat.

My knowledge about working in a resort-style environment

like this was negligible. When I lived in Madang my family and I would frequent Smugglers Inn, a local tourist resort, for dinner and swimming activities, but it was nothing like the Chevron.

I was exceptionally nervous about myself and my abilities. I wondered what I could offer a place like that. I didn't have the skills right at that moment but I knew I was a quick learner and I would learn what I needed to know. I had to get through the formal interview, first. Someone believed in me enough to offer me this chance and it was a chance I took.

I can remember preparing for the interview. I wore the only suit I owned. I had just bought it a few months ago to attend an engagement party. It was a white skin-tight skirt and double breasted jacket that layered nicely in the front. It was by all means what you would call, a snug fit. It comfortably wrapped the curves of my body in its soft fabric. I liked this suit. I felt good in it, sexy even. My accompanying dark, strappy high heels were slightly too tight and constricted my toes, unnoticeable to others, but somewhat uncomfortable for me to walk in. They were at the time my only option beside my thongs, shoes I didn't consider to be an appropriate selection, so I slipped them on. I felt a bit like Cinderella going to the ball and my confidence stepped up a couple of notches.

I took one last long look in the mirror my eyes scanned for any imperfections. My lightly applied makeup perfectly matched my suit. I was happy with my reflection. I needed to at least look professional, even if I didn't feel it. I remember being particularly anxious, yet definitely excited. The slight twinges in the lower part of my stomach had taken hold a light sweat coated my palms. I started to build the dream, to visualise myself working in this resort. I marvelled at the fun it would be and pondered what I would do, who I would meet. Would I work in the bar, the nightclubs or the restaurants? Maybe, even the large conventions centre, which would be awesome.

The whole place was alive, bustling, like it had its own pulse. It was exciting just being there. I recollect meeting the manager of this five star resort for the first time, with hope and expectation in my eyes. I knew that if I obtained this position it would secure a future on the Gold Coast for my daughter and me and this had the potential to radically change the course of my life.

I was met at reception by a very proficient, well-dressed manager and a lovely, short-haired woman in her late thirties who wore a pink low-cut dress. I was escorted to an office and offered a cold drink, which I declined, my nervousness made my hands shake and I was concerned I may spill the drink over myself or make a mess.

We spoke for over an hour. During this time they both attempted to make me feel at ease, but my hidden apprehension prevailed anyway. Our conversation appeared to flow smoothly and positively. I still felt the volley and torrent of questions were more like an interrogation. I was lucky that I could think on my feet and more than once was glad I had the ability to expand stories to fit the necessary requirements of the interview process. After the formalities were completed, the manager said his goodbyes and thanked me for coming then left me in the care of the small, warm and friendly supervisor, who I warmed to straight away.

She directed and physically escorted me through the shopping precinct into a beautiful tropical barbecue area. I saw a paradise with overhanging palm trees and customised, concrete garden paths bordered by garden beds full of colourful flowers and small green shrubs. I was surrounded by it and the ambience of the place overwhelmed me, it was beautiful. This was the hub of the resorts recreational area. I also noticed well-tended large palms towering over and sending deep shadows over one of the two very large, crowded pools. Waiters in black shorts and pink floral shirts carried trays of drinks and tended to the many lounging men and women sunning themselves in the numerous plastic deck chairs on either side of the pool.

In the centre of the beautiful sculptured garden, stood a large open, wood Balinese-style hut. I saw and heard a barbecue plate as it sizzled and erupted; red hot flames danced and licked aromatic steaks and sausages. My eyes scanned and tried to process the whole scene as it unfolded before me. It was better than I had imagined.

My attention was drawn back to the hut where I noticed a tall, bearded man wearing a white loosely-fitting chef's outfit, as he calmly and conscientiously flipped small, searing, bleeding steaks. Another tall, dark-haired man in a pink, floral shirt and black, tight shorts leaned over the counter. They both cheerfully laughed at some insignificant, yet obviously humorous, topic.

I passed them, trying not to draw any unwanted attention, whilst my hungry eyes consumed the scene. My heart accelerated. The sound clearly and forcible announced itself loud and clear in my ears. It's quickened pace forced intense heat to flood throughout my body, which flushed my cheeks as blood coloured my face. I couldn't take my eyes of the stunning, muscular male before me. I wondered who he was. Did he notice me, I certainly hoped so.

I found I could not focus, my centre of attention was completely engaged on the man in front of me. Everything else in my world faded into the distance. My peripheral vision acknowledged, but couldn't register the words that were spoken by me escort, they just hovered around me lost in the breeze. Somewhere in the back of my mind I knew I should be listening to these words as they were important and would impact my life, but I couldn't do it.

The man in the chef's outfit noticed me first. His reaction was simple and primal. He looked intently at me, and then he leant over the barbecue counter and spoke directly into the ear of the dark-haired man. Both men turned and scrutinised me for a long moment of time. Their eyes blatantly looking me up and down, they surveyed the scene before them then whispered words passed between them. I obviously had become the focal point of their discussion. It felt like the bright stage light focused directly on me the main character in the Chevron stage play and the audience stared.

I heard a shrill whistle as it pierced the still air. It caught and absorbed my attention and a smile rose to my lips. I knew it was intended for me. I couldn't be sure who actually issued the shrill note, but I secretly hoped that it would be the dark-haired mysterious man. Either way it made my heart miss a beat and made every cell tingle within me. My face lit up as fiery flames flickered and crept up my neck and wrapped around my cheeks and turned them a blazing red.

I allowed my long, lustrous, dark mane to fall forward to partially conceal my face and cover some of the obvious awkwardness I experienced. My eyes dropped to the ground and firmly refocused on the heavy grey concrete beneath my feet. I noticed I was quickly being led out of the area by my escort who was disgusted at the antics of her staff. As we left the area my senses and reasoning returned and I realized that the woman was still talking. Her words became clearer, sharper and more coherent. She was offhandedly apologising for her employees' behaviour. I didn't mind, not at all, in fact I found it thrilling. My interview was over. I can remember I longingly looked back over my shoulder to have one last look, and then walked out the door.

She had provided me with clear instructions as we parted. I was to report back tomorrow for an induction, and commence work the same day. I was thrilled. I had done it! I didn't know how, but I had done something I didn't think was possible; I secured what I considered to be a decent job.

As I drove home, I contemplated the encouraging interruption of those two men and my heart fluttered slightly. I wondered if I would see them again. However, I knew that I needed to keep focused, simply because I needed this job to help secure a positive and productive life for myself and my daughter, and I could really not afford any form of distraction from that goal.

Chapter 20

My first day was full of laughter and fun. I was the new kid on the block; an employee who wore a low-cut pink dress, and one who everyone wanted a look at. Managers visited, staff dropped in, and curious customers questioned me and then gossiped about me openly. None of it could dampen my excitement. I was just thrilled to be working and to feel accepted by a really nice bunch of people. Days turned into months and my casual status provided a lot of money for our household and I started to feel more comfortable and secure.

I ended up working very closely with the two characters I had seen on that first day. The chef became my very best friend. He was charismatic, charming and funny, and the other one was an attractive, tall, quiet, dark-haired man who eventually stole my heart. The three of us spent nearly every waking moment together; we worked, played and partied hard. This life suited me and I felt I had finally found somewhere where I could be accepted. I felt contented. I would say I was even happy to some extent. *Whatever that, really meant.* Do any of us really experience true happiness, or, is it just something demonstrated in the movies. For me contentment was enough. My life was better, far more positive, more constructive than I ever recalled.

A few uneventful months passed filled with work and the creation of relationships. However I started to reflect on my life and its direction. I had some serious reservations about my choices. My new life encompassed elements that completely terrified me, like my budding relationship with John. I seriously doubted my own ability to maintain any sort of positive relationship. I was concerned for both our welfares as I doubt *I* had the capacity to keep it alive past a few years if that. My history spoke for itself.

I knew I liked this guy, John, liked him a lot. I just had difficulty believing I could do something remotely constructive with him. In my mind, relationships and the long term timeframe didn't go hand in hand, what's more was the thought of it scared me. Back then when I thought of relationships I always remembered the anguish I saw on my dads face that day at school, and a deep ache flowed into my spirit.

I internally questioned if John would still like me and want to be with me if he really knew the real me or would he leave like my mother did. At the time I had no idea what a real relationship was like, I know I doubted my ability to be in one. I wanted to try but I was so scared at letting go of what I knew was real.

I liked my new 'straight' friends and I loved living on the Gold Coast. My daughter was settled and she had made some friends. Despite all that and the security that surrounded me, I couldn't stop the overwhelming desire to run back to the familiarity of everything known and comfortable.

As I look back I can see I lacked the skills to adequately deal with some difficult situations or people. Talking and listening were traits I found hard when it came to conflict management. What I was good at was running away, avoiding, rather than trying to work through an issue. For me running was a lot easier than being put in a situation where I had to self-reflect or change.

I realised whenever I turned away from these hardships I never got to encounter what lay behind that particular door. Unlike Alice in Wonderland I sometimes never even peaked through any of the keyholes, so I missed experiences that I may have benefited from.

The Gold Coast picture I had created was just another one of those doors. The question was whether or not I could commit myself to stepping across the threshold and venturing inside, instead of hovering around the fringes. From the distance I glimpsed a land full of flourishing open plains of opportunity and destiny but in the background I saw the distinct outline of a terrifying active volcano which threatened the valleys below with its engulfing red hot lava.

On this occasion I leant forward and put my eye closer to the large key hole. I could feel the cool air tickling my nose as it flowed through the opening from the other side, but I pulled away before I could ascertain the future. What I did instead was rattle the key in the lock damaging the mechanics of the device.

With my key firmly planted in the lock I pushed John away. I turned into a manipulative bitch and made life hard for him. My negative actions and dominating behaviours caused us to split up. Retrospectively I thought I was unworthy of John and the life he offered. He was too stable, too kind and too nice to be with someone like me.

During our brief time apart, I reconnected with a guy I had once known from Madang. We were good friends previously, but had never really been together. At the time a spark sizzled between us, but we were from opposite ends of the spectrum. The only common ground between us was location and parental association. Our fathers played in a social band together, and we spent night's together, killing time.

I had not seen him since 1980 and a lot of things had changed for me since then.

His phone call came, quite unexpectedly and at the right time. He asked to see me. I was stunned he had located me, yet, curious to see him again after all these years. We got together and spent the night trying to reconnect, unsuccessfully. We talked about everything, we drank a lot of alcohol, but the spark between us no longer lingered. It had died in Madang, along with my vitality and radiance, and we would never see or speak to each other again.

Not long after my brief interlude with my policeman friend, John called to reignite our relationship, a fire burned deep within him and my absence would not put it out. Feelings between us both lingered. For the first time in my life I put real faith in something unknown to me, something I couldn't control. I weighed up the options of returning to Yeppoon but I chose instead to stay and see where the life on the Gold Coast would take me. Risky for a person like me, but I threw caution to the wind and stayed.

I did put a personal unspoken caveat on the decision, I gave it a twelve month timeframe and the limitation of taking things slowly and not making any future plans. I had rolled the dice and as they tumbled down the long velvet number covered crap table, I didn't place any monetary bets but in my heart I played the lucky seven.

I remember I rang my daughter's grandfather, as I didn't want to speak to Jades father, and told him I would not be returning to Yeppoon. It was an awkward conversation, where he wished me well and said they would see us again soon. I explained I had met someone and did not want, ask or expect support from his family. All I sought was space to see what numbers landed on the table and time to play my full hand.

I was weak, and I knew it, where Jades father was concerned. It mentally disturbed me how strong his emotional hold over me was. I knew my resolve could falter at any time if I spoke with him, so I didn't put myself in that situation. I was genuinely scared of the profound magnetism that life had on me. However what I did know was that time away would help me get stronger like it did in Townsville. Townville was a trial run before the real deal.

When I finally said yes to John to reconnect, I observed something powerful grow within me. I felt the bonds that held me to my old life *slowly* disintegrate. They were replaced by steel reinforced concrete pillars which sprung from a deep, strong foundation, John's foundations, based upon his more positive relationship experiences. With every moment and day that passed I grew stronger and my self-esteem soared. Inside me a tapped well was released. I was liberated from my oppression and Yeppoon faded into oblivion and became a fleeting memory. As the pressure dwindled I found courage to try things, I found courage to believe, to hope and to trust and I learnt to embrace the greatest of opportunities.

I was not perfect. Seeds of doubt still lingered, but as time passed, I found it easier to suppress them, conquered by a new determination to succeed at the life I had chosen. During this time I stripped off the clothes of my old life, discarded them like my winter wardrobe in summer. Time healed some of my wounds and a new person emerged. This persona may have always been there, but maybe had been invisible to the naked eye, covered over by layer upon layer of suppressed by feelings, situations, attitudes and perceptions.

Momentum carried the three of us forward at a rapid pace. My summer wardrobe rapidly expanded, filled with fragrances of hope and optimism. Each new summer dress I wore symbolised a positive experience, a conquered crisis, a triumph over a difficulty. As my outfits increased so did my self-esteem, which cultivated more confidence and optimism. It became a cycle of positive energy.

We all entered a realm where love was mutually offered and accepted, and where distinct boundaries lay.

Optimism replaced negativism.

Chapter 21

A good twelve months before leaving Yeppoon my father reached out across the rocky chasm that separated us to forge a new bond, a new relationship. It was rocky at first and I was doubtful but we soon settled into a well-established and acceptable routine. Neither of us could go backwards and neither or us wanted to. There was too much damage and too much change between us. We did however restart where we left off, picking up the pieces of a mess we both contributed to create.

I remember the first day he met Jade; she was one and just walking. Jade and I were at Roslyn Bay Harbour preparing for our trip to Keppel Island. The sun was tipping in the sky but it was still hot and bit at our exposed skin. Jade wore a blue sun hat which tied under her chubby chin and a pair of blue bathing pants. My father stood at the fence his fingers wrapped around the wire whilst his forehead was imprinted with the diamond patterns of the fence. Silence prevailed as Jade stood one side and dad on the other. A lone slow tear slid down my father's cheek which was quickly wiped away and was followed by an accented hello. The moment lingered as they stared at each other and the day moved on.

I saw dad a lot that final year, especially when he moved to

Yeppoon. Regularly I would walk along the hard sand pushing Jade as she sat quietly in her stroller, around to his flat where we would talk and consider the future. Our conversations never touched on past events. I think it brought too much pain for both of us, so it was a topic that would not be discussed for a few decades to come. When I decided to leave for the Gold Coast he was saddened but I could also see he was relieved I had decided to leave my life in Yeppoon. He didn't actually say the words but I knew he was thinking it. On quite a number of occasions he had been witness to the many arguments and violent clashes Jades father and I were regularly in. He had even enabled Jade and I to live with him when I had vowed my relationship was over, only to return, and dad would dutifully deliver me back into the hands of my partner and the saga would reoccur again and again. So yes I believe he was more than a bit relieved I had finally made the decision to live a life outside of this relationship.

His final words to me before I left stayed with me for a very long time. They continued to plague me for months. His words caused tidal waves of questions to roll around in my mind. I couldn't comprehend the meaning behind his actual words "I am praying for you" I didn't understand what that actually implied. I wondered why he would say that to me. My father 'the enigma'; he was so hard to understand, this was just another spanner he threw in to the mix to keep my wondering.

He was so different than the man who had raised me, it was disturbing. The transformation I had glimpsed was nothing short of a miracle, it was simply amazing. I wondered what had happened to him to change him so much. His anger, his drunkenness, his selfishness and the pain behind his eyes were all gone. He demonstrated something I longed for. What I saw was internal peace. Joy radiated from his face, it replaced the veil of pain and the mask of suffering he once wore.

I wondered but never asked how he stopped the storms in his life. I needed to know because mine raged constantly, sleepless nights plagued me yet he slept like a baby. I knew my internal life was in complete disarray, governed by negative talk and I didn't know how to calm the storms but he had done it, the question was how.

In the early months of my Gold Coast life I thought often about my dad's life and the changes I saw. He showed me what a dependable relationship could look like. He also taught me about forgiveness. I often contemplated the fact that people who love each other such as families offer forgiveness to each other. Forgiveness for everything—well, most things—the question for me was if I could find my circumstances forgivable. The answer was a resounding yes.

Our last meeting replayed in my thoughts and lingered for many weeks. However, like all things, the memory eventually receded into the gloomy dark corners of my mind, overtaken by life's activities. I just knew I like this new guy who was my dad.

The Gold Coast was a healthy choice for us. It had certainly offered a positive environment for Jade to grow and she flourished under these conditions. In spite of this I started to doubt my relationship would work out. I thought it would eventually end up being meaningless, with unfulfilled expectations just like my previous one. The problem was I had hidden secrets, secrets like my drug use, my days as a prostitute and the lies I told to maintain my secrets.

There were days, sinister times, when my mind persecuted me. It hurled insults at me about my dark past which wounded my self esteem and made me quite depressed at times. During those times I sought solace in my father's promise: "I am praying for you." I didn't understand its meaning, but I knew it was meant to uphold me somehow.

I tried hard not to think about my family, my parents and brother who I hadn't seen for a few years but memories of them sometimes just appeared. Even though we shared a very unpredictable, explosive and unstable relationship, I loved them. The history that bound us together was fraught with anguish, grief and hurt and resulted in a lot of conflict. None of this changed the fact they were still my family.

As I look back on our family situation, I can see where we went wrong, and why we all became so estranged, but when you are living in a situation, it is hard to see a single tree in a thick forest. I don't think any conflict should be a contest between parties. Rather, it should be used more as an opportunity to grow and learn. Unfortunately, this did not occur in my family. A battle of wills ensued, where neither side conceded, whereas, if we had learnt to communicate more effectively and listen to each other without judgment or criticism, we all might have changed the dynamics of the family as well as our thoughts and attitudes towards one another.

We could have learnt to be more accommodating, more flexible, more adaptable and communicate differently. Resolving conflict is rarely about who is right or wrong; it is about acknowledgment and appreciation of differences. I found it was more about unfulfilled expectations. I had expectations that were not filled and I guess my parents did too. I don't think I acted like they wanted or needed. I didn't feel loved or wanted. Initially I chose to punish my parents, but, what I really did was punish myself. I withheld myself from them not allowing them to help me.

Reconnecting with my father taught me the real meaning of forgiveness. I came to realise that it is always important to understand that we are all capable of making mistakes, and we do, I know I have. We all suffer misfortunes in life whether they are due to our own hands or someone else's; it is simply a fact of life.

We sometimes act on misunderstood or partial information. We do and say stupid things that we later regret because of our emotions and insecurities, and in the process, the collateral damage is people, and usually, you hurt the person you love. There is a saying that says, "hurt people hurt people". I know I did. I believe that it is up to us, as individuals to break that cycle, and that is what my dad did. He had the guts to come forth and identify and admit his part in the wreckage that had become my life. He reached out to me, he offered a hand to help heal me and I had the courage to take it, I found out when we choose to forgive, we change, and others change around us. Situations change, and that is certainly what happened to me and my parents. Learning to forgive them both was not easy, and it took a lot of ongoing work on my behalf. They had hurt me deeply and I carried a lot of hurts with me. As my father altered his attitude towards me, my behaviour also altered. I found I was more accepting of him and more forgiving, and deep down I realised I had missed his influence in my life and my daughters.

I also realised that blaming others for what was happening or has happened, doesn't get you anywhere. When I blamed others, I noticed I pointed a finger at someone else, but three always point back at me. When I stopped blaming my parents for everything that was wrong in my life, I actually started to heal, and I was able to take some positive steps forward emotionally.

I had lived with both guilt and blame which were equally destructive forces in my life. I hated being chained to the grudges and hurts of my childhood. I wanted to see the world through clear glass again, not through the dirty glass that I currently viewed it through. To do this, I knew I had to forgive myself. My actions of the past were done and could never be undone, so I needed to find a way to live with my choices, and deal with the guilt that came with them.

Forgiving my mother took a lot more time and effort on my behalf, because she simply didn't demonstrate the remorse or sorrow that was obvious with my father. She reached out to me the day my father threw me out, offering me a place to stay and for a brief moment in time I accepted her offer. However when I went to Brisbane she was living with another man who was not as accepting of me and I left to return to Rocky days after I arrived. A few years later her relationship ended and she later moved back to Rockhampton.

My relationship with her was casual but I was always reluctant to truly trust her intentions. I found myself questioning and searching for hidden agendas. However, in time, forgiveness filled my heart and I learnt to trust them both again.

Over time I have leant that my perception of difficulties aren't always a reality and if I broke them down piece by piece, it helped me to understand the underlying causes and helped me to reason a possible solution. Knowing this helped me when a negative thought came into my mind or I perceived something that made me feel pessimistic about my circumstances. I was far from a seasoned traveller in this area and sometimes I didn't succeed with it either.

Chapter 22

I had made my decision to stay. The allure and fascination of the Gold Coast had charmed me and I was committed to a dark-haired, well-built, broad-shouldered, quiet young man named John. My past still hung low over my head. It threatened to reveal itself and I knew I had to find a way to uncover it without shocking John. I was frightened if I didn't do it soon my new life would collide with my old life and I would be judged on the actions of the past before I could offer some sort of explanation.

John and I were like lightening and fire, a mix of two negative reactions. He was like lightening, me more like fire. Both of us brought baggage and heavy burdens into this union, but we forged forward anyway.

Lightening is beautiful to watch, brilliant in stature and power, bright and fast. 70% of its powerful flashes occur internally and when the negative particles meet, they form a very jagged path splitting the sky in two. The man I loved was just like this. He had a brilliant mind, he was confident, had direction, goals and dreams. He was powerful in his own right, majestic even. Yet, he kept himself closed off from the world surrounding him with cloudy barriers, like a safety net. He was slow to react as he internalized his anger yet at the same time he could move the dark clouds overhead and you knew he was not happy.

At the time of our union, I was more like fire. I constantly manoeuvred and manipulated the world around me to achieve my goals and to feed my internal furnace. My temperament could be a blazing hot tornado or it could be calm smouldering ash. My verbal, coiling flames could easily ignite anything. I was also able to propel searing balls of heat from my eyes letting you know I was not happy. I was sometimes like an unstoppable blazing firestorm that stealthily stalked and devoured its prey. As you can see I had a fiery temperament but I was also quite passionate about things and people. I did and still do however, lack diplomacy. My tact was a bit severe at times, my thinking could be rigid and my perception rather destructive. I could be judgmental, intolerant and critical.

In the beginning our lives focused around work, drinking and socializing and Jade. She came to work with us and the Chevron became her second home, everyone loved her and we all shared custody of her. They fed her, watched over her, played with her and entertained her and she loved it. On our days off we would take her to the local park or the beach where she would play for hours and hours. She was a happy and contented child and was never any bother to us.

John was a great father; he had a patience that I never had. He took her fishing, taught her to ride her bike and how to swim. She followed him everywhere. When our shifts changed and we were both placed on permanent night shift he sometimes took her to work with him and she would watch TV and drink post mix soft drink and eat chips in the closed public bar whilst he tidied up. Then she would curl up in our Kombie van and sleep until it was time to go home.

The problem of working in the hospitality industry for me was it fed my addiction and it certainly fuelled and encouraged mine. I knew I consumed more than my average share of alcohol but I didn't think it was a problem. At that time I wasn't prepared to give it up. I was having what I considered to be too good a time. It was something both John and I enjoyed.

We both worked regular rostered shift work and at times we were asked to work double shifts. We made a pact that suited us both—whoever finished first would wait at the bar for the other to finish. This was sometimes very dangerous as the staff often spiked our drinks and before I knew it I was 'off my face' so to speak. John and I would always meet up after our shifts and usually we danced and drunk the night away in a local Surfer's Paradise bar. Staff at The Chevron was offered one dollar drinks at the night club and most of us frequently overindulged ourselves as we debriefed after a long day.

One of those drinking sessions, assisted by over-exuberant work comrades, resulted in my overnight incarceration. I had just finished a long hectic day working in the pink elephant bar and went up to wait for John. I remember ordering my first drink, my favourite ouzo and coke, and the bar staff kept topping them up just as I liked, but this time I couldn't hold my liquor and needed to go home earlier than usual. Either John was later than usual or the staff had been really heavy handed.

We lived only a few blocks from our workplace. So I thought I could make it if I drove really slowly. I left my workmates and drove erratically home. The problems was I drove up the Gold Coast Highway the wrong way, for a short distance, and nudged a post box before parking. After I had fallen out of the car, I was greeted by a curious police officer, who received a mouthful of abuse about my rights to privacy, and that he should mind his own #$%^&#@ business.

I was informed of all of this later. My recollection of the whole event included sitting in the staff bar drinking Ouzo and talking to my friend, the chef. I had planned to wait for John as per our arrangement; however, I embarked on a treacherous journey, driving a lethal weapon.

I found out later John finished his shift shortly after I left and was completely unaware of the events that transpired or my whereabouts.

I remember waking up and finding myself lying on a very hard surface, a bit like a concrete floor. My eyes were blurry and unable to focus, my tongue and throat felt raw like I had spent the night yelling and screaming, my mind was fuzzy and at first I couldn't comprehend my surroundings. When my eyes could focus I noticed I was lying on a concrete cot secured to the wall in a small, windowless, open-plan, besser block room with bars across the only opening which faced a long brightly lit hallway. I was in jail.

I slowly sat up and tried to recall the details of the night's antics, but they wouldn't come forward, drowned in a sea of alcohol and the brain cells were swept away with the tide. A young girl sat in a cell directly across from me. She stared intently at me and assessed my movements. My legs were slightly unsteady, shaky as I rose to meet the uniformed officer who offered me a piece of cold toast lathered in vegemite and a cup of sweet luke warm tea in a plastic cup. I accepted these hand-outs, but was unable to consume any of them. I was more interested in the freedom that potentially awaited me at the end of the presented phone.

I was informed I had made quite a scene and I would not be released unless I paid three hundreds and thirty dollars, which was an outstanding fine I had been issued in Townsville after I left. My only option was to ring John, inform him of my situation, and ask if he could raise the money. I dialled the number, it was picked up immediately. His voice was tense and abrupt as he asked where I was. When he knew where I was our phone conversation became very short, one-sided and filled with suggestions and condemnation. A compromise was recommended and a deal struck between us. He was irritated, disappointed and frustrated with me all at the same time, but he came for me, paid my passage and released me from my incarceration.

A lesson was eagerly taught but this student was not yet willing to learn. I was initially embarrassed and filled with remorse and guilt but when we arrived home all these emotions were totally forgotten, replaced by the silent call of my inner being, an appeal for the 'hair of the dog.' I was being summoned to ease my self-inflicted pain and suffering, a request I was unable to forgo and I spent the rest of the afternoon drowning my sorrows much to the disgust of John.

I faced four charges as I left the police station, and a couple of days later, I was in court, ready for my well deserved sentence.

The court room resembled a large auditorium; rows of seats filled the room resembling a university lecture theatre. The judge presided over the proceedings from a podium located at the front. Numerous offenders like me occupied the hard plastic seats, awaiting judgment.

I stood before the judge who openly questioned my life skills and imposed a tough sentence. The judge took my licence for nine months and ordered me to pay nine hundred and seventy five dollars, both were a challenge and hard to bear. The loss of my licence was a very tough warning as it stripped me of my independence and freedom. It was a lesson I only needed to learn once, and it was one I would never repeat. The loss of my freedom to drive hit me the hardest; it prevented me from living my life the way I wanted. It restricted my social life and forced me to rely on John for all my transport needs which disempowered me and removed my autonomy. This situation irritated him just as much as it frustrated and displeased me. But guess what it still didn't change my drinking habits.

The transport situation was difficult as I needed to work and get Jade to the babysitter. At times John and I didn't have the same shift and it annoyed him to have to drive me when he didn't really need to go anywhere. It was an awful period of time. It actually forced us to move into a flat closer to work, which meant that driving was no longer necessary for either of us. This decision alleviated the tension that had formed between us.

Eventually I was eligible to get my licence again and life returned to normal. During this time our relationship grew far beyond just being room mates and after two years together we started to discuss marriage and children. I suppose this was a natural progression for a connection like ours. We loved each other. We shared a deep, profound companionship and had begun to create some lasting memories. However, our relationship was far from perfect. We both had communication issues; both of us had suppressed unspoken and unshared hurts which were sometimes corrosive to the relationship.

My un-revealed history was a persistent dark horse in our relationship. It always seemed to be there and I knew I needed to reveal it one day. His critical nature also brought major problems into our union. I was quite happy to maintain the status quo, changing the symmetry of our lives really concerned me, and my fear of marriage and the level of commitment it held frightened me. Previous visions of my parents' failed relationship saturated my beliefs and altered my overall philosophy about the stability of marriage. However over time, the fairy tale romance and the Cinderella story lingered in my thoughts and altered the inner feelings that conflicted with these stories and turned my sceptical thinking around.

I realised if I was to triumph over my fear of what marriage represented to me and this relationship, I would need to expose my secret identity and uncover all my classified activities. I didn't want to enter into this level of commitment with secrets that could potentially ruin our relationship later on. Marriage is hard enough without having secrets like I had and I wouldn't marry him without telling him the truth about who I had been.

The idea of unearthing my deeply buried, past petrified me. I knew it needed to be revealed, if we were to have a future together. Nevertheless the prospect of resurrecting my old skeletons brought forth a lot of apprehension and concern. I wondered how he would react and what he would think of me once he knew everything. Would he run for the hills? I tried to put myself in his shoes, but he came from a very different background than I did so it was hard for me to imagine how he would react. i hoped he would listed to everything I had to say and not make a decision before I had an opportunity to explain things.

Chapter 23

I didn't have much time as a date had been set for us to wed. I needed to give him the chance to listen to my story and then have the opportunity to make a decision about our future together. I would not lie to him; the time for withholding my story was over.

I remember that day like it was yesterday. We woke to a brilliant light as it illuminated a new day. It warmed the morning as we prepared for a sizzling barbecue breakfast and a laid back, sun-drenched day on the beach. We purposefully chose our position so we could keep an eye on Jade. I noticed she had chosen to wear her favourite pair of blue and white striped swimming pants again. I had offered many times to buy her other brightly coloured swimmers, but she refused, wanting to live in these well-worn ones instead.

I watched as she carried her bucket and spade and impulsively and eagerly ran towards the beckoning sand. I smiled as she fell hastily to her knees, the red plastic spade hovered beside her, poised to enthusiastically build any creative sand structure she envisioned. All the while her blue eyes constantly sought our attention and approval which I provided with a simple nod.

I mentally reviewed my surroundings, my eyes taking in the

scene like a panoramic snap shot. I gauged the conditions of the moment wanting to use the right time and the right place and then I revisited my internal checklist ready for my disclosure. To the bystanders we appeared like any other young family out enjoying the day. John, an innocent, unsuspicious man stood beside a sizzling barbecue plate and turned sausages as his child laughed and happily played in her own magnificent daydream. Standing tall and towering over all of us stood the majestic Gold Coast's famous Magic Mountain. The picture portrayed through the camera lens was delightful and peaceful. I wanted to remain suspended like this forever.

But I knew I couldn't. So, I positioned myself nervously in front of him, his arms naturally reached out to embrace me. I snuggled automatically into his chest but quickly withdrew and held his gaze for a long silent moment. I needed time to put the right words together and I wondered what sort of verdict would be pronounced today. I wondered if he would he rule in my favour. Could he possibly see reason and offer me leniency, or would he judge with prejudice and intolerance? My life lay in the balance and in a moment he may tip the scales that would cause me to fall to the ground.

I had selected him as my mate therefore he needed to know the real me. There was no other option. He had won the battle and my heart was the prize. Losing him now would leave a wound deeper than I dared to think about. An ache I would carry for the rest of my life.

His tender eyes searched mine. I saw hundreds of questions as they manifested in his mind but they stayed behind his stare. None of them were spoken. He just waited for me to speak. A long still silence hung in the air between us. I felt its weight and as it grew with every second. Eventually the words were revealed, filtered from my overactive brain to my slow responding mouth. As I opened my mouth a rapid burst of rambling words exploded like a forced computer download, data was processed, collated and displayed, all my past indiscretions were revealed on the screen awaiting assessment. The download ceased and my eyes dropped unable to focus on the analyst. I couldn't dare to look at the face I had grown to love. I just waited for the judgment. The judgment my mind had prepared me to hear.

It was a hard task to complete and when it was done I felt so relieved. No more secrets, it felt great like a weight had lifted off my life. All my hidden secrets were fully exposed, out in the open, they would no longer have the hold over me that they previously did. I would no longer feel their continued presence lurking in the back of my mind or fear the threat of revelation, I was freed and I felt it.

I looked up and watched his face change as the emotions surged through him as the data was processed. I knew him well enough to know he would be trying to rationalise the facts and stories I had presented to him. I witnessed many reactions as he mulled over my words. As I stood in front of him waiting for a response I realised both our values and principles were under intense scrutiny.

Finally he looked at me, I felt his grey eyes as they pierced every inch of me. It felt like I was being stabbed by hundreds of hypodermic injections all at the same time. I waited for the words to fall; words I knew would crush me. It would be over; there would be no absolution for me. I saw it in his face. I braced myself. My body was tense with apprehension, ready for the blow to come. I wondered if he would speak to me, the stillness was numbing, I wanted to yell at him to say something, anything. The outside silence was deafening but I was drowning in my own thunderous internal self-condemnation. If only he would speak. What made the whole scenario worse was he turned away from me and continued to slowly turn the sausages. At that moment I thought I would go mad.

I needed a distraction and I glanced at my daughter. I marvelled at her innocence, her youthful joy and unbridled happiness. She brought a smile to my lips and a gush of emotion touched my eyes. I hoped I would not have to relocate her and create a new life for us, it was not what I wanted but I knew it could be a possibility. We would both manage, she was young and adaptable, I just didn't want to do it.

I had laid myself bare to John, stripped off all the protective clothing of the past and now I stood nakedly before him, open and waiting for his response. He finally spoke. His voice was hoarse and thick with emotion and his eyes showed the depth of his feelings. I looked up at him and listened to the words that completely surprised me. His words were simple, straightforward yet clear, it didn't matter. What truly mattered was that he loved me.

I was shocked by his response. My confession was fully heard and totally understood. Both mercy and compassion were offered to me and I embraced them as well as him. Tears filled my heart and overflowed from my eyes, love had saved me and I welcomed it.

He did, however, put a stipulation on our relationship, one that I had no problem abiding with. He never wanted me to return to that life and the drugs I had taken, if I did our relationship would be over. He had offered me a chance I never thought I would ever get from anyone and I questioned why I didn't reveal my secret sooner.

An enormous wave of relief swept over me, its swell surged over every inch of my being, it drenched me with infinite freedom. I felt completely liberated. Life became limitless. I wrapped my arms tightly around him, pulled him intimately towards me and nestled my head closely into his exposed chest. I have heard the saying 'those who are forgiven much love much' and my love for this man mushroomed. I looked up into his face and I expressed my love and thankfulness to him and made a vow that I would keep until this very day.

Sometimes people reach a cross road in their life and they can spend a long time lingering there, unwilling to chose either path as they know the wrong choice could end something they had grown

familiar with. I had no problem in this instance, I made a definite choice to leave the past behind. For the past is just that, in the past, it can not be changed and looking back that far is never a cathartic experience. I had chosen a new life and the expedition had begun. It was a road less travelled in my life. It was a path
completely unknown to me, no footprints guided me. It was up to me to leave my own marks in the sand.

Not long after our discussion that gorgeous day on the beach late October nineteen eight seven we decided to get married and in January the next year we did indeed marry. It was a magnificent fun filled day shared with our family and friends at the Chevron hotel.

A few months after this event we moved to Rockhampton as John had secured a management position. This was a big decision for all of us and as I look back I wonder why we chose to do it.

Chapter 24

We are going to take a leap forward in time and leave part one here but one more tragic event occurred during that year, one of notable significance. The tragedy occurred in October, nine months after our happy day and seven months after our relocation to Rocky. It was an event that shook and weakened the foundations of our newly formed union. John's father was diagnosed with cancer and subsequently died a slow and painful death. At the end stage, John flew to be with his family and sat by his father's side, day after day, witnessing the pain and suffering he endured right to the end. Shortly before his father passed away, John's employer fired him for being away without an end date.

John returned to Rockhampton to no job. The loss of his father and the regret of our decision to move away—when we knew his father was ill—caused John's world to crash around him. The bricks and mortar that once held his life together fractured and as he was struck by overwhelming grief and sorrow, both of which consumed and filled every crevice of his life. His tortured soul scorched all his other feelings. I found there was little room left in his tightly coiled life for my daughter and I. He pushed us away, made us outcasts in our own family as he stood alone outside the family circle. Jade and I became independent bystanders, powerless to comfort him. We watched his life unfold on a distant stage, most of it I saw played out on a drunken platform. All we could do was sit back and observe his internal eruptions and continue with our lives and hope he would emotionally come back to us in time.

For a long time, I watched and waited as John slowly clawed his way back to our family. I lacked the skills to help him recover and deal with his grief, therefore felt useless in the whole process. John took on a part time position at the local swimming pool as a life guard and this somehow helped him battle his internal demons and dislodged them from their previously dominant position in his life. What he did do was transfer his unhealthy grief and depression into an obsession with healthy exercise. He started to run, and he would run for hours. The weather never seemed to faze him, he ran in the pelting rain or the searing heat.

We never really know which lives we influence or how or even why they are influenced. From my perspective it appeared that my father's encouragement must have inspired John to emerge from his dark and looming depression. In nineteen ninety John sought direction, and whilst we lived in Rockhampton he and my dad spent a lot of time discussing career options. John wanted a career with meaning and for a time his aim was to follow my father in his chosen path—air traffic control, but after missing out on the intake John decided to join the Army and we were moved to Toowoomba.

This move isolated me. It isolated me from my family, the people I was just getting to know again and it prevented me from rebuilding a sense of family with them. I also found myself with no support systems and I was left to raise Jade alone on an army base with no friends and no job prospects. It was a hard blow.

John's new position and the Army culture was a stressful change for all of us. John's long hours, coupled with his frequent trips away, resulted in him becoming more introverted, distracted and withdrawn from the family unit. His job was very secretive and he was not allowed to share his work with me, I found this quite hard to understand and this made him withdraw further from me. He spent long hours with his workmates debriefing and drinking in the bases 'boozer'.

Army life certainly put a hold on us rebuilding our relationship which had been seriously damaged after the death of his father. I felt like we were at opposite ends of the pole. I craved company and he was away sometimes more than he was home and when he was home he was not mentally with me, so I started to create a social life 'outside' of the army culture. I secured a hospitality job which enabled me to meet new people and regain some independence. I fostered meaningful relationships with others outside of our marriage, relationship that John was not part of. This isolated and divided our family further and my marriage really started to suffer.

When John was home, communication between us was quite limited. We were two people who shared a house, with no common goals and no common purpose. I wondered what had happened to us. But I soon realised, I was living a life that resembled my parent's relationship. It was one I had vowed not to copy when I first entered into this marriage.

I guess the frequent separations, our fragmented goals and shattered dreams, as well as our apathetic responses, resulted in both of us building two separate lives and contributed to the loss of what we once both cherished. John began to drink heavily and the army way of life encouraged it. It reminded me of the Madang culture where my parents used to drink and party all the time and look what that did. I remembered the damages this had done to my family and I tried to stop John from taking the same path and destroying my life again. But this was a mistake my opposition only made him drink more.

The more he drunk the more my life changed. I no longer felt the same desire to drink and party like I did on the Gold Coast. I guess because I had no one to do it with so it became less of an influence or priority in my life. I think as I watched John suffer during his time of grief it made me realise there was more to life than partying, family was important too. I decided to go back and study and attended evening classes at TAFE to get a certificate in exercise physiology. These lessons changed me further, they enlightened me about the importance of maintaining a healthy lifestyle and the benefits it could bring.

A couple of months into this course, I decided to become a vegetarian and adopt a real healthy lifestyle. This was a life John was not remotely interested in actually he was completely opposed to it. He knuckled down and so did I. Our compromise included both of us doing our own thing and he continued on his path and I continued on mine.

His absence and our family estrangement and constant conflict made me increasingly unhappy. I tried to refocus all this unhappiness into work and I took on more and more hours and spent more and more time away from John. The result was I became a workaholic. I traded my addiction to drugs and alcohol for the achievement of goals.

I had become a fitness instructor who taught up to thirty classes a week, worked weekends at a local golf club and managed my own catering business. I would coerce, push and direct myself to achieve, achieve and achieve. This just caused me to become physically and mentally exhausted.

A distinct wedge grew between John and I. We spent more and more time with others pursuing our own interests. Separating would have been an easy option for us both at this point, as there was no glue that held us together anymore. Our marriage was basically over in principle, it just was not yet formalised on paper. We did actually part for a brief period, but for some reason we didn't separate permanently.

In nineteen ninety after John and I had temporarily separated and reunited, a young family moved in next door to us. I found myself drawn to the young girl's charismatic personality. Her name was Sue, and she was younger than me with two children and pregnant with another. There was something very different about her. She stood out from the rest of the army wives. Serenity, happiness and peace surrounded her, yet her living conditions were exactly like mine. Our husbands did the same job, our houses were cramped and confining and both of us were parents.

The difference between us was not apparent on the outside but she had something I didn't. What I noticed most about her was her ability to see the positives in everything, even when life was turbulent and lonely. Her passion and commitment to her marriage and children was unmistakable and quite remarkable.

We spent a lot of time together and we talked a lot. At first just over the fence, then over a quick coffee, and later I found I spent a big part of my day with her. She really interested me. We shared our experiences and discussed almost anything. However, I didn't tell her of my deeply hidden secrets of the past. Those were darker topics I would not share with anyone. I placed them away in a bottomless cavern, unattainable and out of sight.

During one of these sessions, I came to realise just how much patience and empathy she had for others—something I had never considered in my self-centred existence. I wondered why. I cared about people in my own way. I just didn't display it the way she did. I wondered what was so different about me.

The more we talked the more I found myself comparing myself to her and others, especially those that appeared to be really happy. It was not that I was really unhappy with my life, I just didn't have the contentment and peace that others around me did.

John and I were getting on really well but . . .

Sue opened up to me one day, and explained she was a Christian. I questioned what that meant. She described how she chose to live her life with hope instead of in fear. A concept I had never considered before. I feared just about everything. I feared losing my marriage, being broke, I feared all sort of things. This concept seemed unreal to me. She went on and stated 'faith was knowing the things which we expect, but are currently unseen, will come to pass'. I didn't understand her words. They might as well have been double dutch, for I could not grasp their meaning. I needed time to digest her statement. I mulled the words over in my head for weeks trying to find its true meaning, before I could come back and debate this philosophy with her.

My analysis came back to the belief that people always have a choice in life. We can choose a life full of fear or a life full of hope. However I realised it is just as hard to choose a life full of fear, as it is to choose a life full of faith. She said that faith teaches us that we are not the centre of the universe, but something bigger directs events around us. Wow! This blew me away, and once again I went away challenged and contemplative.

One day, unexpectedly, she quite matter-of-factly informed me that she was praying for John and me to have another child. Her next statement took me by surprise, as it was completely outrageous, but somewhere in the back of my mind it sparked a desire and hope. She told me I would soon fall pregnant and have a son. I thought this was laughable since we had been trying on and off for years.

Incredibly, a couple of weeks later her premonition about my pregnancy came true! This made me question everything I thought I knew and believed in. My pregnancy made me question a lot about myself and about her philosophy. I believed in a higher power, but a

God like she knew, that was something totally different, something unknown. When my child was born and I saw it was a boy, her words stirred deep within me. They reawakened a belief system that I heard about once born from a time I spent with my dad. I began to think that maybe, just maybe, there was something to this God thing.

How could I not believe? Something wonderful had occurred, because a baby boy, a promised child, lay in my arms. As I gazed into his beautiful face I started to understand what she meant when she said we are not the centre of this universe. The world did not revolve around me or my little unit, but there was something much, much bigger in the world than I had ever imagined.

Over the years I have reflected on our talks and the seeds she planted in my life. However, at the time her seeds were sown on barren ground, they were unable to produce deep roots, and the plants they produced were unproductive and fruitless, and like my father's words before them, they faded into the background of my life. I was simply just not ready to hear them or understand their full meaning.

It wasn't until much later that I realised that a hand had been offered to me, but my arrogance and pride overruled any sound judgment. These traits prevented me from pursuing something I desperately needed: guidance and wisdom.

I witnessed Sue's life, I witnessed her joy and listened to her wisdom. I saw it daily as I observed the way she lived and interacted with others. She had shown me a life full of promise, hope and grace. However, when our lives parted, the cares of the world triggered a case of amnesia, and I forgot everything I had previously seen.

As a result of my ignorance and lack of desire to change, I found myself in a continual cycle of destruction. My life was like a yo-yo. I was up one moment and down the next. I was unable to find a balance like the one Sue had shown me.

For the next ten years, nothing would change. Our location would, our jobs would, but our lives didn't, we were trapped in a cycle neither John nor I were ready to change and life was often tough.

I was just like the Eveready bunny—a battery operated bunny who just goes and goes and goes. I spent my 30's and early 40's working, working and working. I also studied as I tried to find myself. Work became my primary focus and I lost sight of everything else in my life. I thought all my achievements would be enough. I thought this would bring me fulfilment, but I found the more accolades that hung on my wall, the emptier I felt. I forgot who I was and I was mad at myself. I placed my worth and value on achieving tangible and idealistic things. I put unrealistic expectations on myself and then got angry for not being able to get off the treadmill of accomplishment. What I needed to find was rest.

But of course I didn't.

I became more and more autonomous, self-sufficient and independent. I isolated myself and lived my own life. I simply pushed my family away and lived my life selfishly and lost sight of what truly mattered. These years were surrounded by turmoil and hardship simply because I failed to listen to an internal voice which told *me* to change.

I refused to explore the possibilities of changing myself. I was trapped in my defiant, self-defeating frame of mind. I would not venture into or believe in things unseen or unproven.

But life has a way of making you change and one day, the cold surface of a sledge hammer struck me in the back of the head and it forced me to stop and listen.

Our family in happier times in Sydney (1972)

In happier times on my father's boat and a Night out with the family at the Madang Hotel in Madang (1975)

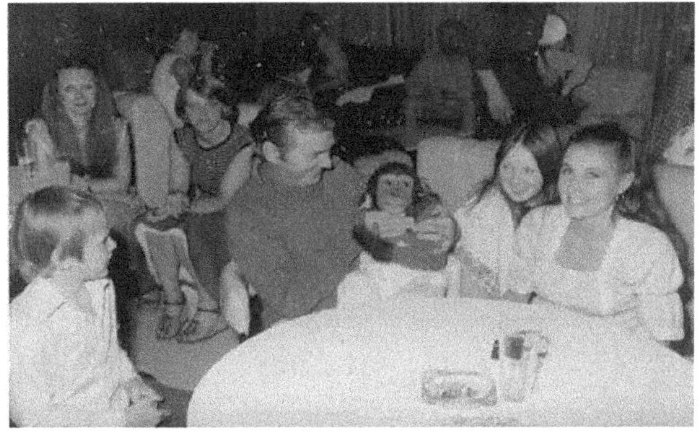

Flying back to Australia after one of my home visits (1977)

St Hildas School Southport (1976)

Part 2

The Awakening

Laurie in Queenstown New Zealand (2004)

Chapter 1

Welcome to the real world

In my early 40's, a light bulb switched on. It glowed brightly illuminating and broadening my vision and understanding of the way I had lived my life. I can remember I began to create new mental pictures based around a life I wanted. I would day dream about how happy I would be in the future, the holidays I would take with my family, I pictured it bright and colourful and vivid. Over time I learnt to focus on a more important heartfelt and contented image of myself. It was a mental picture that made all my other pictures—up till this stage—look like a miserable hollow mess in comparison.

As my mental state became more positive, change started to occur, deep and valuable changes that would carry me through many future hardships. None of it happened quickly. A lot of subtle changes had to take place before I could even get to this stage. Looking back I think it took a good ten years of preparation and learning from the many mistakes I made during my thirties. I guess in my forties I finally realised I didn't like a life full of turmoil caused by my selfish decisions. Decisions like a distressing and costly family move to Scotland after my husband left his army career—I thought it would be fun and we would all enjoy it but it was hell-, three more big family moves and new schools for the kids—I can't even remember how many schools Jade had been to over the years-, and then there was my idea of purchasing a business—which subsequently failed because of some personal conflict and I lost interest.

All of this and much more caused me to honestly and earnestly look inwards. I started to see myself as other people indisputably identified or labelled me. What I saw in the mirror was not the label I had on myself. I saw fear and determination. I also saw complete acceptance and awareness of the hardship of life all in equal measures. However as I really studied myself, I didn't like the reflection I knew others saw. I became aware of the simple truth that I had grown into a middle aged woman who was insecure emotionally and psychologically vulnerable to the impulses of the world. The history book of my past had deeply anchored itself. These anchors had grown strong deep roots which tightly wrapped their spindly tentacles around my wounded soul. Over the years I had fed and watered these roots, encouraging destructive thoughts and memories which just created a bigger world of distrust.

I would often stare at my reflection and ask the same question. The image never lied. "Mirror, mirror on the wall how fair would my life be" and it held back no secrets to its audience, me. The illustration I saw was tragic pictures of my life portrayed as a one continuous act in a movie scene.

During my twenties and thirties all I wanted to do was get on the stage in front of a large audience, wait for the curtain to be lifted, so that I could be applauded for all my achievements. When I looked at the real representation of my life, through the eyes of the mirror, I realised I wasn't as good as what I thought I was. The visual representation I saw showed just how driven I was. I certainly had achieved a lot in my life, but, as I looked deeper and focussed more on the shadows and the non-descript images in the background, I started to notice silhouettes and outlines of various other shapes. As my vision grew sharper I realised these shapes represented the collateral damage in the wake of my achievements. The bodies bloodied and beaten strewn in the corridor behind me, people I had treated poorly, trodden on to achieve my selfish goals. What I saw horrified me. I saw the faultless faces of the people I loved looking up at me. As I saw this image for the first time as a spectator, I witnessed just how much my family had suffered under my autocratic rule, and a cold chill enveloped me and water spilled from my eyes.

That image haunted me for a long time. I think the catalyst for my internal change began when John took on a short but intense relationship with Amway. Amway promoted the daily reading of motivational and self-help books and tapes, and John religiously adopted these strategies. He continually listened to tapes in the car and left books lying around with the hope I would listen to them and vicariously I did. He often shared positive stories with me, ones that inspired and motivated him and after a while they changed his life. I sat on the side lines and watched him change.

What I witnessed was he became more positive, more open to change, more open to experience new things. What I saw in him all those years ago was what I was trying to do in my forties; he had just started the process ten years earlier than me. The biggest change I noted at the time was his skills as a father. He became a great dad demonstrating a new found patience, empathy and love. I also recognised his self confidence and social skills improved. It was during this time I came to understand the impact positive affirmation and self help books and tapes could make to a person's life.

Even though I was aware of the changes I refused to support him and his quest to build a financial empire for our family. How selfish of me. As I look back on that situation now I know I was wrong to not offer support. I was mistaken and critical of Amway, my judgement was very misplaced, it wasn't really about the products or the selling it was about the positive affirmations and the systems for self-esteem growth that really mattered. But we can not go back and fix a wrong. All I could do was acknowledge the injustice I served him through my stupidity and negativity and apologise for my actions. I would have no idea how my actions and words affected him or the mental injuries I caused him, until much later in our life. He simply never discussed any of his feelings about my behaviour or attitude with me. Truthfully it was not something I even considered until many years later. If I could take my harsh words and criticism back, I would, but obviously I couldn't. I wonder just how many opportunities like this one are presented to us throughout our lives and how many we let slip by us, or simply miss out on because we are so selfishly consumed or too fearful to act. If I had only stopped and supported his journey at that time, I may have prevented myself a lot of future heartache. But . . . . Life is a wheel that continually turns and the present moments continue to devour the past whether we like it or not. I know at times I have thought I need more time in this current moment to understand and experience the lesson or witness something miraculous but before I know it the moment has gone, sucked into the vacuum of the past. At that moment it becomes a passing memory to be relived only in my mind or timelessly verbally shared with someone. It becomes a twinkling reflection that fades with time, like everything else. The darker side of this is the hurtful memories can lie in the murky recesses hidden away, lurking waiting for an opportune time to strike you with guilt or shame. It wasn't until it was far too late that I realised the error in my ways and what I had actually done to John by my action and beliefs.

I did start to read some of his books and I found the uplifting motivational true stories in the numerous books he had purchased truly inspired me. I found they were all principle based with strong threads of ethics and morals and I liked that. But it took quite a few years ten in fact before any of the practices would be adopted seriously into my life. I guess in effect what occurred was a seed was planted deep inside me and it needed time to grow.

Years later I would experience a life defining moment. I read something that had significant impact on me. In 1996 after we had returned from our venture in Scotland and returned home broke and disillusioned I picked up a book which essentially triggered a personal mind-blowing revolution. It became the medium that initiated a real awakening in me. It turned and shone a large fluorescent stage light on my personality, my nature, my behaviour and my attitudes. Then it showed me the same reflection I had seen before in the mirror only this time it was from another perspective. I saw a dramatic and heartbreaking pantomime of how I had affected people around me. As I sat and watched it jump from the pages of the book I was more than shocked I was traumatised by the images I created. It was a simple book with a yellow non-descript cover called personality plus by Florence Littauer. It was my first, but not my last, exposure into the realm of understanding the topic of discovering and understanding the differences between the varying personalities and sexes.

This particular book made me contemplate and scrutinise my whole outlook on life, my belief system, my actions, my perceptions, my faith and mostly it made me re-evaluate my treatment of others. To say I learnt how to really empathise with others through one book would be a lie, this was a characteristic, a feature that took more than just a few months to build within me. It took years. This book started the *practical* process of change. Up until this point I think I was being mentally prepared, after reading that book I understood how to change from a practical perspective. It highlighted and featured my weaknesses and exposed them right in front of me. How blind I must have been. I wondered if I was the only person who went through life blindfolded.

I knew the words on the paper and the ink that coloured the pages spoke the truth. I simply couldn't deny what I knew in my heart to be true. I hated what it revealed to me, but I would not deny it, I knew I couldn't. Once my heavy dark glasses were removed everything became crystal clear. I saw the world, my world, in its entirety. It had been so full of chaos and suffering, yet it didn't have to be. I had lived forty years in a dream state, a perfect hour glass created from my little bubble of reality. This book kicked off a chain of events that would ultimately bring about a true deep change within me.

After reflecting on the books content, I was abruptly stopped by one of life's little truisms, a cliché. I could no longer emotionally afford to continue to go over the same speed bumps in my life. Driving my life at such a frantic selfish pace was costly, mentally and physically.

Chapter 2

A change of direction takes hold

By the late 1990's my family had matured, Jade was in her final year at school—a really costly time as any parent knows. Children in this age bracket have more tangible and sometimes unpractical needs that need to be met. Social outings—*they just have to go to*, school requirements—*they need to attend*, formals and the list goes on and on. My son's requirements were a lot simpler—for now—but needless to say as the century changed so would our household needs change and they did.

We were at a crossroads we knew we both needed more money and time to chauffeur the kids to social events and school based activities, and we also had the Aussie desire to own our own home. In the early 2000's we made some big changes to our household. John replaced his meagre funeral directors income with a government position and a I exchanged my home based part time health and fitness career of fifteen years for a position at the same location. This was really difficult. I had to start at the bottom of the ladder again. Over fifteen years, I had previously worked my way up from an aerobics instructor position to centre management then finally owner operator of my own gym and personal training business. So starting at the bottom again was a bitter pill to swallow.

The new, more stable, positions we had taken were with the state government, working in a local correctional centre. It offered both John and I more time off as well as a stable household income and job security with superannuation and benefits, something I didn't get working from home. We both worked three, twelve hour shifts followed by three days off on a rotational roster. John worked in a completely different area than I did. He was responsible for front line support operating all the electronic systems and centre security, me I was in what is known as prisoner management, responsible for humane containment and looking after the needs of prisoners.

I really liked the roster; three days on followed by three off was magnificent. It provided what I needed, stable income and more time to spend with the kids. It also granted me the *opportunity* to find some sort of work/life balance. People often talked about this work/life balance thing. I never got the concept. The other phrase I would hear a lot was 'work to live not live to work'. To me life was work, everything I did required some sort of effort, driving Bill to soccer required effort, taking Jade to work required effort, cooking dinner required effort, even lying on the beach requires some sort of effort—you have to hold the book and enjoy yourself, so in reality I couldn't work out what it was I trying to balance. On *my* days off I spent time with the kids as planned and continued to train a select small group of long term personal training clients. To me I had a fairly balanced life, I thought.

However not long after I started working at the prison, it must have been late November in 2002 because I remember I had just finished my final exams for my degree, when my life split in two and I realised I didn't have much life balance at all. An event so sudden struck me and forced me to live two very different lives whilst haunting the same body. Neither of them was pleasant or enjoyable but living like that enabled me to achieve and overcome what I needed to at the time. I am getting a bit ahead of myself, but I am sure you will understand the meaning of this shortly.

It wasn't long before the excitement and enthusiasm of working in that hazardous and dangerous environment wore off and was replaced by dreariness and boredom. My three days on shift became like the dismal grey rainy days on the set of my own soap opera. For me Corrections was overly controlled, regulated and highly structured. It was a system that didn't allow for any sort of social conscious, one that I was just creating and learning about. It discouraged innovation, it had rules and rules and more rules, ones you had to obey or else . . . . It was undoubtedly constrained I had to suppress all my creativity as well as my own innate personality. Every day, I had to mentally leave the 'real' me behind at the front gate. I would then pass through the first security screen and pick up the façade that Corrections needed me to be and every day I did this my spirit died a little more.

Emotionally and physically, I struggled under the weight of

this highly structured environment. Over the years I had learnt for me to positively grow I needed independence and individualism not dependency or domination and I got both in this environment. My whole life I had made my own decisions and set my own goals and I found I was unable to do either. What I felt was oppression. It was like I worked every day in a dark enclosed restrictive ditch which made it virtually impossible for me to create any sort of bright futuristic picture. Over time I came to realise that my vision was obscured by the heavy window drapes that covered each cell window. These coverings concealed any potential opportunities not only for me but for the prisoners as well.

After a while I was able to pull the drapes back and really look at the world through the prison cell window. I saw a very different world than the one I expected I saw how weird the place was from this perspective. I struggled with the concept of contentment under that environment. The officers all around me were comfortable with the conditions, satisfied with the money, content with the hierarchy, pleased to be a part of the system which I most definitely wasn't. To me their stance just wasn't rationale. This difference of opinion made me question what was wrong with me. I wondered why I found it so hard to be content like most of the officers around me.

Towards the end of 2004 I mentally battled to go to work each day. The problem for me was I felt as confined by the working environment as the prisoners did by the razor wire that contained them. I didn't know how to overcome the feelings of containment and restraint so I turned inwards and changed my focus to intensive study and I completed the Certificate IV and the Correctional Diploma in record time.

As Correctional Officers, we had many daily mundane duties. We sat for long periods of time babysitting prisoners, who interacted in the playground of incarceration away from society. We watched and monitored everything; we wrote reports, filled in logbooks and drank lots of coffee and I studied. Sound exciting? Corrections was a far cry from its Hollywood depiction. Tom Selleck's portrayal of the prison system in "An Innocent Man" was not what I saw. Communal showers did not exist and they were not hunting grounds, nor were there any George Clooney/ Brad Pitt type masterminds plotting a series of Casino heists. In reality it was dead boring, completely un-stimulating and un-motivating. However, there were also days when I have never felt more alive, more alert and more on edge. Adrenalin coursed through every inch of my body as events unfolded.

We were all well trained and practiced in how to handle situations and stabilise unruly prisoners. We were also well rehearsed in incident management, administering first aid and of course report writing and we did all of these often, daily even. However each situation was always unique. Similar patterns often emerged, but because we worked a rotational roster with different people, in numerous locations with different prisoners predicting incidents was sometimes not possible and we were at times taken by surprise. Clandestine activities occurred often. Illicit drug trafficking, acts of retribution, assaults and power struggles, as well as taboo relationships were just some of these activities.

These acts resulted in a whole of prison response and included daily cell and prisoner searches, targeted urine testing, drug busts and sometimes officer assaults. Both the prison and the officers considered drugs and the paraphernalia associated with drug taking including prison made injecting and tattoo equipment to be the biggest threat to staff safety. This was due to the violence that occurred as a result of drugs and the circulation time of the needles—some 'picks' had been in circulation for two years or more—and the amount of prisoners sharing and using the equipment was high. This increased the risk to staff of exposure to a blood-borne virus through a needle stick injury or potential weapon.

It was one of these incidents that exposed me to the full force of the sledgehammer's blow. Its impact struck me with such might that it turned my whole life upside down. Remember I told you I lived two separate lives simultaneously well this is the time when they really started to disconnect from one another. And here is how it happened.

I remember I was working the last shift of that round and was looking forward to the next three days off. It was seven am, I arrived for my shift and stood outside the control room with ten other officers, coffee in hand as we all chatted whilst we waited for the daily supervisor to facilitate the scheduled morning briefing. The meeting began with its usual review of the previous day's activities and then he explained that intelligence had informed the prison of a suspected drug breach and we all had to thoroughly search each cell and accommodation area.

He placed us into groups then instructed us not to release any prisoners from their cells until we had thoroughly searched the whole area. We were specifically instructed to look for drugs and any drug paraphernalia. Dread filled me. I hated those sorts of days. Those events always irritated and frustrated the prisoners and some became so infuriated with their situation they became physically aggressive and verbally abusive. I understood their reaction. I would not like people dressed like police officers, people I didn't know or like, searching through all my personal belongings and removing anything they deemed not necessary or unimportant. Imagine if numerous uniformed strangers barged uninvited into your home, then made you stop what you were doing and forced you to stand outside of your house on the sidewalk, in full view of the neighbours inquisitive eyes, whilst they meddled and intruded in your safe place, touching and examining everything you owned and cherished. I am sure it would make you feel disempowered. If this was to happen to me, I would most likely get angry and give the officer a bit of lip in the process as I know I did the night of my own arrest years ago.

Our task was straightforward, time consuming yet simple. We were required to strip all the prisoners bedding, thoroughly search the mattresses and pillows, remove all excess linen and clothing then urine-test targeted prisoners. I was externally unobjectionable as this was part of the job I had signed on for, however it didn't mean I liked it, actually I hated this aspect, I found it distasteful and provocative as it usually ended with someone being abused or worse. I knew as the supervisor explained his intentions the day would be slow in passing and would most likely be filled with lots of paperwork and reports. In past event similar to this the prisoners would not be let out of their cells until the sun had started to dip well into its westerly position. I knew the task set would take us basically all morning and the prisoners would be very unhappy with the conditions and treatment.

As I walked with my partners to the prisoner units to commence our duties the correctional resident dog squad caught my attention. Four combat ready officers and two un-muzzled German shepherds controlled only by the tight leather leashes stood awaiting our arrival. Internally my mind screamed 'oh no, here we go'. I can remember looking at my partners with a sinking feeling in my heart, their presence was not a good sign, obviously they were looking for something in particular and had some intelligence to confirm their suspicions, otherwise *they* wouldn't be there. My partners and I all knew the day had the potential to turn horribly wrong . . . . violent, especially when the prisoners saw the dogs and the squad in their units. Sometimes,

their presence calmed the testosterone fuelled anger but I had also seen it go the other way more often than not. I hoped no incident would occur in our unit.

Six officers, including myself, slowly and methodically

searched a block of units and another set of six officers searched the adjacent units. The prison was made up of three areas residential, secure and high security units—residential units allowed prisoners more freedom, autonomy and easy access to their bedrooms, (this was an area prisoners worked towards getting into), secure units consisted of four concrete double storey wings with a fully secured fenced exercise yard. Each housed fifty prisoners. A fully computerised monitoring station sat in the middle of the four wings like a tardis—that's what we called it. It enabled the two control room officer to monitor and record all internal (within the units) and external (outside the units) movement such as prisoner work detail, attendance to educational classes or to visit medical.

The area I worked in was the high secure units; this was usually the first area a prisoner came to after his initial induction. The prisoners in this area were sometimes less compliant, rebellious and demanded a lot more attention as they worked how the prison system worked. Here also there were double story concrete wings, just in a different configuration. The major difference between secure and this area was it consisted of three wings with two sets of units instead of the one area with four units, each high secure unit had thirty two cells—fifteen on the bottom and seventeen on the top, instead of fifty, they both had a very large living area and outside exercise yards. In both areas none of the exercise yards allowed any physical access to the other, however they were visible to one another and prisoner could converse but were unable to pass anything between units.

I remember the morning dragged on endlessly; we finally finished searching the thirty two units, the living area, kitchen and exercise yard as well as conducting the designated drug tests just before lunch. We didn't uncover anything suspicious. Actually we found nothing of any real significance except excess clothing and other items not belonging to the specified prisoner. Those particular items were removed from the prisoner's possession and they were 'bagged and tagged' for return to the stores area where they would be washed and reissued to other prisoners in need. Another officer tightly wrapped all the items in a single white sheet tying it up like a knap sack to make it easier to carry to the supervisors station where it would be further processed then forward onto the stores area.

I was glad *that* part of the day was over. The dog squad had been and gone and only a small skirmish occurred, with one antisocial opinionated prisoner taken away to the detention unit. All up the event had gone *ok*. The dogs actually frightened me with their deafening bark which echoed and bounced from wall to wall. They were all large beautiful looking animals and quite well controlled by their handlers, but they still were really very vicious creatures. They were German shepherds of all colours, ages and sizes which could not differentiate between prisoners or officers and this fact was what concerned me. As officers we were trained not to look directly at them as they passed us, if for some reason they were loose we were instructed to lay down in submission.

Thankfully I never had to actually put this tactic into practice.

After we had completed all the paperwork and reporting schedules for our confiscated clothing, we decided it was time for a much needed and well deserved break. Whilst the rest of the crew enjoyed their steamy hot cups of coffee, I picked up the heavy, awkward white sheet and decided to take it up the wire encased walkway to the control room. I didn't have far to walk forty metres or so, but, I remember the weight and size of the bundle made it difficult to carry requiring constant readjustments. As I neared the control room, the bundle rubbing close to my side, I felt an intense burst of hot sharp pain, like a wasp sting mid way up my outer thigh. I looked down at my leg, then at the bundle, wondering what it was. What I saw surprised me. I caught sight of something long thin and silver sticking out of the sheet. As I focussed on it I noticed it wasn't a needle, but it was an implement sometimes used for tattooing. It had obviously not been secured properly in a plastic container, which was the normal procedure.

I guessed my movements must have dislodged the contents of the bundle making it possible for the sharp implement to pierce through my clothing and stab my thigh.

A second or so later I summoned up the courage to finish my task and I walked without difficulty into the control room. I encountered none of the usual time-consuming barriers that routinely slowed down all prison movement for the gates and doors were all open due to the full prison 'lockdown'. I noticed two officers as they sat side by side managing the buzzing communication systems, monitoring cameras and numerous touch screen computers as they electronically opened cell doors and recorded events as they unfolded within the six units. The well seasoned supervisor sat behind them overseeing all their methodical operations.

At the time I found it impossible to look at any of them as my mind raced with the dire possibilities of what had happened on the walkway. I had little to fear as no one even noticed I was in the room; they were all far too busy. I figured they had most likely seen me on the walkway and realised my task was menial and didn't require any further attention—which was true. I have to say I was very relieved I didn't draw any attention to myself.

I dropped my burden on the soft carpeted floor in the open supervisor's office, located at the back of the prominent control room. I heard the commotion in the next room as work continued unabated. I left the status report on the only unoccupied spot I could find on his large over crowded, paperwork laden, messy desk then quickly and silently slipped into the adjacent unoccupied toilet to check out the seriousness of my injury. I was uncertain and hesitant as I stood in that small unappealing cubicle at the back of the control room. I tried to assess and rationalise the situation from my limited perspective, whilst my work colleagues continued to monitor and record. When I removed my starched uniform pants I saw a raised swollen patch of skin with a spot of congealed blood in its core. I knew with absolute certainty, the sharp instrument in that bundle had caused the small open wound I was looking at.

Possibilities raced through my mind, all my logic became misplaced, replaced by instinctive paranoia.

I sat in stunned silence on the cold steel toilet seat and my mind filled with disbelief and apprehension. The small cubicle closed in around me, crushing me. I thought of many things during those first few seconds, it's strange just how many thoughts go through your head when you stop and listen to them. My family, my life, my health, my friends and how stupid my actions had been.

I knew from my training, many prisoners were infected with Hepatitis C (HCV) and HIV. Up to 60% of them were infected with one or both of them. But, as I sat there all I could think about was me. I wondered what my risks were. No response was available to me in the quiet cubicle, the walls spoke no answers. I considered whether or not there had been blood transference from the sharp implement and my leg. HIV dominated my thinking; it was all consuming in its graphic representation making me question what I would do if I got infected with HIV.

I tried to think of anybody I knew who had come in contact with any of these diseases. I couldn't recall one name. I didn't know anyone. Images of the frightening 1980s Grim Reaper campaign, depicting unsuspecting people from all walks of life as they cowered on a bowling lane and waited for the Grim Reaper to bowl them over, completely shattered my resolve. I recall the small cubicle grew more stifling, more unbearable as each second slipped by. It became hot and oppressive and the air stank with the rancid smell of old urine, crusted on the toilet seat. At that moment anxiety was set in motion, activated by persistent disturbing thoughts. My heart rate rose, my senses more alive than before. I thought I might pass out with the smell, the heat, the confinement as the nausea took root in the pit of my overburdened coffee rich stomach. An overwhelming desire to get free spread over me.

I slowly emerged from the toilet not wanting to draw attention to myself but seeking fresh air before I was physically ill. As I stood at the door panic surged within me like waves pounding the shore line, threatening to knock me off my feet. Tremors unhurriedly crept up my body. They started at my toes and moved up to embrace my face. Each muscle individually collapsed, knocked down like a row of dominoes staggering and falling one after the other in slow moving swells.

The hardest thing about that moment was the fact I was unable to think rationally. I was mentally unnerved by the whole incident. I got more flustered as the minutes ticked by. I can't remember how long I stood at the door but I must have looked a real sight because when the supervisor *did* notice me he summoned me into the privacy of his office. He asked what had happened. Descriptive words quickly discharged from my mouth as I told my tale. He listened intently, processed the problem as a veteran of his years would and then ordered me to go immediately to the medical centre for a full physical assessment.

The medial centre was located in the lower part of the prison, a good five minute walk through numerous electronically controlled gates along a camera monitored steel enclosed walkway. I knew my journey to the medical centre would be quick and easy due to the prison lockdown. However I could slow my pace offering myself enough time to think, away from any potential forthcoming prying question, questions I didn't want to answer. And that's what I did. I slowly wandered alone and unaccompanied down the long, secluded passageways, through the huge steel gates and into the multi roomed fully equipped medical centre.

A friendly nurse greeted me at the door. On that particular day I hardly recognised her, even though she was very familiar to me. Like a puppy I followed her as she ushered me into the reception area. I was on automatic pilot, my body travelled but my mind was trapped elsewhere. It tried earnestly to recall everything I had learnt at 'screw school'—the Correctional College of knowledge as the officers called it—about blood-borne viruses. And even after all the training I had attended, I couldn't recall *anything* except the simple basics about HIV. Time for the moment, had ceased to exist. All I can recall experiencing was a continuum of fear and anxiety both of which dominated that particular instance.

Deep in my mind a recollection appeared. A lesson I had once attended on the topic of BBV's was dredged up. All I could think about was the throw away derogative comments and jokes bantered around the room, born predominantly from a lack of understanding and knowledge, as well as a lack of sensitivity and the adoption of the prevailing social stigma society embraced. I will be honest here and say I am not innocent as I participated and fed these jokes as well. In my defence I didn't know any better, at the time.

This makes me more aware of how people can be misguided, misled by a fear of something. What came through really strongly to me was that Corrections did not embrace a supportive culture when it came to Blood-Borne Viruses. Officers like me, despised the potential risk of infection caused by working in confined spaces and associating closely with infected prisoners. The subject was never openly discussed, but we were all aware prison rates of blood-borne viruses were substantially higher than the rates within the community and this posed a bigger risk to us as officers especially if we were in a scuffle with an infected prisoner.

Social stigma is not unique to the prison system; it is also endemic within the community and many current workplaces. Looking back it is easy to see why. People simply fear things they don't recognise or can't control and BBV's are terrifying when you don't understand the *real* risks or how they are *really* transmitted. My fear was underpinned by my level of knowledge at the time. As I stood in the medical centre in the middle of the prison, all I could think about was how people would perceive me if I was to become infected. I felt I would be shunned by not only my work mates and my family, but also the rest of society. If this was the case then I questioned how I could work and live amongst people who would potentially fear me, fear what I carried, fear what I could potentially give them. I feared it. The many screaming voices in my head asked what I was going to do if I picked up something. They also questioned how I could let this happen to myself. This made me re-live every step I had taken. I remember standing there feeling stupid and foolish for my actions, foolish for not taking any precautions. What ifs and could haves exploded across the minefield of my brain.

Reasoning and logic arrived when the nurse broke through my reflection and asked what I needed. I saw her eyes as they scanned my face and assessed my behaviour. I retold my story, this time including ever detail. She listened intently then led me into a large, well-lit room where a large examination bed covered in a clean starched white fitted sheet stood in the centre. Floor to ceiling shelves decorated the walls. These shelves were heavily burdened with varieties of surgical implements, dressings and medicine bottles. She instructed me to sit on the edge of the table. My legs dangled over the edge of the elevated platform upon which I sat. I undid my stiff uniform pants and allowed them to drop around my ankles which gave her access to my injury. When I looked down at the wound I noticed it had become quite red and the puncture site was swollen and raised but no traces of blood remained, most likely it had been absorbed into the stiff fabric of my pants.

She swabbed and cleaned the area as I waited for her verdict. She smiled and then hesitantly touched my shoulder for the briefest of moments, her soft contact reassured me. Her sympathetic words were spoken softly yet clearly. She stated in her opinion I had definitely received a puncture wound to the upper outer section of my thigh. She explained the importance of seeing my local GP as soon as possible to get a Blood Borne Virus test. I sat and quietly listened as she explained she could have done the test on the premises but the results would have been recorded on my staff file and that was something she did not recommend. She didn't explain this statement however I understood her meaning. I was not about to question her as I was fully aware of the implications this situation could bring about not only for me but for my husband who also worked there. I knew how bad the gossip mill was and knew it could potentially make life difficult for John as well as me. Staff would discriminate, maybe not on purpose, but they would, simply because of a perceived risk to themselves. I really didn't want to open that can of worms, so I told her I would see my GP in the morning.

We talked for some time about the principles of transmission and my risk factors. Neither of us knew what 'the implement' that stabbed me had been used for, although we both suspected tattooing which would mean the presence of some blood, not necessarily infected blood. Neither of us knew, who had come in contact with it or when it was last been used or even if there was any infected blood left on it that could have entered into my leg. Lastly we talked about the potential exposure to the weather; if the implement had been left in the sunlight the virus would be unlikely to survive, thus reducing my risks further. There were a lot of unknown elements I needed to evaluate before I considered the fact of a potential infection.

She spoke sketchily about the actual viruses HCV/HIV, but my mind was unable to comprehend any more information. It was overloaded. I simply couldn't take anymore information in. I just wanted to leave and process it all in my own time. I needed time to be alone to think. I can recall her last parting words of support she simply stated "the risks of contracting something, anything at all, are minimal." I wanted to run. I wanted to scream at her, at anybody "take this away from me" but, I was trapped in the middle of a scenario I didn't want to be in at all. There was no escape for me. There was no easy way out. All that was left was the reality of what had happened and the future decisions I would make.

She presented me with an option to go home, or stay and finish the day. Every bone in my body and every internal instinct told me to run, to leave this place, but a powerful personal petition held me in place. I reasoned through a quick check list; home alone to wallow, with too much time to think. I would be alone with the blackness of my thoughts and the voices that created hurtful scenarios as I waited for a doctor's appointment. Or, I could pass the day quickly and return to work. The landscape looked brighter more beneficial with the second option. I chose to stay instead. I rationalised I had three days off the next day, so I knew I could deal with the situation then. I completed all the formalities, signed the necessary paperwork and left the medical centre. The slow walk back to my unit offered me time to think, time to clear my head and put on the face I needed to wear to get me through the day. The journey also provided me with time to make distinct future plans which would start the next day with the test.

The supervisor was far too distracted by ambiguous events as they slowly developed in the units. He had completely and thankfully forgotten my personal incident. It was the best way to slipped back into the workday without drawing attention to myself. This was probably the only time I was truly grateful for prisoner tension occurring on my watch. None of the other officers noticed my absence or my return either as they were on high alert to a pending incident. So I casually slipped back into my allocated position like nothing adverse had occurred, and continued with my duties, no one but me the wiser.

Shortly after my return my early morning prediction came true. The hot, unhappy prisoners newly released from their small air-conditioned cells had become very noisy, demanding and disruptive. They had been locked away for over eighteen hours without access to coffee making facilities or any food preparation facilities—during the lock down periods we fed them pre-made ration packs consisting of sandwiches a piece of fruit and a cup of tea. All that pent up energy was released along with the pungent odour of stale sweat and unclean male bodies; it filled the workstation as it was pumped unfiltered throughout the whole unit.

As the day progressed the officers grew more and more annoyed as prisoners paraded their troublemaking activities in front of them. The prisoners knew offensive and challenging behaviour would bring trouble, the dog squad was only a phone call away but I think they most likely wanted the attention. A break away rebellious group, in another area unfortunately stepped right out of line; they pursued and taunted an unsuspecting young victim and viciously assaulted him, this caused absolute mayhem within the unit. Prisoners not wanting to get involved scattered and hid whilst officers pulled their personal duress alarms. High pitched sirens rung in all of our ears as vigilant officers signalled for immediate assistance. And there I was right in the thick of it all, caught up in responding to the needs of others and forgetting about my personal plight, just like I wanted.

Chapter 3

Homeward Bound

"Love is a miracle, a vision to see"
Sheila Walsh

It had been a very long and tumultuous twelve hours but it finally came to an end. Like every other work day, we securely locked away and counted each prisoner, participated in the daily debriefing session, then waited for our own release. The supervisor, totally distracted by the incidents, the assaults and the required reports, never inquired as to my condition or my incident. All was thankfully forgotten for the time being. The last responsibility of the day shift included all area supervisors communicating a status report to a section we called 'master control'. Master Control coordinated all internal and external prison movements and controlled the entire electronic system during the night shift. However no staff were allowed to leave the centre until all prisoners were secured and accounted for and all areas had transferred electronic control to the overall night commander. So every night the high secure sectional staff waited by the closed steel gates for the voice that offered freedom. I heard the words which issued our release and officers of all persuasions scurried through the opened security stations to their waiting vehicles, eager to return home, me included.

As I drove home my thoughts and reflections returned to the chaotic day's events. I deliberated on the testosterone fuelled prisoner fight and the injures which occurred, a split lip, a black eye and other facial bruising followed by a physical battle between blue uniforms and prisoner browns and the long accompanied and handcuffed walk to the detention unit where the perpetrators would stay for a few days to cool off. I have to say I was truly glad that day was over.

My car pulled into my street and I noticed how particularly beautiful the yard was in the dim summer light. The large circular orange moon hung low in the sky, just above the horizon,—it settled slowly this time of year-, it awakened the sleepy nocturnal native wild life from their daily slumber. The moons' reflection bounced of the stagnant water as it lay dormant in the shallow easement that bordered our two acre property. It was really picturesque. I can remember as I slowly turned the car into my long gravel driveway all the memories and feelings of that day revisited me, they flooded back, like the fast flowing waters of a Tsunami. I fought hard to keep control of my emotions; I couldn't afford to succumb to the same level of anxiety that I had experienced earlier that day as I knew I needed a clear head so I could explain everything appropriately to John.

I parked the car in the garage and for a few moments I sat and thought about the right words to say. I felt like a real idiot, my actions had been stupid. I should have checked and rechecked the security of the bundle, I put myself at risk and I felt foolish for it. I wondered what John would think of me, I was sure he would think I was as stupid as I felt when he heard my story.

Out of the corner of my eye, I saw movement. John had inquisitively come out of the house to see what I was doing, why I remained seated in the car. He casually opened the driver's door then persuasively stood beside the car, his eyes searched mine for an explanation. Before I moved from the car, the words came. I bit down hard on the bullet that represented my day and I spat forth words like gun powder. I dropped my personal bomb. It exploded and shrapnel surrounded this unsuspecting man and an emotional gloom hung in the air around us. The silence that followed brought with it the full impact of the incident and once again the blast hit me in the face and fear detonated and wrapped itself around me.

I saw his usual lopsided smile fade then return a second later, the way the rising moon does when it passes behind a small cloud. He took me by surprise, yet again. His reaction to my story similar to another story I told him long ago, on a beautiful sunny beach on the Gold Coast. He reached into the cold vehicle and purposefully grabbed my hand. His large warm fingers engulfed mine. He guided me out of the car to stand close to him, the body heat welcoming and inviting. In the dark silence of the garage he drew my trembling uniform clad body to his and wrapped his big muscular arms around me, blanketing me in warm hearted hospitality. He leant forward, his soft lips kissed my tear stained face and I knew once again we were as one. His solid, unwavering presence comforted me.

Even in the darkest of moments in our lives, a declaration of love can bring hope and the gift of faith. His positive affirmation blanketed me like a soft warm layer on a cold winter's night. He stood firm and declared that together, we would meet this head on. Together, we would conquer whatever was dealt us.

Together, hand in hand, we walked into the house, united and with a set purpose to overcome whatever would be thrown at us.

Over a light scrumptious candle lit dinner—a variety of flavoursome tasty cheeses, sun dried tomatoes and stuffed olives all in a enticing array—along with a glass of light red wine, we discussed the whole distasteful scenario in detail. Together we pulled it apart, assessed every aspect and analysed everything. Here with my dependable husband, in the safety of my home, I didn't feel as troubled or apprehensive as before. After hours of conversation, both of us assumed the chances of getting infected with a blood borne virus was very small, impossible even, and for the briefest of moments both of us dismissed the whole scenario.

As per my schedule, I made the appointment and saw my local GP. There was no concern in his voice only professionalism, as he heard my horrible tale. He explained it was highly unlikely I had picked up anything. Nevertheless he thought it best to go through the testing process, even if it was just to put my mind at ease. I gathered the paperwork and drove the short distance to pathology lab and a proficient phlebotomist took a sample of my blood and sent it away for the necessary test including HIV, HBV, HCV as well as syphilis.

My GP wasn't overly concerned. I felt I had closed the window on my doubts and any residual uncertainty I felt was only a small current of air let in only by the voices from the dark passenger within.

Time progressed fast and before I knew it, I was back at work for another round of three days, three days of monotony, boredom and demands.

The first of three concluded, uneventfully and I was eager to get home. That night I was the maverick guiding the mass exodus of blue uniforms as we all converged on the front gate. I reached my car and sat quietly for a few seconds watching car after car as the hurriedly drove towards the exit. I switched the radio on, Billy Idol belted out one of my favourite tunes. I turned it up nice and loud. The words to 'white wedding' blasted in my ears, vibrating the small rear car speakers. I sang tunelessly along with every word as I started the car and set my sights on John at home.

I allowed peaceful thoughts to cleanse me of my day in prison. Somehow the oppression I carried all day whilst working in that environment was released when I walked through those front gates. The air seemed cleaner, no way near as foul. I allowed the music I played on the way home to spill from my open windows and permeate my whole being. It helped me rid myself of the heavy burden of working under such an authoritarian institution and by the time I arrived home I usually felt much more relaxed.

I remember arriving home and simultaneously walking into the house and freeing my body from the constrictive uniform I was required to wear. I walked down the slated narrow hallway into the spare room, its door hung open, hungry for a friendly occupant and inviting me to disrobe. As I entered half undressed I yelled my usual welcoming greeting to John. I unceremoniously threw my clear plastic work bag on the blanket covered large double bed—all work bags needed to be made of a clear plastic compound that visibly displayed everything officers brought into the centre. Another regulation . . . . I waited for a response as I indifferently hung my uniform on the hangers ready for the next day's use. I didn't have to wait long as I felt John's presence behind me.

Smiling, I half turned. He stood in the hallway. In the dim light I noticed an anxious, distressed person, not the man I expected to see. He stepped forward into the room and grabbed me by my shoulder and pivoted me to fully face him. His green-grey eyes penetrated and pierced me with a silent, intense stare. He cleared his throat. I knew he had something important to tell me. The way his mouth twitched and trembled, I knew this was not a good sign. I saw emotions there that I had not seen for some time, a combination of anguish and anger. His voice was soft and kind, but also very direct. He said, "the doctor has left numerous phone messages for you to urgently contact him." I quietly listened to his words, knowing they were of significant importance, and tried to find and comprehend their hidden meaning, but couldn't. I silently wondered why the doctor would want to speak to me.

Suddenly the past resonated again in my thoughts.

John had saved all the messages for me. I ran down the short narrow hallway hastily brushing past him. On the way to the kitchen I passed two doors standing open, side by side. One door led to the other spare vacant bedroom and the other guided you into our small humming office. As I moved past them, I could see the fluorescent lights as they illuminated the many objects residing there, none of more importance to me than the telephone. I picked up the cordless phone lay strewn haphazardly on the counter. I could feel John behind me as he closely followed me watching every move I made.

The window of my past, the one I thought I had closed, flew open and brought with it a cyclone. The phone seemed heavier than normal, I guess burdened with a torrent of news it would soon pour into my ear. The numbers my fingers touched burnt and sizzled. The flood gates opened and the torrent of questions began. Could I have picked something up from the incident at work? No, surely not. I couldn't have. My reservation was why the urgency to call him? What had happened? Was this about my test results? It couldn't be! We had discussed it; I had been reassured time and time again by the prison nurse and by my local doctor that my risk factor was minimal. Nearly impossible were the words I recalled. I guess the word 'nearly' is just that, nearly, meaning that there was still a small risk. I didn't think of it in that context. I just presumed

I would be fine and in the 'impossible' category, not the 'nearly impossible' category.

My head spun a whirlwind of thoughts all jockeying for a position to be answered and processed. Apprehension was quickly swept away by fear. Hot rushes of adrenalin ascended and surged throughout my body. My skin became coated in a light lather of sweat and my muscles tensed. Before I even spoke to the doctor my mind had emphatically persuaded me I had been infected with HIV. It was the only possible answer for the doctor's calls. My world started to collapse around me.

I imagined I was infected with tiny invaders who threatened to overthrow my mental stability. They marched and conquered all areas of logic bringing graphic scenes of disaster, death and suffering. I thought this is it, I am going to die, it simply could not be anything else.

The darkness descended and swallowed me.

Chapter 4

A mirror shatters

I had no other choice but to listen to the recorded messages. I didn't really want to hear the words that would spill the truth. I was scared. In my mind I already knew what he was going to tell me, I had resigned myself to the fact that I had HIV. I can't explain why this thought dominated my mind, most likely because it was foremost in my knowledge bank, thanks to the eighties advertising campaign.

The cordless phone gurgled and words like molten lava spilled in my ear. He required a call from me as soon as possible. In all the years we had known him he had never called our home so I knew this was a deadly serious situation. Johns face spoke louder than any words could; worry was etched in every one of the lines on his face. The doctor's tone was obviously troubled, flustered even, behaviour completely unlike him. I looked up at the clock the hands pointed and held steady at seven o'clock. I considered the time and presumed it was probably far too late to call the surgery, but I tried anyway I had nothing to lose.

I doubted I would get a response but this didn't stop me. The phone rang, It was an unrelenting distant tone in my ear. To my amazement, the phone was answered.

A light, cheerful voice responded and enquired about my needs. I explained who I was and that my call was in response to three requests from the doctor to call. She listened intently for a few moments and placed me on hold for what felt like an eternity. It became a moment so far stretched in time I couldn't see or even imagine when it would end.

Out of the blue, my call was suddenly redirected to the doctor's office. I was startled to hear the voice of my regular doctor. I never imagined he would still be at work at seven pm. I thought another doctor may have taken my call and offered an explanation as to why I was required to call, but I found myself talking with the man himself. Shock and disbelief flavoured my tone as I spoke with him. I tried to be light hearted with pleasantries but he was not having any of that. He was serious and concerned and once again I revisited my thoughts of the past.

He explained he had something important to tell me, but it had to be done in person. He wanted me to come down to the surgery first thing in the morning. Those instructions didn't sit well with me and I told him I couldn't wait that long. I explained I had to go to work in the morning so would not be able to come down until after this round at work, unless of course I took a sick day. I didn't want to do that as it would draw unwanted attention to me and this was something I couldn't afford to do especially since I had obviously picked up something.

There was no way I could mentally wait until the next day. I needed to know NOW, right now and I told him so. I explained I was already extremely stressed, emotional and tormenting myself, thinking the worst. Sleep would be virtually impossible, as I couldn't go to bed with an unknown burden hanging over my head. I continued to coerce and manipulate him, overcoming all his objections with my quick rationalisations.

Eventually, he broke under the weight of my persuasions.

I used terms like, "I've got HIV haven't I? How long have I got?" I bombarded and assaulted him with these questions until I heard his agreeable and friendly Egyptian tone bite into my barrage. He said to me, "you really need to come and see me tomorrow." I answered him, "what is going on? Do I or don't I have HIV?" His reply brought me to my knees. He said, "NO you don't have HIV. Your Hepatitis C (HCV) test came back positive, but this doesn't mean you have HCV, we will need to do the test again to make sure." I was silent; I had not even considered HCV. A part of me was a bit relieved, but I didn't know what HCV was.

Words evaded me; they floated in the air around me, caught in the flakes of dust. I stood temporarily frozen in time. I became a wax statue, as thoughts soared and glided effortlessly through my mind from beginning to end. Synapses fired simultaneously, as they all tried to reason and process this very raw, but very important, data. HCV, what was that. I tried to find some knowledge from my internal data bank about what it was exactly. I knew it was related to drug use, and I had heard it referred to as a 'junkie' disease, but I had no idea what it did or how it affected a person.

The penny dropped. A quiet cry from the past resonated from its deep concealment. It gathered momentum. Dark voices rose out of the depths and described familiar past images which hit me like lightening, temporarily blinding me. I yelled back at them I was not a 'junkie', but when I glimpsed the reality of the landscape before me, in fact I was, or had been. I just didn't identify myself with that label.

Discerning this fact released a different sort of internal invader. An invader which made the previous dark voices appear ordinary. It was a sinister being which had been with me for a long time, but had been long forgotten and very much suppressed since Sydney and later in Boarding School. This dark passenger rose up from the threatening pit of my soul and commenced its accusatory malicious statements. It attacked my character from within. A critical and judgmental dialogue commenced, 'you deserve this because of what you did all those years ago.' 'You can't hide any thing'; 'this is your punishment for trying to suppress those memories', 'trying to forget who you really are'. 'See . . . . you will never amount to anything.'

I mustered my last bit of strength and quelled the voices to vaguely hear the doctor say he wanted to make sure the diagnosis was correct by ordering another test. He wanted to be sure. Sure of what? What did that all mean? Was there some level of doubt to the testing process? I didn't have the mental capacity to ask him that at the time, but I would later learn, much later in fact, that you can show a positive result if you have been exposed to the virus, twenty percent of people are somehow able to automatically clear the virus with their immune defences. Even though the result was positive it didn't necessarily mean that person was infected. I wished I had known that fact early in this whole process as it would have saved me a lot of torment. But I wasn't to come to know this fact for many months.

I slid down the wooden cupboards. My rubbery legs folded beneath me unable to hold the cumbersome weight placed upon them. I struck the icy, unyielding, slate floor. My hand still held the phone in a tight grip. My vision blurred as a steamy fog threatened to overcome me; air trapped deep in my lungs was unable to escape and caused my breathing to stop temporarily. My voice returned in a hushed tone. I told him I would visit him in the morning and then our connection was lost.

The trumpet blew; I was forced into the arena, my armour completely stripped from my body. I stood naked before the crowd resigned to the words that I believed sealed my fate. I was left speechless, dumbfounded as I sat on the floor. And then I felt something else, something totally unexpected. A wave of pure self revulsion overpowered me and inside I crumpled with horror. I had become a lump of un-sculpted clay, waiting for the remoulding process to begin. I needed John to come and reshape my life to the way it was before this phone call. Part of me believed this was all a mistake, just a bad dream, a nightmare I would soon wake up from but the logical and rational part of me knew better.

Did I hear him correctly? Did he say I had Hepatitis C? My mind found it impossible to wrap itself around the words hepatitis c, it just kept asking 'what the hell was that anyway.'

I slowly stood and floated across the cold hard floor of the kitchen, like I was a ghost, and placed the jagged dagger that had pierced my world, back into its cradle. The room in which I stood suddenly expanded, the walls blew out as it turned into a super nova, a gaping black hole that threatened to suck me into it. I tried to navigate my way through the space continuum of my brain, but was unsuccessful as a mental haze had descended, blanketing logic and common sense with a vague emptiness. Sporadic questions like shooting stars fired into the deafening silence. Why? What was this all about? What was I going to do? What did all this mean? Was I going to die? What about my family? Why me?

No answers arose from the darkness the dark passenger remained silent.

I had spent years and years creating an image I liked and was used to. I also felt comfortable and safe in this crafted and selfishly fashioned world. That night and that particular conversation shattered my personal mirror. Each shard of glass stole my dreams, my desires and my goals and scattered them in pieces on the floor. My familiar image, the reflection I looked at daily, gone forever, smashed beyond repair. I couldn't conceive of the thought just at that moment, but very soon in the not so distant future, I would recognise the ruined glass signified it was time to create a new destiny, to mould a new life, one that would be based on future pain and suffering as well as lessons learnt in the past.

When you allow your body and mind to relax even for a second, you can be surprised by what can be recalled in this moment. A faint memory came forth of a story once read or heard about Pamela Anderson, I think she had HCV. By all accounts, she looked healthy and happy, I knew she didn't really live a great lifestyle; she partied hard and drunk excessively. Whereas I exercised daily, ate well and didn't drink much. So, I thought maybe these things would stand in my favour. As I began to dwell on this slight positivism the voices whispered in the distance. I knew I couldn't afford to pay them any credibility for they were to damaging.

But they continued to whisper and question my knowledge. They shouted doubt into the most vulnerable recesses of my mind filling them up like fluid around stones in a jar. I knew my knowledge about HCV was very limited. I comprehended the seriousness of the disease, but, mortality, was that a possibility. The voices gathered momentum, my brain drowned in the rapid succession of questions, questions that I had no answers for in that moment in time. From the depths I heard. 'Did it kill people? Would it kill me? Would I become ill and die? Would I suffer? How painful would it be, or become? My kids, how was I going to tell them? What about all the things I wanted to do with my life, the places I wanted to visit, the people I would never meet, my career, my husband?' The voices kept coming, like cannon balls striking an embattled ship. My vessel was damaged and wounded, but I wasn't yet ready to let it sink.

I knew I would fight regardless of the prognosis, I was after all a fighter, I had fought major battles before. However right at that point in time I became aware I had no strategies to fight due simply to a lack of knowledge and understanding. I was starting from a very disadvantaged position. This was not something I recognised or felt comfortable with, but I knew that I did have the capacity within me to learn.

I looked at John, our eyes connected for the briefest of moments, what I saw disturbed me, I could feel his anxiousness, his distress and I saw the dread that dominated his face. The sensation of disgust and self revulsion I previously felt, faded slightly. However it would revisit me on many more occasions in the future and would nearly take my life, but once again I am getting ahead of myself. At that moment I wanted to take flight, to fly away, to just be able to leap across the illuminated roof tops toward the shimmering light of the moon or even hide in the deep crevices between the dark buildings. Anywhere but here.

John stood in the middle of the kitchen, expectation written all over his face, he deserved an explanation, the question was, could I provide a good one. A deep silence lay suspended between us. He had heard everything. His body language demanded my full attention as he waited for the words to come forth between us. Slowly, he reached out and affectionately took my hand in his, turned it over, toyed with my fingers and gently stroked my palm.

He lingered, patiently caressing my hand waiting. Speech didn't come easily. My throat was painfully constricted with grief and my voice was ragged with anguish but the words were finally produced. They stopped when the last single tear slid from my eye onto my thinly covered shoulder. The small damp sensation more unsettling to me than the words I had just spoken.

For the third time in our relationship he didn't offer any judgment or condemnation for the actions of my past. Once again he offered acceptance, love and support. He embraced me. Held me close, tight in his arms and I could hear the steady rhythm of his heart, which offered a deep comfort. We both knew our history for we had created it together. We had fought side by side and supported each other through the adversities life had thrown at us, beginning with accepting my past, his fathers death, the tumultuous years of his army career, a miscarriage, our family upheaval to Scotland, being homeless, being broke, having a failed business venture, my daughters fathers death yet we had prospered and prevailed. Our relationship had been restored time and time again. This would be another test for us. My hope at the time was that we would have the strength and courage to conquer it, like we had done so many times before.

That night we held each other unmoving for a long moment, our bodies wrapped together closely intertwined. I lay tight and comfortable in his arms. How much fitful and replenishing sleep we both had I don't know. I know, I had very little. The minutes seemed to drag by unenthusiastically, they slowly turned into hours and each one brought me closer to the appointment that would change my life.

I awoke from a light rest to the last shadows of night as they were lifted slowly by the light of dawn. I looked over at my sleeping beau. I prayed this would only be a mere hiccup in our lives, but a feeling of foreboding had slowly crept in with the darkness of night.

Chapter 5

Times of trial

A mighty blow had struck us both. We found ourselves in unchartered waters, new territory for us as a couple and our marriage. I knew this challenge would test both of us. It felt like the house I had lived in for the last eight years had turned its transparent windows opaque, the glare from the sun unable to warm our home and for a brief uneasy moment, it seemed like my home was preparing for a disaster to occur. I was unsure if the walls of our home were secure and strong enough to weather the approaching storms. Would they be able to stand up if the storm became a category five cyclone? If we did manage to conquer this milestone together, I knew there would be some residual damage, undefined changes. I feared what they could potentially be. I knew *I* would never be the same, there was no way I could walk out of this unscathed, I was in the direct path and would take a direct hit. My question was what about John and the rest of the family, how would this storm affect them.

That particular morning was a tough one for me. It was a brilliant day, bright and sunny. Not the kind of day you expected to be haunted by ghosts of the past. The air did have a deceptive edge to it; a hint of winter chilled the mood. And it started with a lie, I rang work and told them I was sick and needed a day off, well it wasn't really a lie as I was technically mentally unwell. I had very little sleep under my belt and was very anxious about my visit to the doctor who I knew would be ordering the retest.

My past which included my near self destructive practices had risen and dealt me a potentially lethal blow. Over the years I had practiced positive self talk and conquered and put to bed permanently—I thought—the flow of voices that spoke so negatively. However I realised, I had only stemmed the flow briefly. My old ways had crept back into my life, seemingly overnight. The pending doctor's visit was just the new excuse which enabled them to ravage me.

The doctor's words revisited me and I wondered if I could allow myself to believe there could be a problem with the last test result. The dark passenger said 'No,' and I didn't think I could have that sort of hope in this moment of time. I was totally insane to think "not infected" would be written on the paperwork, and of course it wasn't. The test was proven correct, written in bold ink. I was positively infected.

I wasn't really disappointed. I kind of felt numb. The news didn't shock me, simply because I expected it. That's not to say I was ready for that result, I wasn't. I simply just thought I deserved it.

My friendly supportive GP referred me to a liver specialist, a gastroenterologist, specialising in HCV. I rang and asked for the next available appointment which happened to be four months away. Now this news shocked me more than my actual diagnosis, I found it hard to believe I had to wait that long, but I did.

For me the actual problem was I had no control over my situation, I had no power in the circumstance at all, no access to any information, no brochures or any other resources was made available for me, simply because the GP had none. As an ongoing concern I have to question whether this would happen if a person was diagnosed with any other chronic illness. Can you imagine being told you have cancer and not being able to see someone for four whole months? It was quite a daunting process. I was scared beyond belief.

I actually went and got a second opinion from another doctor's surgery. Visiting this doctor only made the situation worse for me. After he retested me and of course the test returned positive, he informed me that I had a moral obligation to tell my employer. This concept put me into a real head spin and caused me a lot more stress than was warranted. At the time in my much less informed state, I believed him. Not that I listened or took his advice—this was one day I really appreciated my in built obstinacy and tenacity—I didn't do what he told me to do—luckily—I could not conceive of telling the prison hierarchy of my situation. There was just no way I would disclose my situation to them.

The whole initial process of diagnosis was absolutely terrifying for me. I couldn't tell you of one positive thing that occurred, maybe one, the fact I was not judged by my own GP. He demonstrated great support and empathy for my situation, but he couldn't help me. I was shocked and traumatised by the whole event. I felt I was stripped of my autonomy. I hated feeling disempowered, it was like the biggest event of my life was taken out of my control and placed on a festival platter and presented to the master of the situation, the gastroenterologist to assess when he was good and ready. Me, I was required to stand on the side lines of the feast, a silent waitress for four months, waiting for an opportunity to speak and discuss an occurrence that threatened to turn me into a relic. To say I was stressed would be an understatement. Four months is a very long time when you are living in a small room of a haunted house filled with extremely vocal ghosts.

During those first few weeks I felt like I was living on another planet, a land that time and people forgot. I felt so lost, so vulnerable, so alone. I didn't feel like I could share my situation with anyone. I believed no-one would understand. How could I make them understand when I had no comprehension of the topic of HCV. I feared the reaction I may receive when other people found out I was infected and this included my own family. I didn't know about counsellors or support groups back then and realistically I probably wouldn't have seen them anyway. I just wasn't ready to face anyone at that time.

I was afraid of the social stigma attached to HCV, I worked with it every day. I had even contributed to the stigma myself using prisoner jokes and innuendos about drug use and infection rates. The biggest problem I faced on a daily basis was my own internal convictions. HCV caused great embarrassment for me, as it reminded me of my past drug use. I believed if I was to explain my situation to people I would have to inform them how I got infected and I was not able to talk about that part of my life.

I regretted being involved in these jokes and innuendos because in reality who was I to judge when I had once done the same thing as the prisoners. I joked about drug taking behaviour and HCV, how hypocritical of me. The difference between me and some of the prisoners I managed was I had just not been caught and convicted. Living in denial of my past does not excuse my actions and maybe that was why I was slapped in the face so hard with my own diagnosis. My holier than thou attitude needed a readjustment and believe me I got it. At forty two years of age I started to really understand the difference between empathy and sympathy, both of which didn't come naturally to my type of nature. Yet I found myself infected with the same BBV as sixty percent of the prisoners I managed. I felt the same fear, the same anxiousness, the same pain as they did, the difference was I had power to do something about it, they didn't. I had access to my choice of doctors and specialists when I wanted, they didn't. However they had an advantage over me, they had people to talk to, other prisoners to share their fears with and seek information from, there was no judgment between 'brothers' living with HCV in prison. I doubted my officer 'brothers' would share the same level of understanding or tolerance with me, so in that fact they were better off than I was.

In a very short time, my life had radically changed. I looked out the same window, on the same street, but the light had changed, it cast an isolated silver shadow instead of the previous brilliant waves. The moon which had once bathed the outside scene in its subtle glow was now hidden behind a large cloud and the landscape looked pitch black. I was, a short time ago, a happy, content woman, but, the outlook of my life had changed, it was covered in a thick murky fog which obscured my vision and made me emotionally defenceless and weak.

From where I stood at that point in time I had a total understanding of Forrest Gump's quest to run around America. I understood where his focus was, as I had the same focus. I wanted to stop the grief and to stop the pain of life and the circumstances its deals all of us. I understood the driving force that made him get up one day and run and run and run. I too felt that pressure, it compelled me to run. Run from the disease that burdened me, run from my life and everything it brought with it. Run from the constraints of my work and the people I worked with. Mostly I wanted to run from my family because I didn't want to burden them with my disease, my death, my ongoing chronic illness or the threat I posed. I just wanted to run off the end of the earth if that was even possible.

The question I asked myself back then and I still ask today is, 'if I didn't find out about my diagnosis would it have been any better', 'is it better knowing you are infected or not.' Now I am not talking from a physical point of view because that goes without saying, of course it better to know, but from an emotional point of view, I am not so sure. The range of emotions I went through just in those first few weeks was traumatising in itself let alone the years that followed. I felt things, emotions I had never felt before. They were intense feelings that ranged from severe anxiety, fear, phobia to exultation, blessedness and joy, some evidently good, some noticeably very bad.

The only true realisation I had during those first few weeks was that I had no other choice but to play the cards I was dealt. The question that burned on my lips constantly was, would I hold a winning hand. I had never played black jack before, but I had been forced into a game already in full swing, experienced players sat at the table and as I joined them I realised I had to play the game of my life. The stakes were extremely high and I was completely out of my depth. I had no option because I was obliged to play against my will. My only hope was to find a very good teacher somewhere along the way, someone who would be able to direct and support me as I ventured further into the game.

Chapter 6

The insidious vines of my past started to rise from the decaying ground in which I had buried them long ago. They wrapped tightly around me. Their tiny tentacles attached themselves deep into my thoughts and words of condemnation, blame and hopelessness flourished and took hold. Over the years I had practiced and learnt to keep the negative voices at bay but discovering I was HCV positive, weakened my defences and opened my vulnerable mind to the pessimistic pictures they loved to display. I saw pictures of John recanting his understanding, me as a failure, both as a mother and a wife. They told stories of the disgrace, the dishonour and the scandal I had brought into our family and the pain and suffering to come. They questioned, how I could stay with John after all they had shown me, the mental pictures disclosing his true feelings. They whispered words stating he despised me, as much as I despised myself

Internally, as the vines fully matured they brought a profound darkness into my life which gave rise to what I have previously referred to as the dark passenger. The dark passenger was the sinister voice that bought calculated self flagellation, self hatred and self punishment into my world. It spoke embittered words of criticism, blame and conviction and poured these sour expressions into my soul turning it wretched.

Not many of us, who have done something wrong and continue to carry the burden of guilt, go about whipping ourselves, literally opening our backs up and bleeding for the cause. But how many of us pound ourselves mentally, severely criticising ourselves with our own inner self talk. I don't know which one is more damaging, one is physical the other is emotional. Physical scars heal. There aren't any bandages big enough for emotional scars; personally I find them much harder to heal.

My personal chastisement came and went throughout the first part of my life, some episodes were long and troublesome, full of rebellion and conflict, others were brief, disturbing but manageable, yet all of them left some form of damage and a mark on my psyche. This self imposed reprimand reappeared more pronounced when I felt vulnerable or had received news like my diagnosis. Every time this occurred it was like my defence system took a frontline hit. This time a HCV missile slammed into my protective barrier it severely impeded the function of the search and destroy turrets that normally protected my mind, the ones that filtered the good and evil voices before they could take root. As my defences weakened the voices got louder and stronger in their conviction.

The vines I found the hardest to defeat were the creeping feelings of physical contamination and internal dirtiness. They sunk very deep roots into my soul and fed on my despair. I felt the filth grow daily; it was like a direct transference of dirty decaying soil straight into the deepest parts of me. My world became filled with rocks and dirt and together they buried me slowly. Each day that past, the rain mixed with the dirt and mud stuck to the deep recesses of my life, coating me in a repulsive filthy layer. It was an internal layer that grew to smother the virtuous worthy feelings I once felt. I had the overwhelming desire to take a large, hard, bristled wire brush, and scrub away this grimy layer, this layer that prevented me from positively moving anywhere.

The problem was I didn't really believe it would make any difference no matter how much pain I endured through the scrubbing. I thought the vines and the dark flowers they produced had taken up a firm immovable residence inside me. I felt lost again in the foliage, buried in the creepers which gave birth to the vine of the past, a past which I had at one time been mentally strong enough to banish and overcome.

A quiet voice whispered somewhere from within me, a question, was there a possibility that I could grow strong enough to banish them again. At the time I doubted it . . . . but . . . .

As my internal war waged, I still had to work and maintain the appearance of a normal life to the outside world. Somewhere deep within me that quiet tender voice whispered words enlightening me to the way my life appeared, it was an absolute mess at this point. I didn't know how to make it better; I had no skills or knowledge how to change it. I just knew I still needed to function at some level so I came to the realisation of how I could achieve that, all I had to do was deceive the people around me, making them believe everything was normal, I had perfected this skill a long time ago, I just needed to do it again somehow. This meant I had to become the old, familiar chameleon again, and that's exactly what I did. I pulled out the mask I had worn in boarding school, the one that helped me get through that hard time in my life and wrapped it tightly around myself.

I would wear this mask for many months. It was not always easy to put on, but I wore it all the same.

The mask was in fact truly hard to wear around the people who really knew me. I struggled to maintain this facade around them. These were people who I had grown fond of over the years and built relationships with. My personal training clients were amongst them, some of them I had trained for many years. I had formed a special bond with a particular family who came three times a week, they had become like my own family and working with them was the hardest thing for me to do. As time went on they could see I wrestled with something personal. In front of them, it became increasingly harder to pretend that everything was okay. So, I made the decision to finalise my business and told them all I was not continuing my business, a decision I would regret for quite some time. Emotionally I battled with this decision and physically, well I cried a lot as I missed them. I wrestled with this decision, but ultimately, I knew I could not maintain the facade with them.

I simply wasn't ready to reveal the truth about my past and how I came about being in this situation. I was after all still trying to come to terms with it myself. Hiding the situation from my own family was easier. My mother and brother lived in Rockhampton and I saw then infrequently. My dad and his wife lived close by but I knew I could avoid them for awhile until I was at an emotional place to tell them. My kids were at a stage in their lives where they were self consumed and I had the refuge of my bedroom when I thought I was about to have a melt down, which I did often, sometimes daily.

My biggest fear was the rejection I thought I may receive from them if they became aware of my diagnosis. I wasn't ready to answer any questions; I didn't have any answers at that time anyway. I simply didn't want our friendship to change, and I perceived it would if they knew everything. The filthiness I felt living in me was how I sensed they would eventually feel about me. I recognised the dark flowers these vines grew would wrap themselves around each of these relationships and destroy them individually. The easiest option for me, or so I thought at the time, was to cut all these people off from my life before they glimpsed a side of me that I wasn't ready and didn't want to reveal.

As I told lie after lie, I despised myself. I loathed what I was doing but I didn't know how to tell the truth to anyone. Remember how I spoke of living two lives well at this point these realities really started to take on vastly diverse courses. The words HCV positive was etched on one alternative face and the word 'normal' was etched upon the other, both were false masks. Technically at this point I fragmented again adopting another face. This time, the face I wore said to those who knew of my diagnosis—my partner only at this time—I was ok. This was a path that would take me on another negatively focused road.

My future hope at this time was that if the day ever occurred when I was HCV free I wanted these three faces to collide and rejoin again, making me whole once more.

As the days flowed into weeks the three masks got easier to wear. On the surface it became easier to display a happy, optimistic person whilst my true feelings lay below. However, internally as each day passed my own roots rotted away slowly. My self-confidence and self esteem plummeted. One of the reasons I chose to behave like this was because I didn't believe anyone would understand, or accept me as a person if they knew I was infected with a blood borne virus. I had no previous experiences to gauge any reactions upon, so I didn't know how any of these people would respond to me. All I knew was I was not prepared to risk loosing any part of my life or any of them. They held me together and I needed them to provide a level of normalcy in a world that was crashing around me.

At the time I didn't know anyone living with hepatitis C, ***no one***, so it was hard for me to conceive people would understand my predicament. The only way, I thought at that time, to deal with my situation was to internalise my thoughts and my true feelings. I believed if I revealed anything to anybody it would make me more vulnerable and unable to positively make decisions. The other side of it was I was not in the right frame of mind to deal with a lot of other people's emotions. I was emotional enough for everyone.

Looking back I can now see my communication skills were completely inadequate. I didn't understand or even know how to process what I was feeling. Deep down, I knew my thoughts were irrational and negative, but I didn't possess the skills or knowledge to change any of them or know where to seek support. I could yell, deflect and manipulate, but actually talk? Well, that just wasn't me. I had spent my whole life—up to this point—believing it would be easier to do everything myself and this situation was the same as every other. My past had shown me that only I could negotiate the rapids of this journey and the future ones. I needed to go it alone, because people were unreliable; my past clearly demonstrated that fact.

I couldn't have been more wrong but . . . . The past teaches us doesn't it . . . .

I knew I had the strength to weather the storm I perceived would unfold. I had done it before. History had equipped me with skills to persevere, and preserve I did. But once again I sabotaged my relationship with John, I pushed him away. You would think I would have learnt from the past, but no, I only seem to remember the bad lesson and forget all about the good lesson. I was as thick as two bricks. John had stood beside me before, he had vowed to stand beside me again but of course *I knew better*. I doubted everything. I doubted his love, doubted our relationship, doubted my survival, doubted *I* had a chance and doubted *we* had a chance. I deliberately turned away from John and the only support system I had at the time.

John had been a long suffering partner as I took years to deal with my many inadequacies, all created out of the depths of the historical events rooted in frustration, disempowerment and rejection. The flowers born of these roots such as my over domineering and self absorbed nature must have been truly hard for him to bear at times. At the time I knew I was reverting back to the ways of my old nature but I found it impossible to stop them. Pushing him away was the easiest path to take and my footprints were already clearly visible in the ground. I could easily follow them and trust in where they would take me.

It wasn't that I didn't trust John, it was more that I didn't trust myself with him. I didn't trust myself to try something new, something unknown. That's what scared me. I feared the path it would take me on. I feared what I may discover and uncover about myself. I feared where John would take me if I allowed him into my real world. But what I mostly feared was the disease and the journey it would take me on. I was unsure I had the strength *or* courage *or* stomach for any of it. My pride didn't want people to see me fail or see my weaknesses either. Was it stupidity, yes I think it was, but I could not see any of this at that time. I just decided to sabotage my whole life instead of entertaining some rational thoughts.

Chapter 7

"Sow a thought, and you reap an act; Sow an act, and you reap a habit; Sow a habit, and you reap a character; Sow a character, and you reap a destiny."
—Charles Reade

As the days progressed, horror stories continued to fill my mind. Visual pictures of millions of sinister, minute and unseen invaders purposefully swimming in the sea of life flowed before me. They fought against the current to hijack and aggressively attack the unsuspecting sentinels that protect and defended my well being. Orange spiky HCV bombs adapted to the natural environment and disguised themselves to easily circumnavigate my body's immune shield with the aim of destroying and occupying the host cell, me. As the virus fought for control of my body, with its attempt to conquer and occupy every cell, the major structure of the body, the liver started to crumble and fail.

HCV invaded my body like the bombs that fell from the American B29 bombers that battered Tokyo in March 1945. Their tornado of flames decimated everything in its path, HCV did exactly the same. The invasion tactics are the same to conquer and destroy. This bombing was the worst in history, it was heartbreaking, catastrophic and so were the thoughts of being invaded and taking over by a microscopic virus.

These and other comparisons flowed like honey through my mind they coated and stuck to every curve and fissure of my brain. Whispered expressions of doom constantly trickled in my ears. There was no escape. I knew the fire bombs approached but I was powerless to flee, incapable to adjust my position in any manner. The dark passenger constantly dripped negativity into my mind. Over time it transformed my beliefs, what I thought was real became unreal, what I trusted, I no longer trusted, what I once assumed became no longer possible. I became convinced John would leave me, I just didn't know when. I wondered why he stayed, there was nothing for him in our relationship especially when I was infected with a disease that potentially threatened him as well. I questioned why he would stay when I was most likely going to die as a result of this infection. What sort of life could I offer him? At the time I believed the easiest thing to do was to get on with life with as little disruption as possible. I saw this as a major life disruption, one that could be avoided, if I left.

The weeks became a real stumbling block. They became nothing more than an obstacle that reluctantly edged forward, slowly, far too slowly for my liking. During those early days I would often go into the bedroom John and I shared and fall into bed physically and mentally exhausted. I would lay in the king sized bed we shared wrapped in the warmth of his arms, his body tight against my back and his face snuggled closely into the base of my neck. Even though I felt safe, my mind would not stop creating feature films. Each night after my husband fell asleep I would open the blind nice and wide above me. The unrestricted wooden slats allowed the rays of moonlight to bounce playfully around the room, I would watch as the shadows danced and twirled like graceful ballerinas pirouetting to the music of swan lake on the walls of my bedroom.

Sleep eluded me on more than one occasion during this early stage of diagnosis. I found some of those nights to be much longer than the stretched out hours of the days that already passed slowly. On these long nights I would pull the curtain back exposing the darkness. From my bed, with the noise of my husband peacefully sleeping next to me, I would stare out into the deep blue night and listen to the creatures of the night as they came to life and mocked the day dwellers. The night was beautiful when it was framed by the stunning gold casing of the window. As the antics of the night came to a close and the moons reflection slowly moved out of view the window, the new day and the lighter colours of dawn replaced the shades night. On many of these nights I would lay for hours thinking and pondering all my options.

The most dominating thoughts were those surrounding my infection. The hardest to overcome were the continual melancholy scenarios of infecting others and the paranoia that followed them. On these dark nights I struggled against the rising tide of despair, but often lost the mental skirmish, to fall deeply into the unfathomable void of depression that lay waiting to ensnare me.

At times I welcomed the dawn hoping it would strip away these unfathomable fears. I wrestled often with the thoughts and fought hard not to be dragged down the treacherous path, but my mind was so weak. What if it was one of my children, even a stranger? I couldn't see a way out. These thoughts created an overly sensitive characteristic to rise within me.

The biggest change began not long after my diagnosis and it was very destructive. I started to intensely examine every situation, every person and thing that surrounded me. I watched everything, exaggerating situations, I nervously studied every reaction, every tonal change in voice, behaviour and attitudes and I sought things that were not really present. I can remember thinking how nice it would have been to have a normal conversation, one without fear of suspicion, condemnation or judgment. Interactions like I had experienced every other day of my life before this event occurred.

As I said before I believed it was only a matter of time before John would make the decision to end it. I thought he deserved a much better life. I knew if he made the decision to finalise our marriage I would simply let him go, it would be messy, but I would not stand in his way. I would not struggle or force him to stay. In my heart I knew it was the best solution, the best outcome for everyone, so I thought. Rain had been forecasted by my internal system, but there was no rain in sight, the horizon was clear. However I still prepared for the storm, I battened down the hatches and stood waiting ready to take that next step. But, the storm never came and over time I realised the forecaster had made a mistake and the predication was false. Each day John stayed, I awoke to another cloudless day and in time the days became a spectacular sky full of beautiful colours.

I hated those reflective nights. I hated waking up in fear all the time, rerunning scenarios and mental predictions that never came to pass. I would have made the worst psychic on the planet. I certainly had lost my touch over the years. I couldn't understand where my mind had gone. I had never felt anything like this before, I had no reference point to focus on, this was all new. Well that's not entirely true, a long time ago—back in boarding school—I had touched on this level. The lift door opened revealing a level of depression and destructive behaviour unknown to me, but I never stepped out, my feet had never met that floor. But this time the door opened on a floor lower than I ever expected, I had been taken way beyond my own limitations, I was in the basement and I was forced to step out and the door slammed shut behind me. What I felt on this level was completely foreign to me. My core was hollow, lost. I had felt something like them as a child growing up but these feelings were stronger, deeper. They penetrated my whole being they gripped me and were unshakable.

At the time I didn't know it but I was in the process of being broken. I obviously had some character issues that needed to be modified and they never would have been dealt with if I had continued on my busy selfish path and not been challenged in this way. However, I would not come to know or appreciate this for a few years yet.

All I wanted to do was shake the feelings but for some reason I just couldn't. I felt I was in an out of control car, driving too fast on an isolated dirt road. Many fallen branches littered the path and the branches jabbed me with feelings of hopelessness, misery and sadness and they plagued my journey often flattening my tires. At the same time a part of me knew I needed to work out how I was going to deal with all these internal thoughts. The question was how. It was a simple question but its presence prevented any action from occurring.

All my life I had possessed a strong personality. I had been independent, decisive and rebellious. The person I saw when I looked in the mirror was not the person I knew. The reflection was just not like me. It was like I had handed my life over to someone else and I sat on the side lines and watched as the strings of my life were pulled by an unknown entity. I think my incapacitation was what made it so hard for me to deal with my diagnosis initially. It was such an unexpected blow. It was a blow that really shocked the foundation of my life.

The problem was I didn't understand where *I* had gone. It was like I was buried under a pile of clothing that smothered my voice. Someone else stepped into my shoes, whilst my feet were still encased in them and they moved my legs, their hands slipped into the pockets of my jacket and took over, they coordinated my life.

I was still there but I had lost power, my jurisdiction had been revoked. I was not able to influence or command my own world. It was quite a weird sensation. Everything still worked the same and moved the same but my mind had relinquished control. All my automatic functions were controlled by the dark thoughts of a new entity that continually squashed my own. These thoughts just grew in strength, each day I refused to take my rightful place as ruler of this being. Why I allowed this to happen I just don't know.

There must have been a few sunny days during this bleak time early in 2005, but I can't recall any of them. All I can remember is the darkness that surrounded me and the ice cold fingers that continually stroked my skin and crept into the recesses of my mind and tormented me. Most of those lingering early days, I chose to witness my life from the sidelines, not really taking any part in it. I sat back in the audience and watched my life as it was played out before me on a distant stage, words drifted on the wind and reached my ears enabling me to hear and understand the content of the performance, but I wasn't ready to take my place on the stage with any of the other actors. I don't think I was ready to start a fight I knew I couldn't win. I guess what I sought was a 'time out' and I stole it.

Chapter 8

Personal reflection

I took two weeks just sitting, watching and struggling to work out my next move and seeking to comprehend the whole situation.

Life is a real cliché; you never genuinely miss what is right in front of you until it is removed from you. If my pantry was empty I would not only crave food but I would get very hungry. What's more I would miss the taste and essence of the food and the comfort it brings. In life I never truly appreciated my loved ones until I thought I could lose them. I didn't value my health until it was close to being taken away from me and I didn't fully appreciate life until I found myself in a situation like living with a chronic illness. What a cliché.

I write this section with a clearer perspective and a great deal more information and understanding, from a future stand point, seven years ahead of where the story is at present. Using this reference point in the story, I can see I was experiencing something known as depression. A mental health condition I had probably experienced in the past, but had not previously had a label to place on the feelings I felt. Nowadays mental health especially depression and anxiety is much more widely understood and accepted.

Up until this point, at forty two years of age, I wasn't familiar with depression. I had no real experience identifying with it, or appreciating the destruction it could cause if not positively addressed. However in 2005 I had a real close encounter with it, I wasn't visited by aliens I became the alien. My close encounter revealed a very personal dance with the nature of depression. It was a dance to remember but also a dance I would like never to experience again. My particular tango shattered my dreams. Whilst I unsuspectingly swayed on the floor and as the music rose in its crescendo implanted dark thoughts flourished in my mind. These thoughts, if I allowed them to would rob me of my life. Depression has a way of slowly creeping into our lives. It steals our sanity, and I believe that is simply what it did to me in those early days.

I think most of us have felt "down", sad, or discouraged when things haven't gone well, maybe failed a test, a loved one passed away, we got divorced, or maybe work got you down. Mild depression usually passes and has little impact on our lives however the more chronic form is a lot more intense and does interfere with our lives. I believe many people who experience the feelings associated with ongoing depression assume something is really wrong or they are going crazy, I know I did. I literally did think I was going round the bend, I didn't understand what was happening, I just knew I felt different, my feelings and my thoughts were so dark, and it was so out of character for me. I had become that alien.

When you look up the word depression in the dictionary it explains depression as being a word that describes feelings such as sadness, worthlessness, hollowness, gloom, frustration and disappointment. It also explains people will experience ongoing unconstructive thoughts, negative thinking patterns like over analysing and excessive worrying, blame and guilt. I only wish I had someone to tell me about all this seven years ago, but I wasn't aware of any of this back then, if I had, I may not have gone on to do the things I did . . . . Getting ahead of myself again . . .

I believe the first stage of death is depression. It has a way of sneaking into your life, filling you full of condemnation, guilt and blame which if left unchecked later leads to sickness and finally death. I read somewhere that all illnesses start off with either mental or physical dis . . . ease or dis . . . stress. My situations and life circumstances up until this point had caused me to become stressed and uneasy with my life, but learning I had HCV made these feelings go in to hyper-drive.

On many occasions I allowed and greeted the vast dark clouds to cover me in the gloomy shadows that would roll in and obscure my view. However, I also welcomed the voices and flashes of understanding that temporarily blinded me with their reason and logic. They visually reminded me of a beautiful future landscape on which I had glimpsed. The sun overhead still provided warmth in my life but the air nonetheless was cool under the shadows of the clouds overhead.

It didn't take long for me to figure out that my silent reflections and negative thought processes as well as the false perceptions which were created by them were severely influencing and changing me, in more ways than one. I was becoming a foreigner in my own body. I started to isolate myself. I perceived and dwelt on the worst in every situation. I started to act, speak and treat others with indifference; this fundamentally altered my relationships in a real negative way.

My relationship with John went from being stable and healthy to being unstable and unhealthy in a matter of weeks. The relationships with my friends in essence crashed simply because I withdrew from them. I didn't answer the phone or go out to meet them, I simply did not have the words to say. During this time I allowed my perceptions to completely sabotage my life.

My diagnosis made me feel like I had been abandoned and forgotten by the world but the fundamental truth was that I abandoned and forgot the world and placed myself in a voluntary protective bubble. What I should have done was share my fears, so people could understand what was happening to me. But I didn't. My life experience changed my perception and I believed I was too messed up to be loved or accepted by others.

Looking back I can see I got confused by the situation I was in, by my illness and the things around it that I didn't understand. At the time it didn't seem fair, it had no reason, none that I could understand. I was placed in this situation with a purpose unknown to me, but I would soon be taught to truly focus on something other than myself. I would also discover how to focus and trust in an entity beyond understanding, something beyond reason. I would be trained not to quit or settle for less than the best outcome. I had been shown how I had focused my life on avoiding, evading and self centeredness and this was about to change. I would learn who I was as a person and to be the best person I could be. I would also come to know the true value and true nature of commitment and courage and it would be demonstrated to me from others.

Chapter 9

Family loyalty

I allowed a tornado with two spouts, called my diagnosis, to abruptly rise from the depths of my life, and annihilation and chaos came with it. Within three short weeks, the foster world I thought I intimately knew became entangled in a vortex and spiralled out of my control; it removed everything that had grounded me over the last 20 years.

The roots that had grounded and underpinned my marriage started to break. I found it hard to lie with my husband as his wife. I tried to remember the sureness in John's voice and the calm positive words spoken followed by the last lingering warmth of his lips. I wanted to rekindle that positiveness and experience the warmth it presented but the blackness of my infection broke the fragile memory and returned me to the bleak reality of life with HCV. My internal thoughts flowed, defined, steady and indifferent. They simply accused me of my crimes as I sat guilty in the dock. I heard their supporting arguments, arguments I could not refute. My thoughts had become my internal prosecutor and they were presenting a sound case against me. I was infected and my presence put others at risk, the line of reasoning was accurate and I had no rebuttal.

Any intimate moments we shared were shrouded in a veil of masked, deep-seated fear. A fear I would infect him. I would not put him at risk so I stopped engaging in any sexual contact. I found it impossible to act 'normally' around him, especially in the bedroom. I felt vile inside and I felt that vileness seep out of every pore and coat my skin, like tar. I believed every time we interacted, his steel grey eyes would drill into me penetrating deep into my soul reading every thought and feeling I had. I thought he saw the darkness. He must have. It was all over me. His eyes gave me mixed signals. I thought he had a hidden strategic game plan, his escape. I was not sure, but, I perceived odd vibes from John. I suspected he was lying to me about something, shielding me from his true feelings I assumed, he was not telling me the whole truth.

There was very little foundations left holding our relationship together. Communication was non existent, we had no sexual relations, no physical contact and I pushed him so far out of my atmosphere he may never find his way back. I thought surely now he would move on. I knew this would cause undeniable pain and possibly be something I would not recover from, but I thought I was mentally ready and prepared for that scenario. For a split second my life was crystal clear, it was a perfect balance of rituals and balance yet at the same time it was so full of chaos and suffering all at the same time.

My life hung in the balance, a grain of sand in the perfect hour glass defying all the odds and remaining in the top half. I was living in a dream state walking in defiance of the odds. However I knew it would not last. I believed it would be inevitable; it was just the time, how long would it take him to go. I thought it would be the best thing for everyone, even the children. With my limited knowledge at the time, I genuinely believed I was going to die, and die soon. I certainly didn't want the children to watch me suffer and live through that experience, especially if they didn't have to.

If I lost my family a perpetual nightfall would settle over my life. There would be no beautiful multi-coloured sunset to brighten my world there would only be a grayness as it simply turned from a soft grey to a darker shade whilst the surrounding breeze got colder. My heart beat a strong and steady pulse for this family. I loved them deeply. They were all so familiar to me, familiar isn't the right word, precious is more like it, these were people I cherished. I felt their warmth, I knew their individual scent, I had a connection to these people and a strong urge to protect them. I would never put them at risk ever.

Losing John would be really tough. I had always found comfort in his arms. I felt safe and warm in each embrace. He was a magnet one I would find hard to pull away from. He had a warmth and essence about him that lingered around me like an intimate whirl wind; it would die slowly when he was gone. I could not afford to open myself up to the conflict of emotions or the inward bombardment, which would arise from his departure. Voices of every tone and inflection would echo in my mind, emotions like terrible loneliness as well as the physical sensations of pain would assault me from every angle when this scenario played out. The mental assault would be the worst and hardest to bear. But I knew staying with him was essentially a dangerous, and potentially deadly, prospect for me, and I believed it would be better if our twenty years together ended.

Time crawled past like a small snail on a long journey. Each day the dawn would grow beyond the open wooden slats above my bed and each day John would rub the sleep from his heavily hooded gritty eyes and fumble for his glasses beside him on the wooden chest of draws. It was another long sleepless night for me, consumed with thoughts of our separation.

However, he didn't leave like I expected and my internal sky became a rising flame bursting through the opening allowing scarlet ribbons to dance around the room. His choice to stand beside me was a decision I did not fully understand. It was a vivid contrast to my black muddy thoughts and the grave task hanging over my head. However in the back of my mind rang the old sailors caution 'red sky in the morning a sailors warning'.

A Hep C tsunami had struck its hardest blow and our foundations had been severely shaken, yet our love still stood. For awhile I was able to send the dark passenger back to the underworld in which it lived waiting for the next vulnerable moment in this journey. I felt I had closed the window ever so slightly on the winds of doom that blew continually. For now it had become a slight draft. Questions frequently pierced through my façade, numbing my mind and exposing my weaknesses, questions like why? Why would John stay with me, was it possible that he loved me that much that he would risk his life to be with me? This thought shocked me . . . it was hard to tackle. The dark passenger had its own philosophy and believe me I heard it.

I closely watched John as he processed everything that happened around him and still he stood firm. His unwavering dedication to our relationship changed how I perceived him. I started to really look at him, and I saw a very different man than the one I had first married. I saw subtle changes, ones I had never seen before, probably because I was always so self-absorbed and career focused, I never bothered to look. I'd never really looked at him. He had matured, grown, and I had missed the whole process.

It was during this reflection phase that I realised I didn't see things how they really were. I saw our relationship and life as I was. John had become a strong person, full of conviction and loyalty to his family. A loyalty I had never experienced before, neither of my parents had demonstrated this skill or anything quite like it. It was odd witnessing it for the first time, it was an unknown quantity like so many others in my world at this time. However this was a positive one. I thought, if he believed in us this much, then I needed to pull myself together, and start to fight as well. Fight, for not only my life, but for the family unit I had once helped to create.

It was time for me to stop feeling sorry for myself and rejoin the world. I had found a sound reason to fight and I would not be defeated now.

The first step was to bring John back into my uniquely crazy world, deeper than he had ever been before. Underneath my smoothly polished shell was another hidden entity, the real insecure me. It dwelt deep inside and not many people ever saw it. If you talked to me long enough you may see a glimpse of the real host within, usually my overt personality kept you at bay or deflected you so you rarely witnessed this. I knew I would need to drop my mask and enable John to witness the suffering and pain I had camouflaged up to this point. And at this point I let go of my third face and allowed John true access to ME.

The second step was to get my self educated because at this point I was riding the largest wave of my life in the dark with silent predators stalking from the depths.

Chapter 10

My internal pain

John and I had another hurdle to jump over.

It was time for John to be tested to see if I had infected him during the course of our marriage, we had never practiced safe sex, we had shared toothbrushes, razors, tweezers and had at times had blood present when either or us had tended to each other's wounds. I tried not to let this scenario crush me, I refused to give way to the dark passenger and I tried really hard not to entertain those thoughts. I had to consciously pull my mind away from them as I could not allow myself to dwell in the thoughts and feelings of an earlier period, there was simply no point resurrecting historical events. It was time to start being operational, moving in a positive direction for a change. I could not allow myself to wallow any more.

The time between the test and the results passed agonizingly slowly, and it was the grimmest of times for me. Nebulous shapes fired bullets filled with guilt and blame at me from every angle and they assaulted me. They trembled under my dim reflected positive light but became a living embryonic being. John would blame me. I knew he would reject me if I had indeed infected him. This would be the first nail in my coffin, and the lid would slam shut nice and tight, snuffing out my life in the process.

I had stepped into the arena and dropped my mask. I was not fully prepared but I stood as battle ready as I could anyway. The first enemy was in sight and I knew the battle would begin soon. Tomorrow's mission loomed, the results of Johns test would be presented to us and a sentence would be pronounced. The first part of the trial would be over.

Sleep had been hard to come by as emotionally I sat all night in the dock waiting for the moment of truth. I had waltzed around sleep for many hours and nearly engaged with it, but, it was stolen from me by the first urgent calls of the wild. Their high pitched shrills snatched me back from a momentary cloudy mist that was ready to embrace me. The night was over and the day dawned and an agonising wait to access John's results began.

We lived in a nice uninterrupted area on 2.5 acres. We were surrounded by an odd mix of houses old and new, brick and tile and wood and tin. Some stood majestically on large open plan blocks others were more secluded. Nearly all of the houses in this suburb had two or more dogs, so as I enjoyed my morning runs, my feet pounded the bitumen to the varying harmonies of the passing baying hounds. This estate was not gated but was bordered by parkland with one road in and one road out restricting access.

It was a suburban quietness only minutes away from the bustle of the main Caboolture township and the local doctor's surgery we were scheduled to visit. As we drove to our appointed visit the air in the car was dense saturated with our thoughts. I pressed my face against the window and tried to pierce the gloom, silently allowing the tears to fill my eyes and gently fall down my cheeks.

Words can't explain what I felt at that moment. The jeers, the sly insults and innuendos that were slung at me from within cut deep but this was much worse. I could handle obscenities, hatred and laughter as I was conditioned to that from working in the prison but this was overpowering. I was filled with a penetrating fear, regret and dread. My life hung in the balance, upon a scale that would be revealed in a matter of minutes.

Apprehension dominated my whole being it merged with my soul as John and I sat together quietly, on the hard cold plastic chairs. The flurry and commotion of the busy surgery surrounded and distracted us. I wanted to be in some other alternate reality, something out of the Twilight Zone, or the Fringe. A reality I was not really in, but could observe from the outside. Young children with snotty noses and crusty eyes peered at us from the safety and security of their mother's side. A TV boomed non-descript daily news directly above us, phones constantly rung and people steadily moved in and out of doctors' rooms. The all-encompassing noise and movement was stifling, yet somehow, comforting in its diversion from my predicament.

The judge was ready to see us, we were next on his docket. The door swung open and there he stood, my heart missed a beat, small beads of sweat slid down my temple and adrenalin surged through my body. What a miracle- adrenalin is. It instantly took away my tired body and replaced it with the young virulent essence of my youth. The doctor looked questioningly at John and me. His rounded shoulders encased in a well ironed shirt and vest made him appear squat rather than tall. A frosting of grey covered his temples, an expression of care and empathy had been etched upon his features from the many years of helping the infirm and weak. His wire encased spectacles were slung low on the end of his long Egyptian nose and he peered over the top of them at us and smiled. He lifted his arm and beckoned us into his oversized, cluttered room. For the first time in days, John grabbed my hand, fully encasing it in his. I turned to look up at him, my saddened blue eyes filled with the tears I could no longer contain.

His steely eyes absorbed mine. Time stood still, the grain of sand that had stood defying the odds toppled into the pit and was filtered through to the other side. There was no turning back the hour glass was on a roll and would not be stopped. The question was would I be buried in the sand and forgotten. I felt the deep penetrating stare as he pierced my soul. My heavily burdened heart pounded furiously in my chest. I was nervous and scared, wondering what he would say to me. My eyes moved to look at his half open, upturned mouth, his eyes far too intense for me to focus upon. He slowly leaned closer to me, his lips grazed my ear. His whispered words resonated in my mind and stilled the stranger within, "it is going to be alright, Laurie, trust me."

I gasped for breathe partly from his closeness but mostly from the words spoken and their intended meaning. I tried to register the vibrations I felt emanating from him as he looked at me, searching for a reaction. What I saw radiating from him was love, real love. I believe the quickest way to understand a person is to look at the fruit of their lives, to listen to the hidden man. John had offered me unconditional love without any strings attached. His words verified what I saw. My head told me I was still unsure, my heart wanted to accept what I had just heard. My head asked what if I had infected him. My heart dwelt upon the spoken word.

Love is having a tender heart and is expressed by how we treat people, how we humble ourselves before them, how we forgive them and how we sacrifice ourselves for another. John did that as his eyes delved into mine and I saw that in them.

My head threw questions at me trying to dislodge the stance my heart was taking. How would he react if the test was positive? Would he hate me? Would this terminate our relationship? How would I react? What would happen to the children if both of us were infected? And the dark passenger rose and whispered condemnation and reminded me of the past. The actions of my youth were painted on a canvas before me in vivid colours. I observed a younger version of myself injecting a drug that had brought destruction upon my house. What had I done, all those years ago? How could I have been so stupid, so selfish? The past has an echo and it finds a way to vibrate around you as a constant reminder. Here I sat with John beside me, an innocent man paying a price for something he had no part of.

I unsteadily got up from the chair and slowly turned towards the door. My feet automatically, yet reluctantly, moved me. My trendy blue Nike runners felt like heavy pieces of concrete attached to my feet. What a predicament I had placed us in! The situation was completely surreal. As I reached the door, I recalled my husband's words and his simple captivating smile, "It is going to be alright." Did he truly mean those words? I didn't know if I would feel the same if I found myself in his shoes. Would I feel the same? I doubted it.

John demonstrated strength of character I had not witnessed ever before; a mighty power shone from him, its potency and intensity, totally absorbed me. Where did it come from? The fruit I saw hanging from his vine was quite extraordinary. It made me reassess our relationship, our life and myself. When I originally signed my name on that marriage certificate I thought I was signing my name in the sand not really expecting it to be there tomorrow washed away with the tide. But as I sat in that chair in that situation I realised that was not so, my name sat beside his and was etched into concrete where the water will never wash it away. No situation, no feelings, no mistakes, no circumstances could wipe away our names. Could there possibly be a fracture in the outer lining of the dark tunnel which encircled me? Was it possible to see a glimmer of light and hope? Was John strong enough to carry both of us through this? I thought he just might be.

This was our moment, a defining moment, one we would always remember. I know we all have cross road moments or what we call light bulb moments in our lives, but this particular one was mammoth. We sat close together facing the doctor expectantly. John appeared to be too calm whilst I was more like a ticking time bomb waiting for an opportune time to explode. I began to feel uncomfortable in my chair; it confined me holding me tight in place. I felt like a prisoner on death row, awaiting my sentence. I wondered why John was so calm, how could he be, it didn't make any sense to me. I closed my eyes and took a deep breath to steady myself, to stop the body tremors that resembled Parkinson disease and to slow the adrenalin flow which accelerated my heart beat and brought a feeling of euphoria. A feeling I would welcome in many other situations but in this moment I needed clarity and lucidity not vagueness. I wanted to understand every word the doctor said. I also needed a quiet moment to interrupt the shrieking voices in the back of my mind before they gathered any more momentum. I needed my mind to be still for just a time.

In the stillness I silently prayed the doctor would hold a redemption card and my mortal sins would be forgiven. I would accept my punishment but this man didn't deserve this, he didn't deserve to be infected, he didn't deserve to live a life with a chronic illness. I deserved it, he certainly didn't. Yet here we were awaiting a potential sentence for an innocent man.

The doctor was sympathetic to our situation. He had limited knowledge about the subject of HCV but he knew people and he cared about both of us. He started by questioning how we were both coping. I couldn't answer him, I looked at him astonished.

Words failed me. I thought, if you only knew the weight of the burdens we carried! I knew he was genuinely concerned about our situation, but every delay was an agonizing blow to me. I just wanted to yell "hurry up! Give us the results!"

All I could rustle up was a simple nod. John answered in long sweeping sentences which amazed me. I thought what are you doing; just tell him you want the results. I was nearly sick with anticipation and anxiety. I could feel my pulse as it flowed heavy and fast through the narrow opening in the side of my neck, nausea rose and threatened to remove me from the only room I needed to be in. I could not remove my eyes from the dancing computer screen. Words hip hopped across the screen as he pressed button after button, it was impossible to decipher any of them, yet I knew the answer lay waiting, hidden there somewhere. Unconsciously my hands fidgeted. My long fingers toyed with a piece of rough fabric, scuff marks erupted on the hem of my black shorts as it was irritated between my index finger and thumb.

Finally, the computer screen stopped its dance and John's medical history opened up in front of me, pages containing columns of facts and figures, unlocked for me to see. I leant forward and scanned the screen trying to process and locate the answers I wanted.

The doctor sat quietly as he discerned the results. Finally he turned to face us. His deep brown eyes peered at us; a hint of a smile touched the corners of his mouth. He paused, and then turned the humming computer screen towards us to allow us to see the data on the screen. Old historical appointments and outcomes filled the page, so much information, it was impossible for me to distinguish the results. John's green eyes jumped from the doctor to the screen and back again. I knew he was trying desperately to detect and recognise something as was I.

His eyes finally settled unemotionally on the doctor, waiting. I wasn't quite as patient as John. I was agitated, my impatience and anxiety grew, it growled inside me, threatening to eat up my determination to sit quietly. He finally spoke, directing all his words to the man who sat calmly and intently beside me. His eyes never left John's face, his full attention channelled towards him. His words flowed specifically and with exact detail. The hammer blade hit the anvil and delivered its verdict. Two sets of eyes focused simultaneously upon me, they penetrated and probed me for a response. I felt the heat of their glances as they searched and questioned me, interested in my reaction to the outcome.

I sat stunned as my mind tried to rationalise the result. How could that be? He was negative, but, how? What did this mean? I never considered that to be a possibility. Of course, I wanted him to have this kind of outcome, but I never believed it would be possible. It was unimaginable, unreal, remarkable and awesome.

I felt humbled by this result. Humbled that I could be given another chance. Humbled that I had not infected him and humbled that he still loved me, after all of this.

All of a sudden, my mind filled and overflowed with hundreds of questions, all fighting to be heard. How could this be? What sort of infectious disease was this? I recalled some risky situations we had been in during our marriage, where my blood had come in contact with his, and still he was not infected. How come? It shocked me, the whole scenario was surreal.

I started to see a glimmer of real, tangible hope. I could see a fracture in the tunnel wall and a tiny ray of light beamed steadily into my darkness. A lifeline was offered, a rope to guide me, and I gladly received it. However, I wondered if it would be sturdy enough to save me before the walls collapsed under the weight of the burdens I carried. Was there now a possibility of some hope for us? Could we actually live together without a constant threat lurking in the background? If so, I wouldn't have to leave. Was that a possibility?

The stale air seemed to collapse around me, sucked out by an overpowered vacuum, and replaced with a beautiful, sweet aroma. The stiffness and tension I had carried for the last few weeks were erased by a few simple words, "not infected." For the first time since this saga began I felt relaxation creep into my cells, like a slow rising mist after the rain on a hot sultry day. I heard a symphony as it played soothing notes inside my head. It brought a calming affect one I had not felt in quite some time. The words not infected surrounded me; they flowed over me blanketing me in the sweetest of melodies. He was not infected, I couldn't believe it.

My senses were alert, sharpened by this new situation. I sat silently evaluating John's reaction. After twenty years of marriage, I could identify minute, but subtle, changes in him. Small, unseen gestures, slight changes in his tone of voice and minor body movements, detected by me, but unrecognisable to others. I waited quietly, intimately trying to decipher his signals. John's face beamed like the sun. Joy radiated from him. He was genuinely happy, relieved by the news, and so was I. A deep full darkness had settled over us for the last few weeks. This had turned our lives into one long cold winter's night, but this news made the sky over head turn from its deep purple into a lovely shade of pale blush. Through the pinkish hue I witnessed glimpses of the rays of sunlight as they waited for the right time to shine and illuminate the weeks ahead.

I dared to smile. I allowed the muscles of my body to relax and I felt pure joy, something I had not experienced for quite some time. I wondered if this would put the dark passenger to sleep for awhile and enable me to work constructively towards a possible solution. As I looked at the people before me, I said a silent prayer of thanks to a God I only slightly knew.

I had not been really close to God. I knew of Him, I had witnessed things and had firsthand experiences of His capabilities, but I didn't really know Him. I guess I was what you would call, "a Clayton's Christian," an on-again-off-again kind of person who practised the principles only when it suited me. My only real experience of going to church was at the Anglican boarding school I attended. There I learnt that if you are too messed up you are unlovable or unaccepted by God. Later Sue would explain that God loved me any way I came. She also taught me He was not mad at me for the things I had done. Through Isaiah 54 verse 8 and 9 God communicates his lack of anger with us. He states 'with everlasting kindness I will have compassion on you" "so now I have sworn not to be angry with you and never to rebuke you again".

I had learnt these things but I just never really believed that the promises in the Bible applied to me, as I was *so* sinful; unworthy in every respect of the word. So, why would He want to help someone like me? Sue once told me that God just wants us to come home, come home to peace, home to joy and home to overwhelming love. She made it quite clear that a feast had been prepared for everyone of us, murders, thieves, liars, adulterers alike for there was no difference or level to sin. In spite of our human nature we are all still acceptable to God, you see all our debts, yours and mine, have already been paid for, nailed painfully to a wooden cross. She stated we are all like a prodigal son and we will all wear a beautiful coat that none of us would ever earn. In that moment, standing beside John as he received his welcoming news I felt God may have listened to my silent pleas and I couldn't be more grateful.

Walking out of that medical centre, towards the waiting car, I felt like I wanted to kiss the hard concrete surface that my unencumbered feet walked upon. The euphoria and relief this forecast brought was a turning point for both of us. We were united in hope, and together, we had overcome our first major milestone. I knew this was only the beginning. I also knew many more hardship lay before us but, as we left that building, I just focused on the moment. We reconnected with each other, melded with the paint on the canvas and became a striking picture, a silhouette of a happy normal couple.

This would certainly be a dance to memorise. I remember the way John looked at me, his face showed understanding, forgiveness and love. I realised all of these traits were woven into the fabric of his life and he reached out and offered them to me. That night we held each other tight, cherishing the time we had, simply picking up where we left off a couple of weeks before. I couldn't have felt more loved as I lay wrapped in the warmth and comfort of his arms. It was a night to remember as it shut the door on the uncertainty and doubt that had been between us and it opened the door on our relationship again, something we both needed. How long it would last I didn't know, but for this point in time I was content and my inner voices were stilled.

We had witnessed a real victory, one I didn't yet fully understand, but it was a victory all the same. It provided us with strength to consider the next step. I wasn't yet sure where I was headed with this whole Hep C thing, but I did know I would need to make some hard and fast plans. John's negative result was an aspect of this disease I didn't understand. To me infectious meant infectious, obviously that was not the case as he was not infected. This meant there was a lot I needed to learn and understand about HCV. I also knew *I was infected* and the journey I faced tomorrow and beyond that was an ominous, snow-covered mountain which loomed before me. I knew that the hardest path was yet to come.

But for tonight I snuggled closer into the warm safety net my husband provided and slept the sleep of snow white.

Chapter 11

Attitude is everything

The days that followed John's visit to the doctor filled me with optimism. I noticed my dependably upbeat personality returned. I was usually like a balloon filled with helium, only a pin could pop my enthusiasm. Negativity did not usually reign in my inner being, yes the voices challenged me and were constantly present but in general I was able to suppress them. If you knew me you would have said I was a positive person with a lot of drive. I was task orientated and got the job done and I could motivate people beyond their own perceived capacity. I guess you could call me a great manipulator, I just did it nicely, or so I thought, maybe John would say something different. I was not quite sure how I acquired these traits but I was certainly glad to have them. They had helped me conquer many hardships during my lifetime. I didn't know it at the time, but these characteristics were qualities I would need for the long journey ahead.

There was a great sense of relief and happiness filtering through our home for those first few weeks after our doctor's visit. We both knew we had passed under the shadow of a cloud and had lingered there for a time, but we were also aware we had shuffled our way back into the sunlight. I can only speak for myself when I say my overall perception and outlook for our future changed. Positive notes, affirmation and images started to spice up my mind, the lovely soft pink flowers of the bougainvillea returned and replaced the negative vines that had threatened to take hold of my life. Their fragrance and essence infused anticipation and hope into our home. This exquisite aroma permeated every room and saturated all the participants in my house. Laughter reigned, but fear still lurked in the background.

During this time, I don't know why, but I started to pray more regularly. I believed I had been given a sign, a symbol of hope when John's test came back negative. I had the feeling that a debt had been paid and I hadn't paid the price. Someone had paid my bill, signed a cheque on my behalf and I was very thankful. How was I ever to repay the deed? I knew it was impossible. I had been given a gift that I could never repay so I just gave thanks through prayer.

At this point in my life my two lives started to battle each other. It basically became a war between my heart life,—my feelings—and my thought life,—my mind—as well as my attitude versus my desires. Even though I had not been on this journey long I had already started to realise it was what I did when nobody was really looking that mattered. How I acted at home with my family, how I treated other people, especially when they were long suffering like John. The question was what I was really doing for these people. All of this I came to understand was the real meaning to my life. It wasn't the masquerade I played, or, the face I showed to the outside world, or what I wore to display myself. It was about relationships. What this journey taught me was to get excited about getting up each day, to be really positive about living regardless what life threw at me.

My daily prayer began simply, "thank you for this day. God, I know I am unworthy to come before you, but I am here asking for your help, I need to be healed. I don't know why this is happening I only need strength and courage to go through it, please help me understand".

Changes appeared subtly, they crept into my life slowly. I found I focused more on positive things. I had found a sound reason to stay, to fight this disease. The best one lay beside me warm, muscular and completely naked. As I lay in our big king sized bed, my mind stilled in the silence I heard the rhythmic breathing of John as he lay peacefully beside me. I lay listening for a long moment staring intently into nowhere just appreciating the life I had. After a while, I started to visualise a hopeful future, full of expectations and a smile danced at the corners of my mouth.

As the days progressed I found it easier to maintain this daily ritual. The golden ball of the sun bobbed joyfully above the horizon of my life, it brought clarity and candour. Meanwhile overhead a clear blue sky filtered down through a casual mist and the household atmosphere and a Hep C strategy swiftly gained definition and sharpness. I simply had to retain the right attitude, an attitude of faith, forgiveness, love and hope. The major problem was coming up with a way to keep the neighbouring voices at bay; these voices tended to be lively, accusing and critical and had previously crushed me. I had to find a way to prevent the next storm from causing so much turbulence to my family and my life.

My previous self-destructive beliefs and attitude had shackled me in the past. I could not allow them to confine or blind me anymore. Our recent good news, as well as the realisation that John was not going anywhere, had released me from the chains which prevented me from positively engaging in my life.

The first strategy in my big comeback was to make the conscious decision that I would fight back. I decided I wanted a life. I wanted a future with John. I would not roll over and let this disease rob me of everything I cared about. It had already stolen weeks of my life. I would not lie down and let it kick me again.

Once my attitude started to change and I started to fight for what was already mine, I was surprised to discover how deeply and sincerely I was loved. John accepted me in my ragged condition, he knew how wounded I was. He knew how rejected I felt. He knew I was carrying an infectious disease yet he didn't hold any of that against me instead he opened his arms to me acknowledging all of this and loving me anyway. John showed me just what unconditional love was, in a manner in which I could understand. He didn't hold my sins against me, he just accepted me.

His actions were something I had never witnessed before, maybe he had offered them to me under different circumstances but I don't think I was ready to accept them. I must have been blindfolded for most of my married life because I had never seen this level of support before.

The second strategy included a vow to learn everything I could about the little passenger hiding in my body and banish it from my life. I chose to stop feeling sorry for myself. As I stood in the arena facing my opponent I stepped enthusiastically forward and picked up the weapons of war. I chose the first part of my defence, body armor made from chain mal which would protect the knowledge I would gain and protect my heart by keeping the love and support of my family close to my skin. I picked up a full face helmet to provide the faith I would need to help combat the mental attacks that regularly plagued me. The sword of treatment still lay in the distance, I was unsure if it was a possibility, however I would start the process to learn and understand the treatment regime and the potential it may provide. Hopefully the battle would be won using this option. I hoped it would deliver the final blow and rid me of HCV forever.

Chapter 12

Formulating a battle strategy

In those early days HCV scared me, it was an unknown entity. It resembled Mount Everest. I stood at base camp looking up at the cold icy steep face, the wind chill factor dropped the temperature further and a low mist hindered me as I tried to plot the best and safest path to take to conquer this ominous disease. After all my years of study I had learnt how to conduct research and compile data. With this ability I was able to systematically examine and analyse my findings—and I ended up with reams of it. I began to have a very intimate relationship with Google, it became my best friend and I spent a lot of time with it—sometimes six hours or more a day—in those first few months. What I did was categorise the data into specific topics such as transmission, prevention, treatments, natural therapies and affects, I also looked at worse case scenarios.

I learnt this tiny body snatcher, my unknown invader for the last 20 years, was totally immersed in my life substance. Its venom saturated my blood. It had become a co-host, a being I shared my body with daily. Until now, we had lived in some sort of harmony.

An unknown compromise had been reached between my body and this virus; a cycle only my immune system understood, and one my mind wanted liberation from. Liberation would come at a high price. I had to make my body inhospitable to this virus, turning it into a chemical playground, a playground the virus could not enjoy. Before I did this I wanted to totally amerce myself in breaking down this mysterious, microscopic passenger I had picked up.

Over the next few months, I found myself enthusiastically consumed with internet research. The internet contains so much information, I read page after page devoted to suitable, reliable information. I was interested in everything: conflicting views, treatments, natural therapies, medical journals, blogs and testimonials. I hungered for it all. I devoured and gorged myself on all of it just like a ravenous wolf.

My life reshaped itself. Over a really short period of time I moved from the embryonic sac—where I had spent the last forty odd years plugged into the matrix so to speak—into the real world. The doctor had slapped my face nice and hard leaving a red welt on my cheek. He tore me from the warmth and safety and awakened me to a very different reality. A reality where disease and viruses reigned. As I took my first step in the new land I learnt to be more open-minded, more impartial, more objective and I had a lot more empathy.

I also stopped the blame game. I took responsibility for the things of the past. I became accountable. I no longer made excuses for my poor behaviour. As I grew I accepted no one talked me into doing anything, I chose to participate willingly in all activities. Being diagnosed with HCV was a direct consequence of the choices I made, I willingly chose to participate in behaviour that was detrimental to my health and the blame lay at my feet, alone, no one else's. I accepted that and that fact alone moved me from a toddler into adolescence. I still had a long way to go to adulthood but I was no longer crawling, I was one step closer to getting up that mountain.

My home life took on a new flavour as I structured the environment to limit transmission. I became clinical and straightforward, I removed my toothbrush from the mainstream holder, I stopped using Johns razor and went to waxing instead, I refused to have sex when I knew I was close to my monthly cycle and I tended to my open wounds and sterilised surfaces continually. To outsiders this would have appeared laborious and challenging but I reasoned I could deal with it. It was a price I could easily pay. My studies had informed me I could prevent transmission if I was careful and deliberate enough not to make mistakes.

There would always be doubt, like a wall I couldn't see beyond. With it came feelings of fear and uncertainty. However John stood beside all these actions, fiercely and valiantly supporting them and encouraging me. I couldn't question his integrity after all he had done, after all he had forgiven. All our past personal pain and experiences had taught me I would do whatever was asked of me or I would die trying. I would overcome this disease and I would not infect any other person especially not in this household. My resolve was a solid as the concrete beneath my feet.

As time progressed and my investigations continued, the papers on my floor piled up and I began to feel more and more in control. The scales swung in my favour. Learning enabled me to formulate a skilled strategy to start the long climb up my Mt Everest. It provided me with the right equipment; I now had my harness and crampons on as well as my cold weather gear and thermal underwear. Wisdom and truth replaced my ignorance and fear and the climb was no longer so daunting. As I grew in both knowledge and awareness, I became less vulnerable to the blistering cold winds and the words that hovered. I learnt to avert and redirect the undertones and the harmful messages they hinted at and replace them with rationale. Learning brought a different kind of maturity and growth within me, it gave me confidence, dignity and enabled me to consider the future and consider the potential presented.

With this new maturity came a growth in my level of faith. For me I found God. For you it might be something else and for that purpose I will talk about a higher being. I came to see the world was full of believers of all faiths who look good on the outside, they put on the right clothes but they lack what it takes on the inside. I witnessed real Christian behaviour from John. He didn't gossip, judge or criticise me, he didn't cause strife in our lives he simply offered his unconditional love and acceptance. I believe this is the true heart of any faith. All I can tell you is that I am not the same person I was ten years ago, I think I am a much better person and that can only be contributed to believing in a higher being.

Religion tells us we are not worthy, that we are too messed up to be accepted by God but the reality is we are acceptable, we are lovable and we can be nurtured if we want to be. I spent most of my life believing I was not worthy of anything. Finally when I came to accept I was worthy and I realised a price has been paid for me, I was staggered by the feelings it brought. I recognised all the things I had done in my life, my drug use, my prostitution, my abortion, my selfishness, my attitude, my behaviour all of it was ok, it was acceptable. These actions were really no different than anyone else's, we all have done wrong things in our lives, yet a price has been paid, paid in blood. In my case it was all nailed to a tree. Guiltless flesh was scourged and torn from an innocent back whilst blameless blood flowed and turned the grains of sand red, all so I could feel a peace and joy that I had never experienced before.

The same God that cleaned me up can also clean you up. There is really nothing like being accepted and loved and seen as an asset not a liability. A grace had been offered to me and this same grace can be offered to you. It helped me in times of need and I know it can help you also. I believe that all of us are searching for something.

I read in one of Dean Koontz's novels 'We are buried when we are born. The world is a place of graves occupied and graves potential. Life is what happens while we wait our appointment with the mortician.' To me life is more than that. I know death is an actuality for each of us however what we do with the living part is very important. I don't know about you but I want to leave a positive legacy behind. I don't just want to wait for the morticians stitch. I actually believe each of us has a lot more to offer to the world around us, each of us has a song to sing. Some of us go to meet the mortician with a song still in us. I spent the first forty years of my life really not living, I was existing, but not really living, if I had continued on the same path I would have met my maker with my song unsung.

It wasn't until I received my diagnosis and found my faith that I started to look at life without my dark sunglasses on. I hope you find something to help you on your life's path. I found what I needed, I hope you do to. Faith helped me understand. It helped me move forward. It helped me learn to love and trust again, and made me feel a part of something special.

The biggest lesson I learnt during this phase of my life was our circumstances are temporary but our character is not.

Chapter 13

Nothing in life truly remains hidden

"Diseases can be our spiritual flat tires—disruptions in our lives that seem to be disasters at the time but end by redirecting our lives in a meaningful way".

~Bernie S. Siegel

My specialist appointment was only a few short weeks away. I had waited apprehensively for three and a half, long-drawn-out months to see this man. I hoped he would relieve me of my burden. I had reams and reams of data. Two large folders were filled with information on the best ways to manage the disease I carried as well as some natural therapies and treatment options. I knew from the information I had collected the treatment options were a product called interferon and Ribavirn.

I learnt Interferon was a protein that occurred naturally in the body in very small amounts. It was a drug that needed to be injected into the fat layers on your stomach or thigh and was used to assist in the fight against HCV. Interferon stimulated the body's immune system and from all accounts made people quite ill with flu like symptoms and fatigue as well as depression, sounded like taking it would be fun. Ribavirin on the other hand was taken in tablet form and was in a class of antiviral medications called nucleoside analogues. It worked by hindering the virus replication process inside the body and it came with a lot of other *great* side effects like a cough, skin irritations insomnia and many others. It certainly didn't sound like treatment would be an easy task to complete for anyone. My research had informed me that *the Pegasys brand* of treatment had a higher success rate. I just hoped when I finally met this specialist he would endorse that particular product.

As my appointment loomed closer I knew we had to inform the children and our family. We had either been lucky or we were great at hiding things, because no one was the wiser. However we also knew we couldn't leave it much longer. Deception is not a good thing to be good at. I didn't want to go through the next year or two being deceptive to my kids, lying to them didn't set a good example to either of them, I wanted to be a better role model than that. Imagine leaving that kind of legacy behind.

John and I were resilient, but neither of us wanted the kids to suffer. Like any parent who loves their children, the last thing we wanted to do was be responsible for causing them unnecessary pain. Nevertheless we knew it was time. Luckily my fervent study had provided me with an extensive arsenal including a wide-ranging array of answers to respond to the questions that I thought would be shot at me.

I was reticent to uncover any of my past to those closest to me, especially the portions I had tried to forget. I had discarded my old life a long time ago, burying it in a steel casket. I also didn't like that decayed person, and I certainly wasn't keen to revisit my past. But, here I was, forced to revive it. I was nothing like that old rotting corpse. I was reborn. I lived a vastly different lifestyle now. My recollections of this old life were both distasteful and confronting. I could see no honour or esteem in any of it.

My diagnosis made me realise nothing in life stays completely hidden or remains in the darkness forever. It seems that everything is eventually revealed, uncovered, brought out into the open, for the whole world to see, whether you like it or not. This was my moment, my revelation. Back then, I didn't think about the consequences of any of my actions, but I was not so naive today. My penalty had caused so much anguish, sorrow and embarrassment to myself and to John, and now I had to face the children.

I felt uncomfortable and humiliated in this situation. The last thing I wanted to do was give a detailed account of the things I had done in the past to my children and to the other members of my family. I would have preferred as I flicked through the pages of my life that they would have been filled with things to be proud of, things I could share and not feel embarrassed or sad about. My story was not the kind of story with a fairy tale ending, their father was in part the prince that saved me, but there was no magic kiss that made my world right. My life was more like a train wreck, carnage spread all over the countryside. Instead the tale that would be told would include darkness, evil deeds, destruction and intimidation and it would all end with an ominous threat.

There was no way of softening the story, the tale would be told truthfully but I would try and soften the impact with love. All I could hope for was understanding. What I needed was acceptance but it was what I would get that totally frightened me. The family needed to hear the whole truth, and they would. For twenty years I had covered my secrets under the ground and had tried to forget their existence. I had moved on but someone had never forgotten. And that someone had other ideas.

A silent unknown detective had reopened my case and the judge demanded a new trial, it was time to exhume my secrets and hand them back to the mortician for the autopsy that never occurred. The thought of this new trial terrified me, it would be a lot more public and the end result was totally out of my hands. I vowed to stand in the dock and tell the truth, I was a condemned person but I would withhold nothing from them. As the hearing commenced and the prosecution started with their questions, I vowed to honestly and openly answer it. I feared the outcome and I knew it would be hard, but I also knew I had to deal with something I had run away from all those years ago. I believe this was one of those critical and essential steps I needed to take.

These last few months of hiding the truth had been

excruciating. I felt physically and mentally exhausted as I put on a mask daily to pretend and cover my internal anguish with a blanket of invented happiness. My dreams had been troubled and lucid. What I saw as I shut my eyes was a cold grey marble marker with my name etched in long flowing letters upon its surface. John and the kids double over in grief as they stood side by side holding each other whilst the bitter cold wind swirled around them on a bleak winter's day. I could not shake the vividness of the dream no matter what I did it followed me throughout the days preceding my big reveal. The future loomed up before me like a giant black hole and a question hovered in its core would the children understand.

I am not really sure why we took so long to tell anyone. I can only surmise that we both were in a form of denial. If we didn't talk about it, then it wasn't really there. Although, it hovered in the corner of every room we visited, followed us everywhere like the proverbial white elephant in the room. I believed we needed time to find a sense of peace with each other, as well as understand our feelings and the impact HCV would have on our marriage, before we could talk to others about it. I think taking that time out enabled us to assess the situation from a lot of different perspectives. I sought knowledge John sought acceptance. Time provided us both with a breathing space to try and acknowledge and understand what had happened. I also believe this space enabled us to assess our future relationship, even though we never discussed it I think it was the main reason for the delay.

I knew the day I would reveal my secrets to the clan was

imminent but before that could occur. John and I needed to discuss our feelings and work out a solid plan for the future so we could offer the kids a solution when we spoke to them. I had all the facts but I had no answers.

The long dark night was at an end, the ashen dawn did nothing to diminish my feelings of dread for the designated morning talk.
It wouldn't be a life threatening discussion but it would be deep, very deep. I knew the content could potentially change the course of my life. My doubts about John's commitment prevailed. These doubts were born out of my own feeling of inadequacy. I kept thinking if the shoe was on the other foot how would I react, would I be able to show as much grace as John had shown me. I wasn't sure how I would react. He had shown me another path and I was still trying to understand and come to terms with it.

We sat side by side, together on the patio, facing the pebbled concrete pool. There was nothing between us but the whisper of the wind and the stirring of the lethargic dust particles in the ribbons of light. In the distance tall palm trees swayed and danced to a gentle unheard song. The sweet aroma of fragrant coffee floated gently around us on a delicate breeze. The sun was high in the sky a bright yellow fiery ball, its rays sparkled and reflected like diamonds on the rippling surface of the pool. Our hands wrapped around the hot beverages as we sipped the strong essence. Despite the sunlight, the air was a little cool, the hint of winter as it prevailed over the outgoing autumn. We sat comfortably in the colourfully cushioned deck chairs our backs moulded with their distinct curves. Silently we savoured the moment, both conscious of the task ahead. The announcement would come in its own time, it would be sombre and sluggish with a vague sorrow yet it may also offer a hint of a new season with new ideas, new suggestions and a new flavour. Time would tell.

I blinked away the urge to cry, yet tears spilled from my eyes despite my stoic effort to prevent them. John leaned over and caught them with his finger stoking my face in the process and the words flowed. I asked about how he felt about sharing a life and living in close proximity with someone in my condition. Was he scared? Did he fear for the children? Was I still attractive to him? We talked about treatment options, cure rates, natural therapies, my options, we talked about risk factors, we talked about our relationship, the future and we deliberated his negative result, both of us amazed and happy he was not infected.

We talked for hours. The sky turned from a beautiful shade of pale blue into a deep blush, the only break in our conversation was the school pick up trip. We had immersed ourselves in a philosophical discussion, a reflective and sincere sharing of our feelings, our fears, our hopes, and together we cried. As the sun set and turned the sky a lovely shade of purple a bond was created between us. A bond that would not easily be broken. It would not be forgotten by me even in the darkest hours. I would put it aside for a while but I would never forget the words spoken that day and the promises we made to each other. For this talk made me a believer in marriage and restored my faith in people.

This day would be with me for all eternity and when the day came when I really needed to stand by the convictions made that day I would recall the agreement we made to simply stand by each other no matter what happened. It was a mutual contract between us, a bond to uphold the family unit in times of severe trouble. John would stand beside me. His eyes and cold focused conviction jolted me back to reality. He would not be my Judas. He would be the warrior that vowed to care for me and I finally realised I had made a serious misjudgement of his character. He was not a betrayer in the guise of an angel, he was simply the real deal.

Even though I felt more settled, I found it impossible to make any future plans. The smooth-tongued mortician lingered in the background and my persuasive dream still followed me. I was far more aware of HCV and its potential to eradicate its host—me—with cancer or liver disease or both, which made me more perceptive about the likelihood of my own death. I understood the risk and protective factors, but I didn't quite know how the disease had affected me personally. I could have cirrhosis or serious liver damage at that moment and not know. I knew these were the two biggest threats to my life.

Knowing this made it virtually impossible to plan or think about what tomorrow may bring, for a goal orientated person like me this was a really big change. It challenged the whole constructs of my personality. I thrived on goals, getting the task done, achieving was my number one priority yet here I was unable
to mentally make a single long term goal. I am talking about a

person who on New Year's Eve creates and systematically plans the whole next year using both short and long term objectives with specific timelines to reach a detailed target. Now I am not talking ambiguous goals I am talking meticulously thought out and precise goals. Not only do I write them down I turn them into a highly visualised picture so I can have it right in front of me. So not being able to continue with this should have been a red flag not only to those around me but to myself. Living day to day with no purpose or being mindful—living in the moment—as it is called was in my case easier said than done. I would become better at it as time went by, but it was hard to break a forty year old habit. I had turned myself into an adrenalin junkie and like any drug addiction it was a habit that was very hard to break.

In those early days I lost control of my world, circumstances had forced me to relinquish the reigns of my life and it sometimes felt my life didn't feel real. At times I felt like a fictional character in an elusive story, a spectator watching a series of scenes in a play, a play I was the main character in however I had no scripted lines to learn it was a pantomime that was ad lib. My responses and actions were custom-made to the scenes I found myself in.

At night I would lie in bed desperately seeking sleep and solace from the characters I played during the day. But I would hear the familiar cries of the Australian bush, the possums noisily disrupting and upending the natural balance on our front veranda and the curlews high pitched scream like a child's cry alerting it parents of its desperate needs, as they filtered through the half opened window above where I lay. The noises always crept nearer to my window as if they knew I was listening. Their lamentations brief yet disturbing keeping me from any slumber I may have enjoyed. Always between three and four in the morning the wailing came alerting the wildlife to the awakening of the day. In summer this was followed by a consistent pounding on the glass, a booming crash when a nesting bird continually battled fiercely with its own mirrored reflection.

I never awoke refreshed only more haunted by the prospect that someone else was in charge of my destiny. I had lost total control of my life. I wasn't scared about this prospect, maybe a bit perplexed. What I really struggled with was when it occurred to me that I could be taken from this earth at anytime, swiped form the earth in a Godly blow. My days were actually numbered, this was a concept I had not really dwelt upon before, it lingered in the background like a dark shadowy mist. I was forced to confront and accept my own mortality.

At forty you think you are pretty indestructible, not like you were in your twenties because you had everything back then, but in your forties you don't or I didn't dwell on death and dying or sickness, you are living it up making the most of life. The reality of it is death is all around us it lurks in the atmosphere. Regardless of what horror or happiness transpires in our lives the mortician has our number and one day it will be time for him to call.

It made me think, maybe life was a bit like a performance review. I wondered what the assessment criteria contained. Was I being assessed on my behaviours and attitudes and if I didn't fit the bill, what would be the result. Was HCV part of my reprimand, was this the rod that would spare me from further punishment later on. I had not a single answer to any of these questions. I wished I didn't have to go through this but I couldn't change anything.

The past can never be changed. However if I had a time machine I would have gone back and rewritten a few things, altered a couple of details but that is impossible for now. I knew I had wasted so many days of my life focusing on what I did wrong in the past when I should have been expending my energy on the things that were right in front of me, the things that mattered. I can't change what I have done or the things I have lost or the people I have hurt all I can do from this point forward is focus on the time I have left. I didn't have the best start in life like so many other people but I would have a much better finish.

I think that day on the veranda as we watched the sun sink slowly into the western horizon burning from a fiery orange towards a violet as the heavens darkened above us was the turning point for me. I had uncovered all my inner feelings, my uncertainties and my reservations. I placed all my cards flat on the table and fully exposed my hand to John. I laid the inner parts of myself out before him, something I had never done before. I had no secrets left within me.

Twenty years ago he was a young untested inexperienced man, but that day I saw a warrior a true soldier. A man who stood to defend my honour and the reputation of this family. He had progressed through the rites of passage and somehow I had missed the experience. Realising this shocked me, I couldn't work out how I had never seen the changes in him. I really must have been blind.

Those hours spent by the pool that day sincerely connected us. They opened my eyes to his concerns and personal fears, as well as enabled me to see the real man I was married to. I really saw the changes in him that day. He was transformed. His sympathy for my plight and his pure determination to stand by me boosted my commitment to overcome this speed bump. As I listened to him speak, my loyalty and devotion to our relationship strengthened.

What stunned me the most was just how easy it was to talk to him, to tell him how I felt. I was able to rationalise my thoughts without any judgment, condemnation or criticism, and I was able to listen to his enlightening responses. I was embraced, surrounded by tenderness, not blamed, just loved and accepted. I had discovered someone I could really trust. This level of communication, had never occurred between us ever before, and it felt good.

His words throughout the conversation implied that he did want to stay with me, and he did trust me. He stated he was in this marriage for the long haul and would not throw the towel in now, just because of a slight rough patch we faced. Our marriage vows were permanently imprinted on his heart. He had said yes to "in sickness and in health" and he chose to support me through this battle.

Chapter 14

A one way trip

A few days elapsed after our talk, and we both felt confident and comfortable enough to talk to the children. The strategy had been formulated and the date had been set. As the dawn rose on the new day so would our secret be brought to light? Timing was of the essence.

The night before our big reveal, I hardly slept; it was impossible to sleep. No amount of bubbles or salts in a hot bath could help me sleep that night. I had tried everything rescue remedy, exercise, yoga, meditation, if I had had some prescription medication maybe I would have resorted to that but I didn't. Nothing I did seemed to work. So I thought why waste all that energy lying in bed staring at the dancing shadows playing on the ceiling.

I slowly manoeuvred my bulk out of the shared bed careful not to wake John and pulled on my black lycra running shorts and oversized t-shirt. My comfortable well-worn adidas shoes sat waiting expectantly at the back door. I easily slithered my feet into them without untying the laces. I slipped out of the warm cosy house and walked down the open eighty metre drive way, gravel crunched and spluttered underneath my weight as I passed over it. The chilly air bit at my uncovered bed warmed legs but I barely felt it. Crisp air stung my cheeks bringing a rosy glow to my face. My breath created little puffs of steam as my pace increased but they quickly faded, absorbed into the atmosphere to be reused by someone else. Thirty minutes later with the final tones of night fading, replaced by the pink and yellow tinge of the dawn I returned to my house and the familiar rush of after exercise euphoria.

Our children, the oldest, my daughter who was so much a part of the life I lived before, reminded me of the sun. She possesses a natural charismatic beauty. A warmth and vitality blazed from her. The energy she emits supports and influences the lives around her. My youngest reminded me more of the earth. Solid with incredible depth and power, multi-layered and profoundly thought provoking. He also possessed a fierce intensity and diversity, as well as resilience. Both of them remarkably different, unique in their own way.

Our family life and the seasonal changes we all experienced were governed by the deep connection between these two children. The sun had nurtured and provided light to the earth when the storms of life had struck previously. She had guided him and kept him safe during the hardship of life in Scotland and then our return to Australia. She had also nurtured him during the troubled times of our business venture. Now as they were older they drew on each other's strengths. They trusted in each other and offered support and encouragement when things were tough. I hoped their alliance would stay with them as they uncovered the truth and headed into the stormy weathered that lay ahead.

The four of us together made up our own unique planet. A home with a culture only we understood and felt comfortable in. together we had created it, nurtured it and accepted it. Our home was one where we shared creation, development, history and affection and our lives would always be perpetually intertwined. I trusted this would not change after they heard my story.

My love for my children poured like the rapids of a Niagara Falls, consistent and outpouring. The powerful emotions I felt for them engulfed, embraced and accepted everything they did. I could not allow this situation to change our relationship. I loved them far too much to have that happen. My sole purpose was to preserve the peaceful and calm waters of the environment we currently lived in. I wasn't sure how that would be done but I would try anyway. My wish, like any protective mother, was that my words would not cause either of them any further distress or pain. They were adolescents, one was a young adult, I really just wanted them to continue to positively grow and prosper, not to be burdened, with my worries. Their lives held enough of their own challenges, and setbacks as they travelled their own course through life.

I believe life is a succession of moments all strung together in one giant necklace. For me I believe it is a one way trip. I knew I only had one shot at this. I knew every word spoken could never be taken back. So I needed to be mindful and choose my words carefully, in an attempt to make the children feel as secure as possible.

Both their lives had just begun. Their paths were still being crafted. I did not want my words to extinguish all that we had formed over the years. If this trust was lost, it could cut a path of destruction in all of our lives. Trust is a fragile concept, something that can be lost in an instance. The last thing I wanted was for the kids to start to erect negative and destructive strongholds in their lives like I did as a child.

I also didn't want to betray either of my children by being deceitful or dishonest. I hoped their hearts would not harden at my words or their backs turn towards me. I vowed to try and endure this situation, and everything else that would occur, from this point on, with as much grace and dignity as I possessed.

My youngest child Bill lived at home with John and I on our sprawling two and half acres on the northern outskirts of Brisbane. He was a fourteen-year-old youth, who still possessed innocence and a keen openness to experience the unbound world, he lived in. At that age needs are simplified not like the needs of a fully grown adult based on the demands of work, the world, friends, acquaintances or a growing family. His life just needed time and a comfortable safe space to grow and mature.

This sensitive deep child was fated for better things his intelligence was more intended for the comfort of a warm classroom surrounded by familiarity and friendly faces not for the cold uninhabitable and dangerous terrain of the world I was venturing into. This was my journey, I was sorry he was dragged into it as collateral damage. He didn't deserve it, his innocence didn't warrant any kind of penalty.

Bill was just commencing his life's journey, his path was not even mapped yet. Hints of his forthcoming trek were coloured lines on an atlas hung on the wall with pieces of blu-tak, but the marks lacked any clear direction or focus; he was still finding his feet. I hoped my news broadcast would not hinder his travel plans, the last thing I wanted to do was to create an unstable and turbulent time for him.

He had grown up knowing a very different person; only a hint of that old Laurie remained by the time he entered the world. He grew up in a stable secure home surrounded by people who loved him. We were not perfect, I would never win any parent of the year awards but the home we created was much better than the home I grew up in. John brought a stability to this unit I could never bring, he grounded us all, he kept all my nomadic inclinations to a minimum. Sometimes I did win—like out move to Scotland. However in most cases he tackled and knocked down my constant desires to up root the family and move and try something new. Me I was more impulsive less rationale and got us into some trouble like purchasing a business that nearly ruined us emotionally and financially. Together we balanced each other out and were able to raise our children in a diverse and flexible home.

Bill knew nothing of the person I was before he came along. I never discussed it or even hinted at any of my previous antics to anyone. It was a topic never talked about in the house. I no longer entertained any thoughts of what I had done. To me the chapter was shut on that part of the story, it was written a long time ago by a much younger less experienced version of me and was not relevant to this day and age. A new chapter was opened when I met John and the story was still being created.

However, this night the bed time story would be vastly different than the usual tale it would be a personal account of my memoirs. My narrative would not be a fable it would be a horrible saga full of a sequence of events including deception and trickery. I would not be able to speak of the fairy tale ending he would want to hear for I was unsure of what lay ahead.

I wondered when he listened to my account of events gone by, how he would react. Would he withdraw? Would he be able to understand? Could he accept the story without judgment? I hoped as I displayed my journal that through his innocent untainted eyes he would be able to comprehend the words and understand the hidden messages lying underneath the black ink sprawled across the ancient paper.

His reaction to my testimonial is what scared me the most. At fourteen he was at a very tender age where the influences of the world over rule rationale. I feared the emotional alienation that potentially may occur once the details were revealed and clearly understood. His mother was an ex drug addict with hepatitis C, an infectious disease that may have been passed on to him at birth. His withdrawal would be a pain no medicine would ever cure; it would be like losing him physically from this planet to an unknown world. If this occurred my life would become a windowless, cold, empty, dark room, one I would be chained to for the rest of my life.

Like most bad things that happen in life the timing was right off the mark. He was at his most vulnerable. His life was moving in unfamiliar territory. He had recently experienced a change in schools, with this came the loss of all his childhood school friends and familiar surroundings, add to that hormonal changes. If this all happened a few months in the future, when he was feeling a bit more settled the affect may have been minimised, but no, that's not how it all pans out, is it.

On top of the bad timing his melancholy nature meant he was prone to withdrawal and depression. He was also analytical, thoughtful, and very thorough. Detailed, perhaps is a better word. I used to think he was completely unenthusiastic, but came to realise he just needs to understand the purpose behind the task. All of this aside, I found him to be self-sacrificing and extraordinarily loyal. So the right approach was crucial to ensuring a positive outcome.

Chapter 15

Words from Heaven fall

"A flower has to go through a lot of dirt before it can bloom."
—Author unknown

As the scarlet sunset turned a nice light shade of purple, the shadows lingered and darkened through the kitchen window where I prepared a succulent roast beef dinner, with browned, crunchy-baked potatoes, served with mounds of emerald green peas and moist, juicy corn; his favourite meal. I watched as the purple turned into pitch black, it felt like a fist had clenched my heart and wouldn't release it, the pressure was immense. Terror gripped me. I was drunk quicker on it than if I had taken four shots of tequila in quick succession.

Full darkness was framed by the gold embossed edges of the two large glass panes. I turned on the overhead down lights and the sullen light was replaced by a glorious glow. I plated up the scrumptious meal and together we sat at the table, each of us awkwardly toying with our food. An arctic fog of apprehension slowly swirled around each of us, our thoughts frozen. Silence lingered and hung heavily in the air. Each of us waited for the first words to cut through the icy environment. The sun had hardly set but I knew my time was running out, like sands through a cracked hour glass. I believe most of us think we have it all together, I did. I believed I had my life all mapped out, planned in a way that was meaningful to me. But in reality I didn't. I have in the past failed dismally at many things, my relationships, my work life, my parenting skills, my health was a mess due to choices I had made and here I sat trying to find the right words to destroy a loved one's life. Destroying my own life was one thing but hurting an innocent child was another. Every one of the failures I experienced gouged a bigger hole in my heart a little more each time I went through another one.

I think we all go through life in a complete daze like being plugged into a world like the matrix where our physical bodies are abused by machines whilst our minds are manipulated to believe the artificially created world around us is real. I can truly say I really didn't pay any attention to the details of the prevailing substance of my life. I missed so much, which was blatantly obvious as I sat before my son. I had lived my old life anesthetized with booze and drugs or a cocktail of both and as I got older I found comfort in ideology.

All my life no success or achievements I obtained could fill the hole in my heart, the emptiness prevailed. I couldn't bear another failure with my son sitting right in front of me. How could I say what I needed to say, could I possibly find the right words. I genuinely couldn't start the conversation, like a coward I sat and continued to toy with my food as one slow tear etched its way onto my blank canvas.

I heard hushed words as they echoed around the room. I felt the ventricles of my heart collapse into the deepening emptiness. They words stung my cheeks like a hard backhanded slap, they left an imprint I had no idea how to erase. The tension in Bills voice was evident, he was noticeably agitated yet his expression

was clear and his question was specific. He needed to know what was going on, he declared our awkward phony behaviour had to stop, he couldn't handle the sham anymore. His question was like a boomerang, circling around the room, it needed to be caught but not by the original thrower.

I wanted to peer into a crystal ball anything for some clarity, to make out some clear images, but from this position any vision I had was blurry. I paused, my throat completely dry, Bills eyes burned into mine waiting forcing me to look down. My shoulders slumped and a low sigh escaped from me throat clearing it, but still no words came forth.

Fear slipped into every cell of my being. Fear of his rejection. I didn't want to revisit the cruel memories; the snapshots that flooded my brain in that moment, but I knew the words would eventually be told and they would rob me of breathe and make my body want to crumble. My heavy heart was clenched in a large fist. I lifted my eyes and gazed at him and John, the silence gathered, building between us. If I could, I would have encouraged the moment to stretch, grow and linger between us but I knew it must end.

I placed my fork next to my untouched, gravy-covered meat. My eyes reached John and silent words whispered crossed the airways. As a model dreams of a beautiful face, a rally car driver of his speed I dreamed of a life where my family and I were without this misfortune without the forthcoming hardship. A flood of salty tears quickly pooled, then gently fell over my eye lids and tumbled down my cheeks. As Bill witnessed this seldom seen action, fear and panic rippled across the skin on his face and settled there. His voice was shrill, he basically screamed his new question. It hung in the air with the last unanswered one. “What is going on?”

My throat constricted. John rose to the occasion his voice resounded all around me as he started to explain my epic story. The one sided tale commenced with a brief concise introduction, the words Hepatitis C and infection floated between them. I sat quietly and mutely wept unable to intervene as the saga was told. The warm intimately spoken words appeared innocuous and laid-back on the surface yet underneath the sounds held an intense meaning that was understood.

As I sat there silently I felt like I was losing my mind. I needed to find my feet, stand up and stop being such a whimp. Water flowed freely down my cheeks as I raised my eyes to meet my sons. I searched his haunted face. The worse thing I could do was offer no explanation at all. I knew there were things I wouldn’t tell him not tonight but it was my chance to get it off my chest, maybe the fist that clenched my heart would relax its grip just a little.

I looked at the cringing boy on the other side of the table; he slumped deeper into his chair as the time spun a web between us. I cleared my throat, a rumble that caused all four eyes at the table to turn and focus on me. My voice was delicate and pathetic as it offered him a detailed account of what I had learned. All the hope I could convey at this stage was my appointment with the specialist in a few weeks.

He became very still and very silent, a fourteen-year-old boy in emotional turmoil. A whirlwind with chaotic winds had struck his safe place, the damage was still being processed but John and I could see the first signs of damage as traces of fear blended with the tears lingering on his long eyelashes. He twirled a steel fork between his thumb and forefinger, as it teased and prodded a lone green pea. Unexpectedly, he stood up, staggered slightly, found his balance, and then left the room. His favourite meal sat cold and uninviting untouched. A hole was left at the table which fed the emptiness in my heart. His silent quick withdrawal left John and I speechless. He entered his room, slipped between the sheets of his double bed, and refused to communicate or socialise with either of us for the next two days.

What a predicament I found myself in! A predicament I knew I had brought upon us. This situation was entirely my fault. My sinister passenger thrashed within me, a drowning being fighting for life. It flung debris at me from every angle. What had I done to this family? What had I done to myself? How could I ever redeem myself?

Without conviction and principles to act as my mental warden my mind became an anxiety beacon drawing in negative emotions, thoughts and feelings. I had chosen very poorly in the past. Twenty odd years ago I had flown too close to the sun and I got severely burnt. My free will had created this situation for good or for bad and I found myself dealing with a bad case of sunburn that I should have dealt with ages ago. One of the open wounds was my existence; my being in this house threatened my family. I just didn't know what to do about it. However the dark passenger had a very vocal opinion, I just couldn't let the message filter and stick to the surfaces of my mind.

Looking back I can see the troubles in my life came from dwelling on the previous disasters and forgetting the potential life offered. I was blindfolded by my own desires, unable to see the promises and gifts before me. Living a life with excess fear or concern as well as having too much faith in the wrong ideals and details previously caused all my suspicions to come to pass. I would not allow myself to fall into the same trap again, I would fight the passenger and its evil sayings and I vowed not to fall to its malevolent tidings.

As I sat at that table, I felt completely alone, the vacant seat opposite me was an excruciating stab to my already weakened heart. I wanted to escape. Even a small mental diversion from the reality of all of this would help. But, I felt so tethered, completely bound to the unfolding situation. I wanted to be that free black haired proud stallion as it raced over the large open grassy plains, the one from my childhood imagination, not this restrained, tightly reigned mount.

Questions echoed and resounded inside me. What could I possibly do to help him? His needs totally escaped me. I didn't know what to do. I wanted to take away his pain; the pain I knew I had caused. I would take it all, if I could. What sort of mother was I, to do this to a child whom I loved more than life itself?

I didn't think anyone could possibly understand the heavy yoke I carried, or the toll this all took on my life. I wouldn't talk about these feelings to anyone. I couldn't. I wouldn't let any of my family see this vulnerable side of me. They relied on me to be the strong one, and that was what I would try and portray. But, if they only knew what was really going on inside me, I think they would be shocked. In reality, I felt weak, pathetic and undeserving to be a part of this family.

I left the table, unable to meet Johns face to stand outside on the veranda, alone. Tears clouded my eyes as I stood on the patio. I found it nearly impossible to see through the thick mud my gloomy thoughts had created. Evening had settled in but there was nothing in the way of the night's usual beauty, not that I could see. The blackness simply grew darker and the wind grew colder. Through my watery veil the landscaped changed and I witnessed the brilliant glow of a big yellow moon as it floated amongst the many sweeping clouds. Stars shone vibrantly overhead, and the entire landscape before me was illuminated.

Laurie Smyth

As I looked up at the moon through my blurry tear stricken eyes, it dawned on me I couldn't conquer this journey alone, I simply didn't have the skills to overcome it. The sky glimmered above me. A flurry of messages carried on the wind reigned down upon me caressing my skin with their soft touch. They spoke of true meaning and of hope. The moons afterglow illuminated by the rays of a dying sun lingered and subtle warmth surrounded me. The moon has no light of its own it simply reflects the brilliance and radiance of another planet, the sun.

As I contemplated this fact I pondered how I could reflect confidence and commitment when it refused to dwell permanently in me. I figured I had to learn how to convince people around me I was going to be ok, especially the children. People don't like it and they don't cope well if they are confronted with negativity. I needed to take a leaf out of the moons book and borrow someone else's confidence and enthusiasm, just until it became real to me. I had worn a mask for many years, but, it was a long time ago. My old friend the chameleon would need to be resumed from the grave in which I had buried it and I would have to learn to mask my pain once again, this time for the sake of a family I loved and didn't want to hurt. I simply couldn't let the members of my family see the pit I continually cycled in and out of. It would scare them, just as it scared me.

The pit was sometimes dark and sometimes very deep and often I spent my life hovering on the edge waiting to topple over. Over the years I learnt to take some steps away from the danger zone but the pit never left me. It was at times shallower than others. During these easier times I didn't wallow in its wiles long, whereas, other times I was trapped in its negative clutches as it clawed at my back reopening old wounds. At this crucial time with my son trapped in his own pit of turmoil I could not tolerate its beckoning cries. I forbid it from entering my mind and by doing this I knew a personal battle, an internal war, with my own mind would begin. I dared not lose this one, if I wanted to help my family.

However, my emotions were so fragile, like the soft flowing petals of a dandelion. The white hairy pods with their dark small centres can easily be picked up and tussled even by the slightest of winds. I knew I had to somehow cease the cyclic behaviour I had experienced for many years. What I needed to do was learn how to fill the pit in, cover it in quick drying cement so my name would forever be etched upon its surface but it would not have any power over me. My behaviour and attitude whilst in this pit was completely unhealthy, not only for me, but for the rest of the family.

As I silently stood on that glowing moonlit patio I promised the heavens the pit would be closed. I wasn't sure how, but I knew it would be done. I would need help and I would need strength to complete this task so I sent a silent little prayer to the heavens, asking for help. I simply asked for guidance to move forward, it was a simple cry and uncomplicated request. How many of us pray in times of need? The problem is if we ask for something and don't believe in the answer then what's the point. Prayer comes with belief, ask and you shall receive it the Bible says.

I battled with this, one because I didn't think I was worthy and two, I didn't believe He listened to me. But I am not alone in this thought. Luke 1:11-16 tells a story about a man who prays earnestly for a child. An angel visits him and informs him his petition has been heard and will come to pass, well like me, this man didn't believe him. You see both he and his wife were old, possibly passed the years of child rearing. His wife did get pregnant with an infant named John. But due to this mans unbelief the angel supernaturally shut his mouth so he was unable to speak for the duration of his wife's pregnancy. I wonder how many times I have prayed for something but my disbelieving mouth messes up the plan and therefore misses out on something great. This prayer was far too important for me not to believe in. I needed help. I wanted to be healed, to be with my family. I didn't want this kind of life not now not ever. I felt backed into a corner with no other way out but to believe this time. I stood on that patio, a broken woman. Tears flowed evenly down my cheeks, rivulets of salty water formed into streams. I knew I had once again entered the arena but this was a battle like no other. It was one I was not fully equipped for even though I wore my full battle regalia. I had entered into an ancient battle one from which HCV had sprung, it had been the champion many times before and was very adept at survival in this kind of savage environment. I couldn't beat it alone, I knew someone else had to step into the arena with me and fight back to back with me if I was to walk out with a victory.

Seconds passed. A still calmness descended upon me, a peacefulness which transcended all rationale understanding. Words filtered down touching me, infusing with my mind. Random thoughts trickled into my head like rain drops. They offered assistance, provided direction and brought awareness. Unspoken words revealed themselves to me, like a gift, offered from a higher power. These were not words I would have thought of. I felt an overwhelming feeling of love like warm protective arms wrapped themselves around me. That night I realised I needed to walk in faith and mix it with love whilst preventing life's distraction from taking my focus away from what really matters, otherwise I could miss out on the healing I so desperately desired. Entertainment and my own selfishness were the two distractions that kept me from believing in many things. I had lost my overall purpose. John still held fast to our marriage vows he proved that to me just a few days before. What had happened to me, it was like I was a lost sheep, scrounging around on the hillside alone. Yet love prevailed in our house despite my short comings.

That night I had a taste of real unconditional love. John had also shown me love recently so why was it so hard for me to love myself. Other people loved me, why couldn't I see the person they saw. I have heard it said you can't give away something you don't have. But I felt such overwhelming love for my children so how could that be true. Over time I would learn how to love myself and therefore love others unconditionally. I would also learn how to focus, for without focus I couldn't succeed and my heart would be divided between the distractions of life and the things that mattered.

On that veranda surrounded by the pool fence and the wildlife chattering in the background I became conscious of the impossibility of being able to fix this situation. I had no skills, but God did. If I was to mentally get through this, it would require His strength, His power, His love and His direction, because I was useless. I didn't understand how to achieve this. I only knew I needed to let go and try something different. I would not give up on my family, not now. I had to follow my own heart and get out of the queue where everyone else stood. This was my personal journey and I couldn't be worried about being wrong. I needed to put my whole heart into making this work and I made the decision to trust in God. Sometimes the only time we find out if we are right or wrong is when we step out in faith.

I needed faith as my youngest child lay in that room, tormented. I would not turn my back on him when he needed me the most. And my daughter was yet to be told.

Chapter 16

Reawakening

My son withdrew for a whole forty-eight hours. For him, this lengthy phase of self-isolation enabled his mind to have a quiet time to process and comprehend the new, unidentified terrain we presented before him. It also provided a moment in time for examination and calculation of all the options. He needed time alone away in a safe haven so that he could reset his life.

To a casual spectator if they viewed this scene, it may have resembled a room filled with serenity and tranquillity. They may have detected a slight level of discord. As his mother, I witnessed the true underlying current that raged and churned within him, as he lay like a statue, face down upon his bed.

During those long forty-eight hours, I was like a ghost, cold, trapped between two worlds, one of self-provocation and one to placate my child. I sat at the side of his bed and gently touched and smoothed his blanket-covered leg. As I sat with him, I questioned what I had done. My behaviour and its consequences had caused so much pain to the people I loved the most. Why didn't I consider that before I shoved a needle in my arm?

Internally, my own personal torrent of rain tried to drench me, soaking me in self-pity and condemnation, but instead of listening to the torment, I focused on transmitting strength and positivity. This action kept me out of the rainstorm that loomed overhead. An electric shock collided instantly with the negative words that threatened me. This was my son. This was not a time for self-indulgence or self-pity. It was time to really start to practise the reflection tactic I had been shown.

I had to put on my protective rain coat and get out of this entire negative deluge. I knew I had to generate more optimistic thoughts if I was to positively uphold and endorse a vibrant future for us all. As the time progressed, with my words, I endeavoured to convey a positive outcome to him. I also made a serious effort at being light hearted, but I sometimes struggled with my awful performance. How could I tell my son that everything would be fine, that nothing would change, when in actual fact, I did not know if these words were true?

I found I had to lie, then try and believe in that lie myself. I guess that's what faith is about, believing in something that is not really in front of you, but could potentially be a reality.

The hour glass tilted, little by little, until it finally, totally, fell over.

Dawn was only minutes from the horizon to the east. The kookaburras laughed joyfully as they announced the coming new day. The pleasurable sounds took me back to a time when the house was full of laughter and the pitter-patter of lively little feet as they ran playfully throughout the house. As I rose from my bed the stars grew dim and the sky blushed with the rising sun. I slowly walked down the hall and peered into Bills bedroom hoping the jubilant sounds from the native birds brought with them a change of season to my son's room.

And they did. He lay atop of the feather doona fully dressed wearing his school uniform awaiting the day. There was no longer any more need for my quietness so I started breakfast. When I looked at him I noticed the boy part of his face had moved aside allowing the man part to step in. The man was visible but had not yet taken full control, he was slowly capturing the boy part and a transformation was underway. He had unknowingly snuck in during Bills self-imposed solitary confinement. It didn't matter to me how or when it occurred. I was saturated with relief. Joy flooded me and my spirits soared. He emerged renewed and ready to fight alongside me.

He had been shattered but was now reborn, stronger, firmer and more versatile than before. The internal storm of the last few days stilled and his life restarted and moved forward, just like turning on a light switch. A lifeless steel sheath housing a glass bulb sparks to life and a brilliant radiance illuminates the area. Bill awoke that day and his spark had been reignited. His life returned to the mundane, everyday practices of school, friends and living. As I watched this from a distance I was comforted and reassured. My legacy rebuilt his dreams and forged his own precious path into the future.

Laurie Smyth

Time is the best healer. Young people live their lives in perpetual personal expectation and unyielding aspirations, thus, my personal crisis, gladly, became insignificant in his busy world.

If I had the opportunity to pick between extreme happiness and extreme sorrow, I would choose extreme sorrow. For in times of happiness, we tend to forget what really matters in life, and some of us treat life with insufferable arrogance and follow idle pursuits. Yet in times of extreme sorrow, we remember where we have been, who we really are. Our eyes are opened to remember our humble beginnings, and we learn to rely on others. We also learn to trust, and have faith in things unseen, sometimes for the very first time.

Chapter 17

The sun lights my world

It was Jades turn to be told. She no longer lived with us but shared a house with her soon to be husband. I knew that revealing my predicament to my twenty-year-old daughter would be vastly different, but just as hard as it was to tell my son. The situation, language and expressions would need to be adapted to accommodate her personality, as she is nothing like her brother. I also didn't expect the same reaction from her. Actually, I was unsure how she would react to the news. She could easily break down in hysterics or simply step over it and not accept it. Either way her reaction was not something I would be able to prepare myself for.

Her warmth blanketed me and penetrated my darkness. She always made me feel important in her life. However, her sincerity and naturalness sometimes overwhelmed me. She would come out with sayings, beliefs or perceptions that would challenge me or make me very reflective. The thought of losing her due to this situation would condemn me to eternal night. I would be a creature of the night forever damned to wander the underworld alone, lost without the radiance of her glow. I could not entertain this thought, as I would never be the same without her by my side.

My first born child, Jade, was born in a harsh and harmful time, trapped in a spiralling rabbit hole of immorality, destruction and depravity. She never asked to be part of my alternate, immoral life, she was there by default, made to endure a life of hardship. If I had allowed us to have anchored in that life, it could have been deadly for both of us. Thankfully, after six years, I completely disconnected from this port, never to sail into or revisit that harbour again. I chose to shelter and protect her from the harsh reality of the world her father and I shared, and moved her to a different waterfront haven, the Gold Coast.

I thought back to my night on the patio, just a few nights before, bombshells had been dropped on me and then been partially revealed. I had become an emotional believer. My eyes had been opened and a hand been offered which I took. It made me feel safe and protected. I felt it the way you do when you pass your hand high over a candle flame, you don't feel the flame but you are aware of the unseen heat that is generated by it.

For most of my life I had been wandering through a world where I never really felt I belonged or accepted however that night changed those feelings. It provided me with surprising information which became a revelation. Once I had been enlightened I realised I was accountable for utilising this information in the right manner. I would never be able to or want to go back to where I came from. My timeline, thankfully, only ran forwards, there was no way to return to that uninformed naive person I was a couple of months before. I might have thrown in the towel at this point just a few months ago but there was no way I would quit before the race had even begun, no matter how hard the road became.

They say 90% of what you worry about never comes to fruition, so why waste the effort? It sounds easy enough but I found it easier said than done, especially when you are a person with an overactive imagination to begin with. Some nights I lay awake listening to the slow drawn out snores of the sleeping man beside me wishing that my brain would shut down even for a few seconds so sleep could overpower and engulf me. Whoever plugged me into the matrix circuit board gave me an overactive consciousness, one that doesn't unplug easily.

Since my patio experience my efforts to stifle the dark passenger improved daily. The fight was getting *somewhat* easier. I found myself not exerting as much energy wrestling the whispers, but then again, at times my progress was a bit slower than I liked. The words from the song Hotel California often comes to mind when I think about this struggle "Voices wake you up in the middle of the night just to hear them say welcome . . . ." it seems they are ever present in all of us. How we deal with them is the unique part, some I guess fold under the weight of their conviction others fight a constant battle to keep on top. What I do know is none of us can let them get a foothold in our lives because the negativity they bring can be really destructive. I suppose that is why rates of suicide are increasing in this country especially amongst the youth of today. How sad it is to read or hear of a person taking their own life, a waste of potential, a gift the world will never have all because of whispered words that crush the soul.

I vowed to win this battle, even if it took me my whole life. I refused to give in, I would fight no matter how hard the journey got or how high I had to climb I would not give up. My vow as hard as it would be to complete needed the support of my family, especially my daughter, Jade. I didn't want to take this road without her by my side. I needed her optimism and her radiance, as I knew they would carry me through the hardest of times.

Another sleepless night faded into the distance, a pattern I hoped would not become habitual. The first glimmers of the change of day beckoned through the window above where I quietly lay awake thinking. My husband's light, nasal exhalations roused me from the multi-layered, thoughts my over active mind conjured up. I shifted smoothly and effortlessly manoeuvred myself from the bed without rousing him. I easily found my black bike shorts and a short-sleeved T-shirt at the side of the bed where I had placed them the night before. I quietly dressed myself and walked towards the back door where my well-worn favourite running shoes waited for me. I slipped noiselessly out the door to embark on a long, thoughtful run. I flipped back my hoodie and settled the iPod ear pieces in the shallow canals of my ears, the harmonious melodies of Dire Straits filtered through providing me with a regular beat to run to. I needed to clear my head before I met Jade. Running was a great distraction for me, and it generally soothed me, especially when I was feeling stressed or upset, both of which I felt on this morning.

My feet found an easy rhythm on the hard bitumen surface. The cold air bit at my exposed ears and I pulled the hoodie up to provide some protection until I warmed up and didn't need it anymore. As I ran I watched the cloudless, pink day emerge from the deep purple ashes of the night. The red dusk became a yellow and a cold wind sprang from the trees and lashed the hair around my face. I looked up at the sky where the sun had not quite risen and saw a spectacular sight, the horizon was pink from every direction. Not a single cloud graced the sky, spectacular ribbons of purple slowly faded as the red ball rose. This was my favourite time of day; it was quiet, peaceful and absolutely beautiful. I ran towards the elusive golden orb my feet keeping rhythm with the music pumping in my ears. Even though the morning was still cool, sweat beaded on my forehead and upper lip, it trickled down the base of my spine and was absorbed by my cotton T-Shirt.

I ran my customary six kilometres easily. My mind was much clearer but it was still not at ease upon my return. After a long hot shower and a light breakfast—my usual carrot, celery apple, ginger and beetroot juice—I was ready to meet my daughter and deliver the dreaded news.

We were off to the local shopping mall a casual five minute drive from where we lived. The location wasn't the best place to have a private conversation but I had to try and find somewhere quiet to talk to her. I knew there were some nice tucked away in the northern wing of the mall. I thought I could funnel her into those areas if the opportunity presented itself. Neither John nor I discussed how this situation would pan out. We had no appropriately planned disclosure tactics, there was none in this case, unlike her brother who required details and time to process Jade would do that instantaneously. She was more of a free spirit, very different to her brother, and neither of us could predict how she would react to the news. So there really was no good-humoured way to tell her, but to say it the best way we could.

I remember the day well. We pulled into the parking lot, Jade stood beside the escalator happily chatting to a person I didn't recognise, killing time as she waited for us. This was unusual for her as her time management skills were sometimes quite poor and I had been left forgotten on more than one occasion. One particular instance Bill and I had flown to Rockhampton to spend time with my family and I had asked her to pick us up from the airport, not wanting to leave my car in the parking bays there. All the time we were away Bill questioned me about the travel arrangements wanting me to change them because he thought Jade would forget us. I defended her profusely. However when we arrived at Brisbane airport Jade was nowhere to be seen. We waited and waited until I finally rang her, a sleepy rusty voice answered and yes she had forgotten. I had egg on my face and my son saying I told you so. Needless to say I learnt my lesson and Bill still reminds me of it even to this day.

We had shopped and not found the right time to talk. But I

would not let the moment pass without dropping my bomb. We stood beside our vehicles, both cars packed with goodies. I lifted my face to bathe in the warmth of the sun's rays and gathered my thoughts whilst Jade chatted happily at my side. As I turned to look at her, I saw her face alight with enthusiasm and passion.

She wholeheartedly embraced life and loved every aspect of it. Her conversation flowed and enlightened me on her new adventures and experiences, all of which brought pure joy to my heavy heart and a deep smile to my lips. Communication had never been a problem between us. It would never be an issue for her. Her life was an open book filled with amazement and laughter. Silences are rare in her company. The problem I had in that particular moment was getting her full attention so I could speak.

John distantly sauntered in the distance, looking at something he neither cared about nor wanted. He offered us both time and space to have a practical talk. I looked deeply, expressively into her immense grey-blue eyes. As my eyes touched hers, her perceptive nature told her it was time to be quiet. I delicately and tenderly touched her arm, to obtain her full attention. She suddenly fell silent and still. She understood I had something important to say. Her inquisitive eyes flicked towards where John stood and then focused back upon me, as she sought reassurance from her moment of unease.

Our eyes held each other in a sweet tender embrace. They danced a dance a mother and daughter should never have to partake in. I spoke truthfully, my words carefully chosen and still they pirouetted around the subject, jumping from here to there like hip hop artists bopping to the latest rap. I opened the vault of the past and relived the painful details of my youth. I spoke shamefully of the consequences and the challenges that were before me.

As I spoke, I witnessed a contrast of emotions fluctuate and pass over her. Shock initially coursed through her, visible to any bystander, followed by sadness and pain then tears welled in her eyes, her face turned a pale grey, her legs trembled beneath her, and her voice became unsteady. She stood silently for a long time, unmoving. After a long moment, she sympathetically and tearfully embraced me, holding me tight against her body. Her tears wet the flimsy shirt which lightly covered my shoulder. I felt her warm breath, as she whispered in my ear, the sweet fragrance of her favoured chewing gum rose up to touch my nose. A message of hope rung in my ear "it's okay, Mum. Nothing is going to happen to you. I'll pray that you will be healed".

She untangled herself from our embrace, leaving me speechless. I had completed my task, delivered my news. The question was, had it been fully received. It appeared to have been as I witnessed the seasons change upon her face. I wondered if the full extent of the impact had struck her or would it come later. I knew her reaction would be different than her brothers but this was completely unexpected.

This beautiful child of mine lived her life in complete optimism and hope. I wished I was more like her. She experienced life fully. She chose to cherish every moment, build happy dreams and lay down joyful memories. Me, I just got the task done, usually as fast as possible. I didn't stop and cherish, or even view, the surrounding scenery. I wondered just how much of life I had already missed because of this behaviour. I stupidly drove myself to achieve and achieve. I was stubborn, determined and ambitious. *Sad,.. when I think about it, now, as I look back.*

She embraced happiness, whereas I embraced success. I think she chose a lot more wisely than I did. She believed and lived by the fact that hope was a constant fire that burnt in her heart. It was something that didn't go out, even in dark and difficult times, and this situation would be no different. Her hope provided her with optimism and expectation that tomorrow would always be better. She was a strong woman of faith and lived her life according to this conviction. She also believed that her philosophy was to be shared, and everyone else could grasp its concept and embrace it as she did. I loved this innocence in her. I wondered if she would feel the same about me if she saw into the depths of my soul and saw the darkness that sometimes raged within me.

As I recounted and narrated the history of my circumstances to the children, it brought me to the realisation that I needed support emotionally. I knew I wasn't coping well with the situation and I knew I needed assistance overcoming the dark side of this predicament. Seeking help was a concept I had never grasped before. I had always done everything myself believing no one could or would be able to assist me. I thought seeking help was a sign of weakness, like showing your opponent all your cards before you start to bet. Internally, I believed I should be able to deal with my own problems. However, I felt a real, strong need to seek out more personal information regarding my condition, maybe even discuss my feelings with a counsellor. I knew seeing a counsellor meant you had to open up and allow them access to your deeper self. Scary stuff. I also knew they were trained to see beyond what other people didn't, and this also frightened me as I had a lot of baggage locked away. I feared they would judge me, condemn, reject and criticise me. But, my need to seek aid overruled my feelings of fear.

Chapter 18

A great support

One day as I was researching I accidentally stumbled across an organisation called the Queensland Hepatitis Council. Their website was fabulous, up until this point I had been focusing on a site called Janis and Friends. However this organisation specialised in assisting people locally, it also provided support services for family members living and managing HCV. I wondered why no one had spoken to me of them before. Even in all the folders spread across my floor holding the mountains of research, I hadn't come across them. I couldn't understand why I hadn't heard of them, or why the GP hadn't referred me to them. This fact shocked me. I searched through all the data I had collected to see if I had missed them somehow, but I didn't. What I did notice was most of my papers were peer reviewed scientific literature, which is what I was seeking at the time.

After a few days, and much internal debate, I summoned the courage to telephone the service for support and to substantiate my findings. Questions raced through my mind, as I hastily dialled the eight digit number. I pondered how I would begin this conversation. What would I say? Could I really disclose my sordid tale to an absolute stranger? Would they judge and ridicule me? I guessed I would know soon enough. Throughout this journey anxiety and apprehension had become my silent companions; they had become one with the dark passenger. However its voice had faded to a quiet whisper. As the days passed it was easier to not take notice of it, most likely because I had started to have real faith. I was also becoming more and more empowered with knowledge. I think once you understand something you are less fearful of it and this fact alone doesn't allow negativity to rise. How can it, if you know and understand the truth, once the truth is revealed and believed then there is no more room for fear to dwell in you and therefore the dark thoughts have no control or power over you.

I heard a buzz in my ear as our telephone lines connected followed by a persistent ring. In the dull space as the connecting line droned in the distance, my own whispered words tried to coerce me to replace the handset in its cradle. Standing there waiting, I began to believe this was a bad idea and question why I needed help from an unknown party. I also questioned if I needed to get more data as my room was full of information already, how much more would I need. However another opinion, my inner advocate spoke against these doubts and influenced me to refuse their position. I needed help and support and I would get it.

A pleasant softly spoken woman interrupted the wrestling match between my dark passenger and my inner advocate. She casually inquired about my needs and I was left speechless for what seemed like an eternity, my tongue was trapped, stuck on the roof of my dry mouth. I was amazed I had actually placed this call and had stood awaiting a response. I had never sought support like this before. This was really breaking new ground in the Laurie category! My pride was thrown out the window, overtaken by a basic human need. The drawn-out silence between us prompted me to speak. Embarrassed at my slow reaction, I stumbled over my words like a child learning to walk. She intently listened, deciphered their meaning and instantly knew my needs. An intuitive woman I would say, because I doubted even I would be able to discern the message or even the language I spoke. Thankfully, she could, and I was swiftly forwarded to a professional counsellor.

My fears were rapidly and completely washed away as soon as the man spoke. His sensitive concern shrouded me, bringing peace to my troubled world. He genuinely cared. I heard it in his voice. As we spoke his words more than just reassured and eased my worries; they completely banished my previously held doubts.

The competence and composure of the individuals I dealt with at the Hepatitis Council was exceptional. I was on the phone for more than half and hour and it was the best half hour I had spent in some time. When our conversation finally ended I felt entirely at ease with my situation. I was no longer fearful of transmitting HCV to others in my home or outside the home for that matter. Infecting another person was a lot harder than I imagined. The fact that John was not infected was testimony to that fact. Another bigger revelation was revealed to me that day, I had a fighting chance at survival. HCV is not a death sentence if you look after yourself. Even though I had mountains of research, stating facts on survival rates and disease progression, I still didn't believe it was relevant in my case, until I actually heard it spoken directly to me from this man. You could say I was a doubting Thomas. I needed to see it or in this case hear it spoken directly to me.

Speaking to this counsellor altered my perception about life and about the disease I carried deep within me. What did happen was my old spirited character resurfaced, probable much to the dismay of those around me; however there were some subtle yet distinct changes. I lost a bit of my intenseness, my highly dictatorial characteristics softened in gracious way. I am sure those around me sighed in relief. I became less authoritarian and less overassertive, although I think my father still would have referred to me as 'von grupen fuher' but I don't think I quite wore that hat as well as I did in previous times.

That one connection had left me with a positive expectation. I knew I would be ok. I thought it would be beneficial for both my son and husband to experience this service and see how it would comfort and support them. Both of them went into Brisbane and had a personal face to face visit with the same counsellor and both of them walked away with as much hope as I did.

A noticeable, constructive change occurred after their visit. I knew it had something to do with the empowerment and support that was tendered to each of us by the Hepatitis Council. I never inquired about my boy's meeting, as I felt it was a very private occasion, and one I did not feel privy to. I do know the Hepatitis Council had a very positive impact on all of us though, and I was so grateful for the input they had.

Chapter 19

Reflection on life

As an adult writing this story, it is easy to look back and reflect to see that I wasted so much of my life and my energy protecting myself. My isolation from the world prevented me from creating real, sustainable relationships. It was a form of self-imprisonment. I was too scared to actually live and engage outside of the comfort and familiarity of the security of my castle. For a long time, I wasn't consciously aware of what I was doing, however being diagnosed with HCV made me very conscious, very aware of my surroundings and the importance of the people in my environment.

Living a life dominated by fear such as this, is not genuinely living; it is, in fact, just existing. My life was bound by anguish and doubt. In essence, I felt like it was a desolate, lonely highway in an overcrowded city. I lived amongst many people, but I was a total stranger who wore a mask, moulded to what I perceived to be the needs of others. I would only remove my mask in the confines and safety of my castle. Those closest to me, a select few, were able to see what genuinely lay beneath.

Laurie Smyth

I found that you can dwell with many, but still your silent cries, the cries of the heart, are not heard, simply because you refuse to let them be heard. When I finally dared to release myself from my self-imposed prison, I somehow became more aligned with my inner self, and glimpsed a sight of who I could be. Over time I slowly learnt to trust people and I built some meaningful relationships. Like my daughter, I experienced moments of pure joy. I also learnt to laugh for the first time with real meaning, something you can't do on your own.

Learning to live unencumbered by my self-doubts, blessed me with moments of peace in the midst of all of this turmoil. After a while, I learnt that positive, strong roots could grow stronger in my life if I watered and tended to them daily. My life transformed when I adopted this new found philosophy. I was not always brilliant at applying it, but when I did, I was like a climbing rose, bound tightly on a supporting trellis. I gained strength, support and love, as well as the ability to share my pain and sorrow.

I allowed Hepatitis C to initially steal my life, but it also gave me something in return. It gave me much more than it took from me. It opened my eyes to a world I never imagined was possible with John. John became my best friend. We shared a single purpose and a common goal. A true and deep bond formed between us. Finally, we shared the same song, and when I forgot the words, he recited them back to me to keep me focused.

He became the turret in my castle wall. He protected me and nurtured my wounded spirit. He held me in the palm of his hand, provided support and encouragement, as well as assisted my actions towards treatment. He was able to capture and sift through the good and bad in our lives, stack and store everything worth keeping, and throw the rest away, discarding it like garbage.

Our lives became like a powerful symphony, days filled with high notes followed by crashing crescendos. I was up and down, believing, unbelieving, suffering, enduring, yet, John persisted through all my emotions, a sky ablaze with dazzling colour, a truly magical occurrence. As the day grew closer to my appointment I lived the whole spectrum of emotions and John stood firm beside me. He fixed my brokenness and pulled me out of the pit when I fell in and placed my feet back on solid ground ready for the next round.

Together we created strategies to positively move forward and with his help I was able to fully accept my situation. I had found an appreciation and respect for this journey, even though I didn't like it. I came to realise it held some purpose. I may never understand this purpose, but I knew a life's lesson would be learnt if I was willing to sit in the chair and be taught. My education and teachers changed daily, one day my daughter taught me something, the next my son, research was always present and John supported it all. I must have been quite dumb in the life skill department because it felt like I was being fast tracked to university.

Life became my priority. My diagnosis brought me face to face with my own mortality and I discovered a new found passion for the journey I embarked on. I planted tiny seeds of hope, which slowly grew and strengthened over time watered constantly by my inner advocate. I also had a new found respect for my own human fragility. Every moment in my life became more meaningful than the last. Each moment was to be enjoyed, not ignored. I had overlooked many meaningful connections in my life and I vowed not do this again.

I had a sudden realisation that there were many concealed, unknown mysteries that surrounded my life. Life and all the promises it held used to pass me by unnoticed. I now allowed it to linger so I could explore it. Some situations and experiences had already been lost forever, buried in the annals of time, never to be unearthed. These were missed lessons in life which would never be explained to me, and they represented missed opportunities to learn something important. Lessons I would never learn under those conditions again, and experiences I would never get to enjoy, because I filled my life with trivial, insignificant affairs, instead of 'stopping and smelling the roses'. This was a phrase often thrown at me, from many different angles, and one I truly didn't understand or appreciate until I was struck by a sledgehammer. It made me stop and assess everything.

I often ponder how fickle the human soul is. It is driven by a multitude of feelings and emotions whereas the spirit of our being stockpiles integrity and truth. If I was given a choice I would much rather be motivated by the spirit being rather than the soulful being. Life is far too traumatic if the ruler is your soul. We all share the same world which is now ruled by chaos, murder, insurgence, war, confusion and turmoil. I consider this to be simply a rebellion against order as people operate under their own soulful commander and labour towards a perceived level of freedom that isn't real or relevant to this new world we have created. So for me I had to find a better way to find a peace amongst the mess my soulful being had created around me. My life was hyperactive, my family life was chaotic, my work was hectic and I had become a turbulent disaster. Hep C gave rise to my spirit being and allowed me to see order in the disorder. It offered me life not death.

Looking back I can truly say I was grateful for that jolt, it was the biggest wakeup call for me. I can honestly say it changed everything about me. Not overnight, sometimes the changes were subtle as I crawled and sometimes the changes were dramatic as I leapt forward. But, I woke up each day with a new vigour, a new zest, for the day. I was more thankful for every day and every moment. The little things that once bothered me like Johns habit of leaving things everywhere didn't annoy me anymore. I learnt to take a breath and relax a little.

In spite of everything I had done or not done in my life I found a sense of peace. I am no better than you or any other soul seeking restoration and healing. I believe we all seek the same thing to be needed and to be loved and accepted. Isn't this just a form of redemption, one that we all seek? I wonder if human beings are truly capable of offering us this gift. Or does it come from somewhere else? Can we obtain it from within ourselves? I think not. I think we can learn to accept ourselves and love who we are but can we offer ourselves restoration and recovery from life's pain and suffering. I believe we need to seek assistance in this department, I know I did. In my case, all my hard work would have easily been swallowed up and forgotten in my own sea of negativity.

Therefore it must come from a higher being. One that offers us such a gift unconditionally, which is something us mere mortals can't do. Once I realised I couldn't receive the love or acceptance I needed to heal from my human counterparts I started looking elsewhere. I look upwards. I learnt to rely on a God who I believe placed His hand upon my life and breathed life into what was once a decaying corpse.

Chapter 20

Growing in spirit

"Problems may only be avoided by exercising good judgment. Good judgment may only be gained by experiencing life's problems."

—Jim Stovall

Changes don't happen quickly, but they do happen when you persevere, which is what I chose to do. Books by Norman Vincent Peale, Anthony Robbins, Florence Littauer and Steven Covey dominated my study and replaced my once loved Stephen King and Dean Koontz. Like a ravenous lioness, I devoured and analysed every word from these brilliant motivational and relationship books, with the desperate plea to positively influence and transform my life.

I aspired to live a better, healthier, more wholesome life. To effectively do this, I needed to put into practice the teaching of my new mentors. I learnt to get up each day and be thankful for everything, I learnt the art of visualisation and how your thoughts can destroy you. I was aware of that already. These books offered clear strategies to stop them in their tracks before they took hold in my life. It required a whole new outlook, a transformation of my behaviours, my interactions with others, my speech and my thought processes. It was tough, as it challenged my preconceived concepts and ideals.

I visualised myself as a spectator at my own funeral. People milled around as they drank steamy hot cups of coffee and ate moist, freshly baked cakes. They discussed my life as they witnessed it. Who would be there? How had I impacted their life? What would they say about me? What sort of person did they perceive me to be? What stories would they remember? Would the stories possess a positive or negative undertone? Visualising this scenario made me realise, I did not want to leave a legacy that reflected unconstructive, hurtful or critical events. Rather, I wanted people to reflect upon me as a worthy, compassionate and helpful person, someone they liked.

My new mentors openly discussed the importance of learning to trust, as well as demonstrating traits such as reliability, integrity, focus and commitment. Another key factor included the ability to expose your vulnerabilities and seek support. Well, that was a hard one for me. My internal radar didn't like this task. To me, trust was earned by actions, not words. Trusting others required that I let my guard down, and most of my earlier experiences of this had a negative feel to them. Yet my interaction with the Hepatitis Council lingered in my memory reminding me of the possibilities trusting others could bring. My perception was deeply engrained forever etched into the recesses of my mind and based on my previous hurts and fears like the circular age rings on a newly chopped tree trunk. These books spoke of renewing the mind constantly with positive affirmations and thoughts. Their words made me reflect more deeply, as I reconsidered my values and beliefs yet again.

I recalled the day when John and I had an in-depth conversation by the pool. I had completely exposed myself and my vulnerabilities to him and he stood by me. Actually, he rose to the challenge and fought repeatedly to keep me on solid ground. So, my mentors' philosophy did work; I had witnessed it. I recalled another event twenty years ago when John had not judged or condemned me for the behaviours of my past. I realised trust doesn't mean that the person had to be perfect, just that they do their best in the situation they are in at the time, and John had proven this to me time and time again.

The question was whether or not I could trust others outside of my circle. Did I dare to try it?

Stigma and discrimination was my primary fear. HCV in the millennium had the same stigma that HIV did back in the '80s when people were uninformed, ignorant and frightened. They were panicked mostly from a TV campaign and their perception of the reaper taking their lives through a disease that was a 'gay plague'. This led to poor innocent infected children being ripped from child care facilities due to perceived transmission. HCV is perpetually trapped in this same sort of perception. It's referred to as a junkies disease, well what about all those innocent people with tattoos, or who had blood transfusions, an organ transplant all before the blood was properly screened. It is unfair to place them in the same category but society does. And you know what, before I became aware of HCV and the impact it has on your life, I would have thought the same thing.

Knowing all this didn't change the facts, I knew I needed to widen my circle. Maybe even one day down the track form my own subgroup of people with the same interests and beliefs and maybe together we could lobby for something worthwhile—less discrimination and more healthy awareness of blood born viruses.

So far no one had said anything negative about my condition or circumstances. However the thought of telling people outside my comfort zone brought a very different reaction to me. My sociology studies had shown me, society is made of a collection of individuals who form little subgroups with the same opinions, beliefs and perceptions and they operate according to the best interests of that particular unit. Which is all fun and games when you are a part of this type of group, but when something or someone alienates you from the crowd things change and not always for the better. If these people start rallying and take on a mob mentality it can be quite dangerous for the minority groups such as the one I was now a part of. These people as a group can get stirred up by a simple idea or perception that may or not be true and the minority find itself the hunted as the mob is swept into a cruel and vicious psychological or at times physical attack. Even hardened prisoners flee fearing the dangers groups like this may bring.

I have said it before people fear things they don't understand and they tend to walk away from them. I feared things unknown, unexplained areas of my life scared me, yet here I was trying to comprehend the situation I had been thrown into. The last thing I needed was outside condemnation from people who hardly knew me and had no idea what I had been through that had led me to the place I found myself in. It was hard enough living with a virus that threatened my way of life let alone experiencing the added burden of feeling discriminated against, I don't think I could have coped. I was emotionally fragile at this point and one more thing could have just sent me over the edge.

The other concern for me was that John and I lived a quiet life. I wouldn't say reclusive but we were not at the pub every weekend partying or socialising 'out on the town'. We had a select group of discrete friends who we mixed with regularly, which of course had the same interests and beliefs, that's not to say we didn't get into some heated debates because we regularly disagreed about things, but underpinning all that was an appreciation and acceptance of each other's principles. We were all very private people who disliked living our lives within a public arena, opting for a more clandestine, behind the scenes, approach. So coming out with the fact that I had been a drug user twenty odd years ago presented a vastly different character than the one my friends had come to know.

I have tried to paint a picture for you so you may understand some of my reasons for not disclosing my health status to anyone. However I had a much bigger problem, I also worked in a Correctional Facility, where stigma and discrimination was common and widespread. Hepatitis was a dirty word in prison. It was not something 'clean' people got. I didn't think I would ever be able to speak to anyone I worked with about my condition. It was just not something officers discussed, yes we openly discussed and joked about prisoner infection rates but we never touched on the subject of an officer contracting HCV. I considered if I did disclose then my punishment would have included discrimination and intolerance. I hardly needed or wanted any more. My dark passenger already had the monopoly on that aspect.

It is a very personal decision to disclose your health condition, and by law, you don't have to. There are a few exceptions, but in general you don't have to inform anyone. Once again, I would refer you to the Hepatitis Council, as they will support and encourage you, as well as provide you with all the information you need to manage your life with HCV. Words cannot describe just how much they helped me. I will be eternally grateful to them for that.

All of this aside I decided to proceed, regardless of any perceived difficulties. I would not allow my life to be dominated by a fear that may never eventuate so I decided to reach out into my small community and tell my friends.

Chapter 21

Inner demons are not what they seem

I was ready. I knew it was time to reach out to my friends. I had been hedging phones calls for too long, unable to deal with the situation, but I felt stronger and equipped with enough knowledge to answer questions. Never the less, I was still nervous about their perceptions and reactions.

My new found resolve, assisted by Mr Peale, enabled me to set up my first meeting with my friend, a nurse. We had met each other eight years earlier, when I became the manager of the health and fitness centre she worked in. I can remember that first day like it was yesterday. I was holding staff interviews to get to know each of them individually; she was busy so I sat with her on the small stage in the aerobic room after she had finished teaching a class. She was hot and sweaty, her face was a slight shade of pink from the exertion and sweat held her short cropped hair in ringlets around her face. She was an attractive woman somewhere in her mid-thirties. I introduced myself and we talked.

My first reaction to her was I found her quite blunt, challenging even. She was discontented with the world and her life, and I liked her straight away. There was something about her that drew me to her immediately. I think she reminded me a bit of myself. As the years passed we formed a strong and close friendship.

I manoeuvred the car into the parking area and sat quietly as I tried to settle my stomach and prepare my speech. All around me, diligent people with laughing, noisy children pushed food-laden trolleys to their waiting vehicles. I got out of the car and slowly walked towards the heavy plate glass automated doors. I saw her as she stood observing the chaos and commotion of the busy centre.

As I walked into the mall, our eyes met. A strange uncontrollable horror welled up in me. There was no real justification for it yet I was stricken with fear. I wanted to run away. She knew I had something important to discuss and she wasted no time in approaching me. I felt like a condemned prisoner watching as the officers approached to take me for processing before they incarcerated me. She hugged me and then silently directed us to a nearby quiet coffee shop and ordered our coffees. After placing the order she turned to face me. Bluntly, she said "what's this all about?" Before I could respond, my eyes filled and overflowed unexpectedly. She touched my arm and guided me to a table for some privacy.

I stared at her and immediately I knew our longstanding friendship would out last turmoil's such as this. I probed my inner self questioning why I had painstakingly doubted her ability to understand my predicament. She was, after all, a nurse and a great friend. I knew our relationship had been built on mutual trust, respect and support, so why did I doubt it? When I saw her, I knew I could tell her anything. She would accept it, understand and still appreciate what we had.

For the next few minutes, she listened intently as I summarised my plight. I revealed everything. Neither of us touched our coffees whilst I spoke. She stared deeply into my eyes as she processed the information I had given her. A smile danced at the corners of her mouth, she reached for her cup, took a long sip from her now luke warm coffee, and said "is that it? Is that why you have been dismissing my calls? Why didn't you just tell me?" Relief flooded through me like a wave as it turns into the perfect tube fully embracing the ecstatic surfer.

In spite of the warmth of the day and the hot second cup of coffee between my hands I felt a chill ripple down my spine as we informally explored every option imaginable. The sweet taste of sugar lingered in my mouth as our conversation drew to a close. We stood and faced each other as we searched for the right words. She grabbed and secured my hand with both of hers and said "HCV doesn't change anything. If anything, it will make you stronger. You will just battle this like everything else in your life. You are a fighter, and don't ever forget it!"

We said our goodbyes, and I carelessly drifted towards the door. That was easier than I thought. Would the others be that simple? I certainly hoped so. Her positive and supportive reaction gave me the fundamental strength and resilience to run the gauntlet and overcome all the self-placed obstacles that had prevented me from getting to this moment.

I was ready and willing to now run that extra mile. I would tell my other close friends today, if possible. I had painstakingly fought and finally silenced my long suffering, tormenting demons, the ones that tried to keep me isolated and alone. I had won a victory that day one I would not forget.

The task set before me was no longer arduous, the mountainous, rocky, inhospitable terrain now distant, replaced by a pleasant welcoming trail. I told my two other closest friends, and I was met by warm-hearted, affectionate people who offered small yet precise waves of hope, love and support. I acknowledged that the tormenting devils in our lives are never quite what we expect, especially when they are met face to face and brought out of the darkness into the light. Identifying this made me admit, I should never have segregated myself from my friends or family. These people wanted to be a part of my life. I stupidly excluded them.

Self-protection, previously, was the foundation of every choice I made. I saw the world differently now. The world I had created was unhealthy and unproductive. My convictions had battered my life. They had destabilized the fragile essence of it, but I had been shown another way. People do care.

My support team had considerably grown in size from two to eight. This new team overtly turned the wheels of life for me, especially when the darkness prevailed. Their presence was a soft breeze, tender, yet compelling. They brought reassurance and comfort to my unstable world. They boosted my hope and encouraged a release from my personalised self-judgment.

I was greatly honoured and deeply touched when they pioneered the new HCV research centre in my living room. I found myself inundated and saturated with referrals to naturopaths, acupuncturists, Chinese nutritionists and doctors. Literature and research papers now camouflaged and concealed the exquisite dappled grey slate, which once served as my flooring. Piles of paper not only sprawled out littering the floor, but clawed and clambered up the walls as well.

It was exceptional and phenomenal; something I will never forget. The problem was, I had to read it all, then deliberate and debate it with my new learned colleagues. My idle doomsday speculations were totally proven to be unfounded. What I uncovered were gladiators who fought gallantly for my survival. These were professional people who bound themselves body and soul to me, swearing an oath "to endure through this hardship." They became a cohesive group united by courage, confidence and a common goal: my survival.

Chapter 22

A conscious awakening

Living with HCV challenged me on so many levels. It initially fractured me on every level, physically, spiritually and emotionally, but it also brought a deep awakening into my life. It brought major changes, ones that I may never experience under any other circumstances. It prompted me to continually review everything I believed in. It prompted me to trust in people again. It increased my level of faith, not only in God, but in humanity.

I believe life offers all of us choices, choices to remain stagnant, die or change. The cycle of seasons offers options, we can continually repeat them bringing forth nothing new, the same fruit from the same tree year after year followed by the bundling up and hibernation periods where we dodge people and just do the minimum to survive or we can break the cycle by getting rid of the deadwood through pruning. Being pruned is hard, well it was for me. I had to forgive where forgiveness was not earned; I had to become humble when all I wanted to do was shout, I had to drop my negative baggage when my pride wanted to carry it, I had to learn to be peaceful in the midst of life's storms and I had to learn to depend on someone else. This might be easy for you but it wasn't for me. My life had been so autonomous, so self-controlled that all of this was unreasonable to ask me to do, but I did it.

I grew up in a house full of turmoil, and the first seeds of my life started out being planted in this same instability but thankfully over time they died and were replaced. Initially I dealt with situations and people with anger; I just didn't know how to respond to anything. As a result I wasted a lot of my life being angry but in time this change and I found peacefulness. I didn't stop being angry what I did stop was the harmful words I spoke to others when I was angry. How John ever stayed with me I will never know. He certainly was long suffering. He didn't preach to me or try and change me, he lived his message being an example of a peaceful presence. He did it over and over again, day after day, month after month, year after year until I got the message. I saw it in him that day on the patio and I wanted what he had. Taking on this peaceful attitude meant learning how to love. I came to understand I would never change my tormented soul until I wore love like a garment, putting it on, on purpose just like you would a jumper in winter to keep you warm. If John could do it I knew I could to.

At times when I tell people of my story they question how I got through it all. I have no answer for them only that one day a seed of renewal was planted in me and over the years it grew and as it grew change occurred and with it came submission. The first shoot occurred when I forgave my parents and stopped blaming others for my circumstances.

I had spent far too many years allowing circumstances and blame to steal my joy. And whether we believe it or not family brings joy and happiness into our mixed up world. Needless to say I wanted and needed them all in my life especially as I went forward into the next phase of this journey.

I simply couldn't put off telling them any longer I was only days away from my first visit with the specialist and I was unsure of what would happen after that. Time was of the essence and even though it moved slowly it wasn't slow enough and it forced my hand.

I sought to craft the right scene. My historical masterpiece simply couldn't be postponed anymore. My family, my father, my mother and my brother, would be told, and I was scared. Our histories had been filled with great pain, and I was unsure of placing my hand on the hot stove again, but I had to trust in their commitment and dedication to our new relationship.

I come from a very unique quirky family. I guess like most of us these days. My pre 'baby boomer' parents consisted of my proud, untamed father, an impressive, powerful man, noble and imposing in character and commanding in stature. and my territorial and solitary mother who is resourceful and adaptable, with feline elegance and stealth. Lastly, my brother had been born into the era of the 'generation xer's' or the 'latch key babies'. He was an intelligent, alert, loyal companion with extremely sharp, quick wit and a very agile temperament, very different to that funny clown I knew in days gone by. My relationship with each varied considerably and had changed dramatically over time. As my life's situation changed and I grew in wisdom, so did my relationships with each member of this little unit.

Chapter 23

A true portrait

My brother, seven years my junior, was married and a parent himself. He unfortunately was a stranger in my life. My period of earlier forced and then chosen exile from the family prevented me from constructing any strong bonds with my kin. We were two transient bystanders, from the same origin, but our single path had been forcibly divided, and we were sent in opposite directions. By the time I was prepared and equipped to reawaken my relationship with him, it was too late. We had become different people. Our parents' divorce and our separation, along with my choices had altered us, and we had no solid ground to rebuild our relationship upon.

Life had tragically torn us apart. I loved him deeply, as the ties between brother and sister are, but we knew absolutely nothing about each other. We were two grown adults unable to recognise the true value and joy that could have developed between us, because it was stolen from us over twenty years ago. A deep, meaningful connection forever lost in the lines on our faces. Instead, the chambers of our hearts held distance, tolerance, patience and charity, whereas laughter, elation, tenderness and expectations should have pumped through every muscle of our beings.

We had a lost attachment, like a stroke that paralyses the body. We needed assistance to regenerate our bond. Maybe this would reunite us. Only time would tell.

Despite our lost connection, he was someone I could rely on, a pillar of strength in times of trouble. I chose to tell him first as I knew it would be easier than the other members of my family. The unfortunate part in this scenario was both he and my mother lived over 600km away in Rockhampton and I was out of time to fly up and tell them face to face. I would have to deliver the message by telephone which would mean I would have to be mindful of my approach and gauge their reactions during the conversation.

I was not nervous as I called his number, as I knew he would be rational and logical with the news. I announced my situation with as much factual information as I had. I kept the sordid tale as brief and concise as possible. Thankfully, with my well-organized, disciplined troops' support, I had all the answers I needed to respond to the many questions he asked. His response was not emotive rather objective and impartial, just as I expected. However two weeks later I received a parcel from him filled with information and expressions of hope and love.

My mother was next on the agenda leaving my father to last and there was a reason for this and I will explain it later on why I chose to do it in this order.

Laurie Smyth

If worrying was an Olympic sport, my mother's living room would be filled with gold medals. I believe she could represent Australia in the London 2012 Olympics. This trait concerned me. I didn't know how to tell her without causing her undue anxiety and panic. I just knew I would have to talk to her calmly and candidly and hope I could deliver the facts quick enough, before she would gather too many pieces of hardwood and sprint off to construct a bridge we may never cross.

I lifted the phone and dialled her number. I took a big deep breath to flood my body with cool, clean air, to settle my agitated stomach. My warm-up preparations were interrupted by her deep, raspy voice, which disconnected me from my verbal rehearsal. I chose my words carefully to construct a picture she could understand and I bared my soul to her. I was a tiny bird, her chick, with a big song to sing.

The news obviously shocked and stunned her, as a quiet stillness crossed the airways. My words blasted down the telephone line breaking up the primitive darkness of the arctic winter that had suddenly engulfed her, as the sounds screamed around her and tormented her. Through the connected line I could feel the coolness of a black night as it fell upon her warm summer's day. I heard her subtle sobs, and I knew that tears flowed down her cheeks, even though I couldn't see them. She absorbed every piercing arrow, even though they initiated more suffering and painful injury to her heart.

Delivering this message in this manner was tough. The phone

is generally not the best way to clearly enlighten someone of a situation like this. It was, for me, virtually impossible to appropriately impart a message like that using a telephone. I knew the manner it was delivered could be misinterpreted. My tone of voice, as well as the words I used, could change how she comprehended the information. But it was my only option at that time.

I didn't want to cause her undue stress and place another medal on her wall. We ended our conversation with the promise to cherish the gifts each day brought, and not to dwell too much on the destructive forces that may rattle the doors of our lives. I have to say I was quite relieved when this conversation was over.

Lastly, I had to tell my father, the commander of the family. The reason I left him till last was he held a very negative view of the medical profession and I needed all the help I could get to assure him I had chosen the right path. My approach needed to be strategically planned and implemented, so I would not receive a lecture on doctor's failures or misdiagnoses and walk away defeated and discouraged.

A timely event arose: his 65th birthday.

We planned to celebrate this special occasion as a family event on the Gold Coast. I just had to find the right opportunity to be alone with him. As fortune would have it, he wanted to come for a walk with me along the beach the next morning. I knew this was the moment of truth.

I awoke to a cold, dark winter's morning. The red fluorescent numbers on the old motel digital clock advised me it was 5:55am. It was time for my true life portrait to be unveiled. Feelings of uneasiness and restlessness washed over me, as I pulled on my warm gym clothes and my favourite comfortable running shoes. I kissed John goodbye and set off to embark on the last leg of my journey before the next chapter began.

The day had just begun. A ball of flames rose out of the earth, encased in a brilliant, deep-red, fiery halo. It floated carelessly on the horizon. It was a natural wonder which brought a fresh start, and hope, in a world full of chaos. The cool mid-winter wind battered my face, numbing the exposed flesh. Grains of airborne sand struck me from every angle. My hair struggled under its elastic constraint and thrashed frenziedly. It obstructed my view and annoyed me. A couple of fearless surfers in black, full piece wetsuits braved the cold water and paddled out into the winter swells. Only a few valiant walkers shared the concrete walkway with us, which enabled us to talk freely and openly.

We started our discussion with the usual topics of politics and the family, but mainly, we just wanted to enjoy the moment and each other's company. Finally, there was a break in the conversation, and I jumped in and divulged the details of my story to him. He faced me, his piercing stare was like a shout on a crowded train station. His short wispy silver hair jostled around his face and for a time I was speechless. Long discarded memories retuned laden with dirt and pain it made a vivid contrast to the beauty of the gunmetal blue sky laced with streamers of pink and the few wisps of fluffy clouds floating overhead. He didn't understand everything I told him, but he understood enough. I spent the next hour sharing all I had learnt over the last few months.

As we rounded an unfamiliar bend in the walkway, I was touched by a bright yellow beam of light. Sunlight struck my uncovered eyes, and alerted me to our location. Unknowingly, we walked right past our hotel. Dad voicelessly walked beside me, entrenched in profound thought, clearly troubled by the newly presented problem I had placed before him.

I broke the lingering silence by revealing our location and informing him that without realizing it, we had both walked beyond our hotel. Laughter fractured the tension between us. We turned around and leisurely strolled back to our beachside hotel and our comfortable chic rooms.

As we neared the hotel, he finally spoke. He was interested in my intentions. He wanted to know how I was going to deal with the situation and what plans I had made. I informed him of my appointment with the gastroenterologist and of my plans to consult my naturopath. He was content with these calculated future plans. However, he wanted to also assist me with research and access another naturopath's opinion on my behalf.

The task was done. It had been easier than I thought. All my preconceived notions were once again unfounded. I had been accepted by everyone, not rejected and shunned as I thought I would be.

The rest of our weekend passed without incident. No-one discussed my infection, and dad and I didn't speak about the content of our previous beachside conversation. The rest of his birthday was celebrated in a stylish and cheerful style, then we all parted again to our own lives.

Chapter 24

Fears are not always founded

"The only good is knowledge, and the only evil is ignorance."
Diogenes Laertius

My entire immediate family now understood the perils that John and I faced. We had one last quest to complete; John's family needed to be put into the picture. Our connection with them had been quite strained over the years. Expectations not met, perceptions misunderstood and lots of communication problems. All of us were responsible for the lost connection between us. Unfortunately, a detachment had formed, caused by distance, time constraints and personality differences, which led to limited and sporadic association.

I believed the prospect of telling his mother our story humiliated him. I also thought this information may potentially ruin any future relationships between us. His mother had never approved of our union and this had significantly contributed to the problems between us. Over the years, I withheld my own unvoiced feelings of rejection from her and the rest of the family. However, I was also aware all of this influenced John's and my perception of a negative reaction to our news, and this made both of us very nervous.

We wanted to convey our message to her directly, so we could answer her questions and offer her a comprehensive explanation if she asked for one. So, we invited her to our place for the weekend. Four months had passed since my diagnosis, and both of us were very familiar, comfortable even, with our situation. Even so this did nothing to dispel the feelings that rose in each of us.

After she arrived and settled into her assigned room, we enjoyed a delightful and tasty dinner, followed by cold drinks on the patio. We shared glasses of chilled beverages and inconspicuous, ordinary conversation. I could see both John and his mother were relaxed and at ease with each other. A pleasant peace and understanding passed between them, an alcohol-enriched view of the world and life.

It was time for me to leave and allow them some private time to talk. I subtly and tenderly squeezed my husband's shoulder and gave him a reassuring look of support and encouragement. I excused myself from their company and carelessly wandered into our generously-proportioned, brick and wood kitchen to wash the dinner dishes, which were casually stacked in the double stainless steel sink. As I sunk my hands into the warm soapy water I envisioned the flow of conversation, even though it was impossible to hear them in the distance.

With the kitchen clean and tidy, I felt it was time to rejoin the conversation and offer support, as well as provide information, if it was needed.

My mother-in-law sat quietly in the dark, staring deep into the deep moonlit night. Light danced and bounced on the surface of the pool and the stars twinkled high in the sky. Confused tears plunged down her cheeks. Her eyes searched mine. She reached for answers to the questions she would never ask. She simply told me she was sorry. This memory will be forever etched in my memory, because it was at this moment I realised she genuinely did care what happened to me.

That night, we held no schedule. I spoke late into the night revealing the mysteries of HCV and everything I knew about my condition. I believe she left our house with sufficient information to understand our situation, our intentions, as well as her own personal risk factors.

After she left our house, a sense of relief and amazement flowed over both of us. The task was finally complete. We could now enter the next phase of this journey, to meet the specialist and all the surprises that would hold.

Chapter 25

Exposing HCV

I love the words of that song, "time keeps on slipping, slipping, slipping into the future," because it's exactly true. You can't touch it or place it in a box. All any of us can do is leave a mark where we have been. Time doesn't care about any of our concerns or what's happening in the world. It has a job to do and it does it unemotionally detached.

As the specialist appointment loomed, drawing nearer each day, I felt more and more like the only passenger on board a captain less ghost ship bound for who knew where. Each night I would lay my head on the soft feather pillows looking forward to the sleep that would eradicate the eerie gloom that settled around me in these dark hours. The sun had hardly set and it was rising again turning night into day until the last night approached.

I lay on our king sized bed and tried to sleep but it evaded all my attempts to find it again. I fumbled on the wooden bedside table for me watch and looked at the luminous numbers. It was three forty five in the morning, the winter sun would not rise or peak in the window above my head for hours. But I couldn't lie there as the time slowly ticked by. Quietly, I rehearsed the words I wanted to say, the questions I wanted answered. In my mind I systematically went over everything I had previously learnt. I had waited a long time for this day. I should be happy it had arrived but I wasn't I was nervous.

Deep, rhythmic breathing harmonised with the noises of the coming dawn. For me sleep was impossible but my husband could sleep through anything and he lay serene and peaceful beside me, his back turned towards me. I rechecked my watch three fifty seven, it was still hours before my historic trip. I knew a run would settle my nerves, so I unhurriedly slipped out of bed, picked up my clothes, strewn on the floor, and dressed quietly in the lounge room. I chose a long, slow eight km route this time one I knew would challenge me more than usual. I needed time to think. My IPods earphones settled snugly in my ears and the upbeat techno and hip hop tunes synchronized my stride and carried me safely on my journey.

An hour later, I returned, hot and sweaty, to the pleasant aroma of coffee. John stood in the kitchen annoying fragrant meat as it sizzled in a fry pan, bacon. Hmm, I loved bacon, but I didn't think it would be possible for me to eat anything, as my stomach churned with nerves. A simple coffee and shower would be all the sustenance I would be able to partake of this morning.

The hours passed slowly. As I waited a small internal war raged across the meadows of my mind. Rocks flew from every direction like surface to air missiles locking onto their targets. They brought all the positivism down with them as they fell. Fear fell from sky above me and drenched me in a torrent of negatively charged rain.

It was time to enter into the next phase of the Hep C journey. My questions would be answered and I would be able to see the ultimate destination of the ship I was a passenger on.

As we drove the long one hour journey, the four lane highway became a lonely desolate road that fed between a tree lined expanses. Pine trees of all shapes and sizes flanked us chasing us up the motorway. Every now and then an open vastness dotted with ghost like stumps and shaggy bush cover broke the view.

Nothing moved except for a few dried bushes and a bit of tundra left behind after the loggers left with the lifting breeze. This stretch of ground was renowned for its criminal activity and it took on an eerie glow as we drove through it. Murders, rapes and drug deals shattered the tranquillity and peace it should have held. This was the final resting place of a well-known stolen child. The truth of the tragedy was concealed forever within a fragrant cover of fir pines, but he remained etched on a canvas in the living room of his loving family.

I felt so lonely as we drove the last stretch. I closed my eyes and listened to the rhythmical hum of the car's engine. I tried to focus on its tempo to calm my endless theories. What I really wanted to do was run, run through the pine trees, linger in their presence, roll amongst the pine needles, smell the fragrance and feel alive again. But instead my journey continued and finally the pine trees faded in the distance to be replaced by modern architecture and concrete.

An hour later we arrived at the private clinic. We parked the car in an open aired crowded car park adjacent to the three storey building facing the glistening ocean, a beautiful setting. The downstairs area was a bustling private hospital with a large reception desk close to the automated glass doors John and I passed through. After reading the signs I was directed to the first floor where the gastroenterologist shared an office space with a busy oncologist. I walked up the two flights of carpeted stairs and was greeted by a friendly smiling woman in her early thirties wearing an ear piece over her short shoulder length light brown hair. She took all my details and created my medical account with ease. The process had begun and even though I felt welcomed I also felt doomed.

I joined John by the water chiller and picked up the first magazine on the large pile beside me. In spite of its presence in my hand, I found it impossible to focus my mind on it. The words were all muddled, the sentences unreadable and faceless pictures adorned every page. As I sat there in that waiting room amongst all those other faceless people my stomach became twisted like a tightly coiled spring. I thought if I was suddenly released I would spin and spin for hours.

This was an interval I didn't really want. It required all my strength to sit and wait as my body demanded to stand and pace. A familiar and warm hand engulfed mine. It brought forth a slight sense of peace, taking the edge off my inner turmoil. John gazed affectionately at me and said, "no matter what happens, I will always love you."

I leant over and rested my head on his broad, heavily burdened shoulder. In that moment, I recognised that my world was a much happier place when I had someone to share it with. I still found it hard to believe he was still with me. For better or for worse, in sickness and in health, these vows were in fact a reality. Fleetingly in between my anxiety peaks and troughs I realised worry and suffering were self-indulgent and self-imposed, but to understand the real value of happiness, you have to have a true connection with another human being, and I did, this great humble presence beside me. Then as quickly as they came they faded and were replaced by panic.

A short, sturdy man suddenly appeared at the corner of the waiting room scanning the faces. He wore and ill-fitting shirt and stained hospital scrubs an olive green colour. I thought he could have just visited the opportunity shop and picked up the first shirt off the rack, as it hung low over his hips and dropped in folds around his short frame. His deep booming voice echoed around the room alerting all visitors. My name rang out, and his eyes fell on me as I promptly stood up. He casually sauntered down the narrow, carpeted corridor, then stopped and rested outside a doorway. I presumed it was his treatment room. He waited patiently for our arrival. He introduced himself and ushered us into his roomy bright office. I was surprised at the firmness of his grip as he shook my hand upon entering. His smiling face, complete with spectacles, did not display any of the weariness he must have felt from his pre-dawn surgery schedule.

The conversation commenced, he was easy to talk to, candid, understanding and he spoke with sensitivity and compassion. I liked him from the first moment I saw him, his happy jovial nature was infectious and he put me at ease straight away. As I sat and listened to him speak I thought this man would take good care of me. He clearly explained my test results then went on to describe the forthcoming potential scenarios and the options I had.

He did however drop a bombshell on me. As I heard him clarify the fact that I may not be currently infected I witnessed a pure moment of joy like I lifted off the ground and was floating with the fluffy white clouds overhead. And then I crashed back to reality as my parachute refused to open, whispered words broke my spirit again as I plummeted to earth '*you couldn't be so lucky*'. He enlightened me to the fact that the initial test I had was just assessing exposure to the disease not whether or not I was carrying active virus in my blood. A lucky 20% of people can automatically defeat the virus whilst the rest go on to have what is called chronic infection.

All I could think about was all those months of lost sleep I had experienced agonising over this situation and it was all a waste of time. I questioned why I was not told this fact earlier. No answer would return those lost hours, they were forever gone floating away on a wind somewhere.

So I was given another pathology request, this time for more in-depth tests such as a PCR Qualitative (to make sure I had a live virus) and a Quantitative test (how much of the virus was in my blood) as well as a genotype and liver function tests. My genotype test was important, as specific genotypes respond better to treatment and the results also determine the length of time a person is on treatment. I wouldn't know if I was a candidate for treatment until the results came back in two weeks. I hoped, if I was infected, that I would be lucky enough to have the easier to cure Genotype two or three. These two strains only require twenty four weeks of treatment instead of the forty eight weeks for genotypes one and four. Genotype one was the hardest to cure so I didn't really want to have that type.

I was relieved I had spent so much time and effort researching, as I could understand the facts as he presented them to us. It must be so overwhelming going through this process 'cold' not knowing anything. I mean it scared me to death and I had gone into this visit with a lot of knowledge. I could not imagine how I would have felt going in 'cold'. I was amazed to find out that 130-170 million people throughout the world suffered with a form of Hepatitis. However what really unsettled me was the fact that 350,000 people die each year from its affects. These figures blew my mind, but they also put the fear of God into me.

After my visit I came to realise that your average, well-intentioned doctor doesn't usually deal with infectious diseases like this, so their knowledge can be limited. Due to this fact they may give you some wrong advice or send you off in the wrong direction. It is such a complex disease with a lot of varying side effects that are not always fully understood.

We were in his office for well over an hour. We covered treatment options, liver care and disease management as well as the procedure for a liver biopsy. I didn't like the sound or thought of participating in a liver biopsy no matter how quick the procedure was. The thought of being fully awake whilst a long thin tube, resembling a barbecue skewer, punctured the upper right side of my body, then was wedged about half way inside me to take a cross section of liver cells, made me feel quite sick.

Our meeting concluded on this note and an appointment was made for my liver biopsy.

The worst thing I did was research how liver biopsies were conducted. I really battled with the fact that I had to be awake for the whole process; I didn't like that at all. The more I read the more terrified I became. I knew I would have to do something I thought I couldn't do. I became conscious of the simple truth that I was not in control of my life anymore. I was no longer the master of my own universe. Nature had stripped me of my self-imposed title. It frequently reminded me of my foolishness by imposing consequences upon me and removing my health. I detected I would not be back in the driver's seat for quite some time. A new figure, a man I had just met, had taken charge and would be in control of the next instalment of my life.

Everything was complete even the liver biopsy was done and

none of them were as bad as the scenarios that were created in my mind.

As I waited for those two weeks to pass my emotions radically fluctuated, they swung like a out of control pendulum. One moment I was up the next I crashed, there was no even ground for me during those days. My friends rallied around me offering support and positive reminders of good things to come. They stated' the best diamonds are made under extraordinary pressure'. Well, I thought I would be brilliant at the end of this, if that was the truth.

Chapter 26

A door slams shut

The results were in. There was no turning back. A new journey was about to begin, its destination unknown to me. What I did know was it would become a poignant moment, a defining moment in my life. The door to my life of forty-two years slammed shut, nice and tight, behind me. I knew it would never be opened ever again, even if I wanted it to. At this point, death was not my biggest fear, taking the risk to really live and see this through to the end, was. I knew I stood on the precipice, a sheer drop or a large rock face lay before me. Whatever was said during the doctor's visit would determine whether I climbed or fell.

My irritated, unfilled stomach grumbled with pangs of anxiety, not because I felt hungry, but because I was concerned about what was about to happen. I sat in the same waiting room as last time, a little more anxious than the last time I sat there. More was at stake this visit. I tried to fill the void in time by flicking through countless, meaningless magazines. My fingers quickly turned pages without considering any of the actual content. I felt compelled to sit silently, but internally, I felt like I had dropped a speed tablet. My inner furnace was stoked. Sweat beaded on my upper lip, and at the same time, dripped down the small of my back. All my neurons fired simultaneously, cells collided. A leg twitch formed and caused twinges of pain to dance down to my ankles. I just couldn't sit still, my inner being bounced around within the soft encasing of my outer skin.

I looked up and there he stood. He beckoned us into his room. I was trapped in a scene from Ground Hog Day. The truth was about to be revealed. Panic rose up in me. I wanted to run. Did I really want the answers? Was it better to know, or not to know? Any second now, I would have to make a decision. My heart knocked so hard in my chest that it could have fractured my ribs, its erratic rhythm resembled a drunken Indian war dance. My hands were slick with sweat and breathing became shallow but rapid.

A reflection of my first experience on a rollercoaster struck me. I remembered sitting in a carriage, fully restrained, as it slowly crept towards an unbelievable height. For a split second, from this height, I could see the big picture for what it truly was, and then I started the fast descent. My mind wanted only to scream whilst my hands, like eagle's talons, firmly gripped the safety bar in front of me. I thought I was prepared for this moment, but I wasn't ready to hear what was about to be said. I wasn't ready to partake of the penalty I knew was going to be imposed today.

Nothing could have prepared me for the twists and turns of this moment, the feelings and emotions were so extreme. John and I both walked into his homey office. He greeted us with his mischievous and lively manner shook our hands at the door as was his customary fashion, and ushered us to our seats. He walked behind his large, messy desk and positioned himself comfortably in his chair. His unwavering gaze held mine and he became very serious as his computer came to life and my results were posted.

He didn't waste any time and in his matter-of-fact, approachable manner he explained the biopsy results. I had cirrhosis and a lot of inflammation surrounding my liver, plus I was genotype one. My brain quickly filtered through the data and I comprehended this was not a good start. He then succinctly spoke directly to my partner, by passing me as he could see I was trapped back in the previous moment.

He explained I needed to access treatment straight away. Time was of the essence. The state of my disease, at that point, could have caused me to progress to liver failure and subsequent death within a few short years. I couldn't process all this information in one go, and I think that is why he directed this part of the consultation to John. I had no doubt I would do everything in my power to survive this journey, and if that meant sticking toxic chemicals into my body, I knew I would do it.

Tears welled up in my eyes and streaked my cheeks, and I momentarily lost my train of thought. After a few long moments my eyes refocused, and I was able to continue the conversation. Treacherous tears spilled over my eyelids and blurred my vision. Before all this I used to think crying was a sign of weakness, then again, I seemed to be doing more and more of it lately. Irrational tears flooded my eyes regularly, especially on my solitary morning runs. Did that make me weak? I didn't think so. I think it made me real.

I couldn't even glance at John. I was afraid that if I did, I would lose what little composure I had. I couldn't afford to lose it, not in this crucial moment. John acknowledged and recognised my pain. He placed his hand on my knee and squeezed it gently. I still needed answers. The fundamental question for me was about my son. Had I infected him? As I asked the burning question tears cascaded down my face and throat, soaking my white shirt, each word caught in the intense heat of my conviction.

He unceremoniously handed me a tissue from the box on his desk, and continued to explain that the risks were low. There was still a small risk, (2-5% chance), that he may have contracted it from me during the birthing process. I asked whether he should be tested. His response was to ask me if I considered it to be worth the stress right now. Nothing could be done for him as he was not old enough to access the treatments. A thick blanket of disgrace covered me from head to toe as I processed this fact. How could I have done this to my innocent child?

Our consultation was over. I was sent directly to the hospital to commence the treatment regime. I barely distinguished the words as they buzzed in my ears. I comprehended every single note, but I failed to hear the music that was supposed to accompany them.

Internally I wondered if there would be a future for me? If so, what would it look like? A tiny voice silently struggled within me. It desperately wanted to cry out, why, but I completely suppressed it. I couldn't bring forth the words I wanted to say. I was too ashamed and too embarrassed about the predicament I had placed us in.

My mind flaunted scenarios of John's utter disgust in me. I saw John as he enjoyed a happier, more fruitful and less risky life. A better life could be his, without me. I was the only obstacle. At that moment, I wished I was a mind reader, just to glean what was going on in his mind. What was he thinking about? How did he feel about me? Was he angry? Did he hate me? Did he feel trapped in this relationship? I would never know what thoughts passed through his mind, because I never asked any of these questions. The pain of knowing far outweighed the possibility of any positive responses he may have provided me.

Chapter 27

Adversity is the best teacher

I can't tell you exactly when I first contracted HCV. During my life, I have received unscreened blood products, such as the Rhesus injections after the birth of my children in the early '80s and '90s, I have had surgical procedures, been part of mass school vaccination programs and lived and received medical treatment in Papua New Guinea. However, I do believe it was probably 20 odd years ago, when I was self-indulgent and experimental in my youthful years. I can't recall ever sharing any injecting equipment. I thought I was careful even back then, but I cannot remember if I shared any of the other paraphernalia, like the swabs, tourniquet, spoon or the water. So I cannot be entirely sure how I contracted this disease, not that it really matters either way, at the end of the day I was still infected and I wasn't looking to blame anyone.

They say youth is wasted on the young. Well, my younger years were spent feeling infallible and indestructible. I held a watertight conviction that my life would perpetually roll on regardless of my antics. I never contemplated or even discussed the idea of contracting a disease from acts of sharing injecting equipment. How would I have known back then that my historical actions would bring harm to me today, twenty years later?

Those days long gone, a portion of history swept away by time, forever discarded, securely locked away where no one could access or change them. They were painful and tumultuous times for me to dwell upon. Days I would rather forget than reflect upon. But, here I was being punished for something I did back when I was young and impetuous. How could I not think about that time and what had transpired, when here I was experiencing the consequences? Look at the outcome and the carnage my bygone actions caused! The personal suffering I now forced upon not only myself but my family and friends as well. If I could take it back, I would, but this is not an option for anyone.

The silent thirty minute drive to the hospital made it possible for me to reflect and compartmentalise the words that careened through my tightly-wound head. The amount of circulating virus in my body was extensive. The fact that I had cirrhosis staggered me. The whole scenario was surreal. It confounded me. I didn't display any symptoms or show any signs of being ill at all.

Cirrhosis generally manifests with overall fatigue, body aches, mental sluggishness, headaches and nausea, but I exhibited none of these symptoms. I did feel tightness over my right side, and sometimes pain, but not enough to slow me down. If you consider the damage to my liver, then I should have experienced some major bodily manifestation, but I didn't.

This latest crisis was unbelievable, incomprehensible, to me. I felt like I was in a scene from a horror film. The most terrifying event would soon be revealed. A deadly virus persistently prowled and circulated throughout my mortal body, a hidden killer, unidentified by its host for the last twenty years. It concealed itself and lurked inside me, its aim to haunt and slowly destroy its prey, me.

The ongoing tragedy of living unaware of a hidden killer was the heartbreak of unknowingly putting those I dearly loved and others at risk. The prospect of this, should it occur, would be my grand finale, my final scene. I could not live with that on my conscience. I knew that household transmission was extremely low unless our bloods mixed from sharing toiletries et cetera. Still, my husband and I had been in some high risk situations, and, thankfully, he wasn't infected. I thanked God for this saving Grace.

Life is so fragile, a mirror so easily broken. As I pondered my situation, I became conscious of the fact I had taken my life for granted, thinking I would live forever. How naïve was I?

This challenging stumble I had taken had most likely prevented a potentially major fall. I may have never found out about my condition, and contracted liver cancer or liver failure. I needed to look at my situation from another angle. There was always good mixed with the bad, and I needed to focus on the positive aspects. This bitter trial I faced was really a blessing in disguise. It could have saved my life.

One of my biggest regrets was that I had not lived a healthier lifestyle, in some regards I had. I had exercised and ate well but I did still drink intermittently. At the time I was unaware of the potential dangers of drinking even the smallest amount of alcohol. The potentially fatal affects it can have on a struggling liver are immense. Aussies are big drinkers, we socialise regularly, and I was no different. I had most likely contributed to my cirrhosis by my heavy bouts of drinking in my twenties, and then the years of the odd glass of wine with dinner or a few cocktails at a nightclub had most likely fast tracked my liver disease.

Chapter 28

Labelled for all to see

"Nothing is so strong as gentleness, and nothing is so gentle as true strength".

St. Francis De Sales

The hospital materialized before us, bricks and mortar with coloured large lettered signs which directed us towards the parking area. We parked the car and sat, silently contemplating our surroundings. Internally, I questioned what treatment would hold for me? A cure? How would it affect me? Could I really go through with it? How sick would I become? Would I be able to work? I couldn't afford to dwell on these questions, as they made me nervous but I did.

As I gathered all the paperwork to start the battle, I become conscious I could fight no longer; there was no sense to any of it. I gave myself over to the phantoms and allowed them to paint pictures that I would never display. A war had begun against my unwanted passenger and I didn't have it in me to suppress it. John grabbed my hand and we started on our new quest. He had become the scaffolding in my life, the substance that held me together, especially in these dark hours. I don't think I could have travelled this road without him.

Together, we walked down a long, active, yet sterile, corridor. Lively people in nurse's uniforms hustled apprehensive patients into busy waiting rooms. We were ushered into a large, overcrowded room. I noticed a large reception area with a counter covered in numerous colourful advertisements where administration officers bundled and sorted through piles of patient files and sat answering phones and directing new clients. The reception desk unashamedly advertised this was a HCV clinic, and this was my destination.

I felt naked amongst the large crowd. Shame shrouded me. It blanketed me with menopausal-like hot flushes which turned my face pink. Feelings of awkwardness and humiliation manifested. I focused on the ugly tiled floor as a confident, yet emotionally colour blind, nurse gathered my paperwork and asked the final questions.

She pointed to another waiting area and we were once again instructed to sit and wait. I noticed people from all walks of life as they lingered and passed time, waiting and assessing each other. My heart rapidly thumped in my chest as I felt critiqued by my fellow comrades, the depth of my shame was, I thought, obvious to everyone present.

A deep, throaty voice echoed my name around the room. I looked up. A stern, detached nurse sought me. She offhandedly handed me a jar and told me she required a urine sample for drug testing. My whole body flinched. A urine sample? I couldn't believe it. I wanted to disappear, shrivel up into a ball so the searing stares of the onlookers wouldn't remain focussed on me.

I looked at her horrified. What was she insinuating? I wanted to scream at her, to tell her I had not touched any drugs in over twenty years! I hardly ever took a Panadol, let alone drugs. I was mute. Words streamed from my brain to my lips, but I would not allow them to be released. They would be imprisoned forever. The truth had been stated and my name had been called. I was labelled a drug addict in front of the whole room.

My legs progressively moved in the direction of the bathroom. My tense body produced an automated sample and I secretly handed her the plastic tightly-capped jar. She stood in the waiting room beside a small, white-covered table with my sample in her hand. Right there out in the open, she unscrewed the plastic container and proceeded to test its contents! I felt exposed and humiliated when she told me my sample was clear. She then directed us down the long hall to an empty room, where we were told to take a seat. She then informed us that someone would be along shortly. I was too shocked to care about her manner or anything else anymore.

The words of a song my brother's band created rang in my ears,

"I am your refuge, put your hand in mine, and I will show you the

way. I can heal your troubled heart and your life of disarray, all I'm asking is for you to put your hand in mine. When your strength is gone and the storms rage, listen closely and you will hear my voice. I am asking, but it's still your choice to put your hand in mine, and I will show you the way. I can make a brighter day."

I had to focus on these meaningful words, and I needed to continue to place my situation in God's hands. I had absolutely nothing to lose. My life was out of my control now anyway.

We waited in an uninviting, clinical-looking room. Time passed like a snail moving up the side of a large building. The room was cold and clinical its white clean walls folded around me, and for the first time in my life I had a feeling of claustrophobia. I felt the beginnings of a sinus headache as it approached and clung to the front of my face and took control of my right eyebrow. The beating of my heart pounded in my temples and made the pain worse. I mentally had to force myself to stay in this room and continue with this barbaric treatment regime. The pre-filled hypodermic interferon filled injection and the pink ribavirn tablets I had seen at the specialist office would fill my life for the next forty eight weeks. My head suddenly seemed like it would explode and I drew a deep breath of air as I tried to calm myself. As the recycled air hit my lungs I felt the crushing walls ever so slowly release their tight grip upon me.

The only saving grace this room offered was it provided freedom from the noise, freedom from the inquisitors prying eyes, and freedom from the eavesdropping.

As cold sweat dripped and blurred my eyesight I knew my life was in checkmate, my king had been caught by the dark knight. I was incapacitated unable to move. My life was completely overpowered. I felt encased in fast setting concrete as it slowly rose around me. Soon it would fully cover me. I knew I was defeated in every way. I was humbled by a tiny virus and a man who was ready to take this journey with me..

Thankfully, this personal nightmare which I just happened to be the main character in, had a potential end date. I could be liberated from HCV in forty eight weeks. I needed to focus on how I would use that freedom. I knew what I had to do to get there. I knew it would be a solitary, hard journey; one only I could endure. John would support me, but I wondered if I possessed the strength to see it through? I just knew I couldn't take counsel from the dark voices even if they shouted at me from the darkness. I would need all my strength to stay focused on the positive side of the equation; hopefully the healthier voices from my newly found white beam would wage a war and fight gallantly for my mental wellbeing.

Time passed and still no words transpired between John and I. Silence thickened the atmosphere. Out of the blue, a small dark haired woman of about forty entered the room. She spoke hurriedly with muffled words which were indecipherable to my ears. I think she offhandedly introduced herself, switched on the video player, told us someone else would attend to us for the treatment segment, and walked out again. I looked at John, he was as baffled as me. John tilted his head towards mine. Our foreheads softly united. Our

cheerless eyes met in a heartbreaking moment
of connection. He curved his eyebrows into a comical expression, and in a quirky tone said, "great bedside manner." His attempt at humour, in these circumstances, made me laugh and it broke the tension between us.

I knew I was held in the arms of someone who knew my every need, and there wasn't anywhere else I wanted to be. The video thrummed in the background. Its educational contents were a monotonous, boring script interrupted by the ceaseless humming of the overhead, bright fluorescent lights. The treatment demonstration video finally stopped and we sat and stared at the blank screen. I slowly processed the information I had been given. A calm stillness fell over the room. I knew I could not do it. It was physically and mentally impossible for me to plunge a syringe into the fleshy part of my stomach. I was needle-phobic. What was I going to do? Anxiety welled up within me. I tried to speak, to tell John I couldn't go through with it, but before I could, John discerned my internal turmoil. He grabbed my hand and unflinchingly stated he would do it for me.

He had been privy to my fears, and understood the private pain I felt. Together, we had weathered many storms. We were seasoned partners who could anticipate each other's moves. We took refuge in each other's arms when the seas were rough, and he knew I was in the midst of a personal typhoon, a rough patch, and he would step up to the bridge and take over, because he understood I was incapable.

The door flung open. A smiling, new figure entered the room. A small round shouldered sandy-haired older woman in her late fifties strode confidently in. Her arms burdened with bags and paperwork. She dropped her items casually on the long uncovered plastic table standing expectantly in the corner. She then sat in the vacant chair pulling it over so she was placed right in front of us. I thought, "she's got the wrong room!"

She introduced herself as the treating doctor. This doctor did not resemble the classic image of a regular treating physician well none I had seen, at best she resembled a retired social worker or counsellor, yet she was confident and I would later find out extremely competent. But still her name went in my ear and straight out the other one.

Her open manner and warm friendly smile put me at ease immediately. She moved quickly through the theoretical process of treatment, and then it was time to do the practical side. She opened a thin file folder that had been hidden under the bag on the table. It contained a hard copy printout of my medical record and test results; she quickly scanned them to ensure the right dose was prepared.

I was instructed to prepare the syringe, but I couldn't, John quickly jumped in and explained he would take responsibility for this task. As the words floated around me, I felt faint, my heart raced and the muscles in my legs went rigid and tense threatening to throw me onto the ground. Acid in my stomach fought to stay in its place as nausea made my head swoon. I had an overwhelming sensation to run, as well as vomit. My mind and body fought against each other, words against actions as they collided in a battle zone.

As a yoga teacher, I had practised meditation skills. I had learnt how to take my mind away from what the physical body experienced. I summoned images I knew would calm me. My therapeutic thoughts turned to the beach. I brought forth the sound of the waves as they gently crashed onto the shore. I felt the warmth of the sun as it caressed my skin and the gritty sand twisted and clustered between my toes. I visualised the colour and the coolness of the water as it splashed up my bare legs, and I could smell the salt as it clung in the air. I held tightly to this vision and a peaceful aura washed over me.

My canvas was ripped apart by words of instruction, the paint not yet dry, dripped on to the delicate sands beneath my feet. I was told to lie on the hard sheet covered bed, face up. Under the watchful eye of the doctor, my husband prepared the scene, just as he had been shown.

John accomplished the treatment manoeuvre like a cautious dancing step. He lay out all the instruments and readied himself for a new task. The syringe poised and aimed at the pinched fat

on my lower abdomen. I felt a light pressure and a slight sting but nothing else. He withdrew the needle tip and placed it into the disposal bin without re-sheathing the syringe. The deed was done. My first injection completed forty seven to go and the long journey of treatment began.

My head was reeling I had never considered I would ever be in a situation like this. Yet here I was. This wasn't in my life's plan, certainly not in the plan I had created. John's voice startled me as he drove me home. He echoed my thoughts which sent a chill down my spine.

Chapter 29

Passing through the flames unaffected

I recalled the doctor's words as I got up from the bed. The treatment could make me quite ill, maybe not this evening but certainly as I woke to the new day, she expected me to experience some flu like symptoms like headaches and nausea, maybe a few body aches and a slight temperature.

The sunlight darkened. As we drove home the day took on a mysterious melancholy tone as it drew to a close and crept towards the northern world. I didn't stay up late, intuition warned me not to so early into the evening I retreated to the bedroom, turned on the TV to watch a few hours of mindless nothingness as I waited for sleep to take me on its own journey. Before its healing power could embrace me, I lay snugly tucked under the purple cotton sheet, eyes open replaying the day's events. I pondered what the morning may bring. How sick would I be? What would I say to people? I knew I wouldn't be able to hide the fact that I may be sick for a long time. I had to work out some sort of strategy. I knew a chemo ridden environment would demand a sea saw balance be rigidly maintained if I was to survive this ride. This would include a regime of pills, exercise and activity, sleep, good nutrition and weekly injections all to keep a tiny body invader at bay. I understood the careful balance and vowed to stay within these boundaries.

Sleep did eventually come and brought with it a light dream state. Something startled me and my eyes opened to dimness. I dare not move expecting the worst so I lay still and waited. Gradually I became aware that the quality of light was changing. I glanced over at the large curtained window and saw glimmers of a pinkish hue as it tried to venture in through the cracks. I lay quietly for another hour mentally assessing my body, sensing any anomalies. There wasn't any, absolutely nothing was happening that was out of the ordinary.

As the sun blinked on the horizon so did I. I had passed through the fiery flames of my first injection and rose through the ashes, with not a single symptom. A foundation had been laid down and I thought if the following weeks were going to be like this, the forty seven to follow would be a breeze. I rolled over and happily poked my partner in the ribs and jokingly blamed him for not injecting me properly. He rolled over and playfully thumped me back then told me I was crazy and went back to sleep. I wasn't about to waste a day, it was six o'clock the best time for a morning run so I rallied my running partners and off we went.

Once again, I was blessed. My testimony was not like others, as I did not initially experience any of the signs and symptoms that most people get when they start treatment. I have spoken to people that have been so sick they have not been able to get out of bed, let alone go to work or go through the daily functions of life.

I have to say, treatment didn't really disrupt my daily life at all. Well, not in the beginning, anyway. I did a few things that may have positively helped me. One of which was to seek Naturopathic advice and treatment shortly after my diagnosis so for four months I was on a strict regime of vitamin and herbal supplements to support my liver. The naturopath I chose was someone I knew and had worked for previously. I found him to be well-educated and had been practicing a long time. The big plus was I had great faith in his abilities and he was very sympathetic to my plight.

He started me on a regime of supplements including ginger tea, four different types of liver herbs, high doses of vitamin C, hormone supports and vitamin B supplements. Just prior to commencing treatment he put me on CH100 a Chinese concoction of herbs specifically designed for liver problems. I continued on this regime all the way through my treatment. I am not sure whether or not this preparation time assisted with me the lack of treatment side effects but in the back of my mind I know his help as well as my strong constitution and faith helped me during this time.

The first four weeks passed with little disruption to my life, except for the despised weekly injections that my husband administered. I was infected with two strains of Genotype one (1a and1b). Unfortunately Genotype I is the hardest to cure and requires the longest treatment regime. I had prepared myself mentally for that, but I was totally unprepared for the barrage of blood tests that accompanied treatment, such as the week two, four, eight, twelve, sixteen, twenty I think . . . You get the picture. At the end of it, I felt like a pin cushion.

Chapter 30

Facades needed and worn

It was early spring. I reached week twelve quite uneventfully, still able to work, run and going through the motions of living a normal life, all without any significant side effects. The only real problem I encountered up to this stage was administering the injection, which I was incapable of doing. But we had a routine. I would reach the vast prison parking lot were numerous cars with the last of the day shift administration staff would trickle past me towards the exit. I would check the rear view mirror and look around before driving to our spot hidden beside a large gum tree and an abandoned building at the lower section of the prison grounds.

John would wait for me, his cropped blonde hair visible through me field of vision at the wheel of his red Daihatsu charade. I would pull into the empty space beside his car our presence totally obscured by the old prison administration building which dominated the far end of the small parking lot. It was a shabby looking brick structure with dirty wooden doors and rows of filthy windows concealed behind white lacy webs. The best part was it was hardly used, the dog squad occasionally utilized its services but not on a Friday afternoon so it was the best place to conduct our covert activity.

Even before the car's engine was shut down John would slip in beside me. Even though we had this routine well established dread would still crawl up my spine. He always greeted me with a lingering kiss then leant over and unravelled the content of the navy blue cooler bag. Time was always against us. Even in the twenty fist century a deed such as this would be viewed as a possible threat to the security of the prison. John had mastered the process and never procrastinated as he prepared the syringe and the disposal bin. Within a few seconds it was done.

Always we were only left with a short ten minutes before I was required at my post inside the prison ready for the long twelve hour night shift ahead. We would sit in the car and share our days like two lovers on a quiet scenic picnic. And all too suddenly our time would be up and John would grasp the hard plastic door handle, release it and create a space beside me that I would have preferred to be filled permanently by him.

I would then drive into the staff car park and steady myself for the long night ahead and its well scripted duties in an environment where darkness and fluorescent light inhabited the same space.

At week twelve, I was required to have another PCR test, to assess whether or not the treatment had been successful.

I tried not to focus on the fact that I needed a miracle to clear this virus. I was not the best candidate. I was overweight, over forty, living with a high viral load, and to top it all off, I had cirrhosis. I needed my blood test to show a large drop, or even better, an undetectable viral load. If this was not the case, I would be removed from the treatment program. I would have no other options, but to live my life to the best of my abilities, being regularly monitored for cancer markers—alpha feta protein—and subtle changes in my liver profile. There was no naturopathic or alternative cure available to me at that time.

There was a two week wait for my test results, and it was the most stretched out interval I had ever witnessed. My life became like a ice laden jagged ridge of storm ravaged rocks. Two prominent faces emerged my work life and my real life each took on separate entities. I clung to the rigid peaks of my position in the prison whilst hugging the frost bitten grass at home and each was a bleak and blizzard blasted as the next. I was hopelessly consumed with my need to be set free from the harness that constricted my life.

To the world, I used the right words. I wore an optimistic mask for all to see, but I couldn't deceive myself, my own personal, pessimistic pantomime continued. My acting ability pathetic, from my view, but to everyone else realistic, as it convinced many that I was coping well. I spoke meaningless words, none of which I believed would come to fruition. Inside I knew the truth. The words I spoke held no real meaning for me, because I knew I didn't deserve to be freed from my internal hell. I didn't think I had been really bad throughout my life but I knew I had done things I shouldn't so it was easy to believe this was my punishment.

The results returned and displayed what I already believed. A storm rolled in with the sunset bringing with it the ghost blue lights of lightening. It struck the horizon and ricochet the information around me. I was still infected. A glimmer of hope filtered down as the rain struck me; my viral load had dropped dramatically.

Upon reflection this meant the treatment was working, just not as quickly as the doctor, or I for that matter had hoped. I was instructed to continue on treatment for another twelve weeks and the tests would be repeated at week twenty-four. I was sceptical but hopeful at the same time. It was working. I could see that.

My father would tell me to be peaceful in the midst of this storm. Everything I needed lived inside me I just had to dig deep and find it, including joy and happiness. He said "you've got what it takes to be happy living right there inside you, use it". He went on to say "read Colossians 3:15 (*Let the peace of Christ rule in your hearts, since as members of one body you were called to peace. And be thankful*) and 1 Peter 3:10 ("*Whoever would love life and see good days must keep his tongue from evil and his lips from deceitful speech*). He explained I needed to learn how to quell my negative thoughts and my negative self-talk as it was destructive. Instead I should talk positively and learn to believe in what I said. He told me everything has a purpose and we sometimes don't understand the purpose the only thing we can do is search and seek out peace to live with what we are going through. However, he also told me 'don't expect it to fall from the trees above your head actively search for and find it'. My questions still reigned. Would it work? Was I worthy enough to be healed? Did I dare to dream of a life without HCV? Would I be given a second chance? If I was, I would try to make a difference, and I would use this gift wisely.

Chapter 31

Continual commitment

A monotonous exchange of tablets, followed by the Friday injections, continued. I had come to wear the physical mask of treatment. Circles of red, raised ridges camouflaged the lightly coloured skin on my belly, caused by the Interferon. The bruising and red rashes behind my knees hurt as they rubbed on the coarse fabric of my prison guard uniform. My skin had lost its natural glow replaced by an old candle waxy texture. My eyes were dark sunken pits and the hollowness of my cheeks made me look old and haggard. My live-in supporter, John, found it hard to access a new injection site, without having to go over the evidence of its predecessor.

The treatment regime and John's dedication taught me about real love. They taught me about trust and acceptance and to accept who I was. I knew with clarity that John loved me and would stand beside me throughout this ordeal. His acts constantly demonstrated his enduring patience, his genuine concern, and his continual commitment to seeking a healthy, positive outcome for us both. He believed we would make it, and he had hope. A hope that lived and burned deep in my soul also, and longed to be allowed to surface, but I dared not fully unleash it, as I knew that disappointment would crush me.

During the next twelve weeks, I learnt to really pray. I learnt to speak to my higher power like a friend. I cried with Him, I laughed with Him, but mostly I talked with him about my fears and frustrations. I found payer to be a haven from my inner turmoil. I used it when I was angry, when I was frustrated, when I was scared, but mostly when fear threatened to take me. It opened my mind and my heart, and led me to others, who wanted to support me. However, at the back of my mind, I still doubted that God would totally accept me. I was after all, in my mind, a joke. I certainly didn't think I deserved His attention. But, I sought it anyway, simply because I had no other option.

In the Garden of Eden, man was given one commandment, don't eat the fruit from a specific tree, but it was consumed anyway, and it resulted in a fall from grace. We had the laws written in our heart and in our minds, we knew right from wrong and this became our consciousness and still we did the wrong thing. Yet we were also offered forgiveness, our debt was paid. The problem for me was having faith I was forgiven. I had broken every single one of the Ten Commandments Moses was given, so how could I possibly be worthy of any consideration. If I was in charge I would have most likely banished a person like me to the ends of the earth, where I belonged. But instead Gods blood was sprinkled upon my heart and I was forgiven. It was a really hard concept to understand and accept simply because I didn't earn it, I didn't even ask for it but it was offered to me all the same.

Hepatitis C brought humbleness into my life. I felt I had nowhere else to go but look up. I felt trapped but I was released ever so slowly. Initially I was like a wounded lioness. I had been struck a blow that left me injured, alone and starving on the savannah, but I would heal in time. I was offered help to survive the rugged terrain that surrounded me and I took it.

Chapter 32

A wounded lioness

"Our lives begin to end the day we become silent about things that matter."

—Rev. Martin Luther King, Jr

Towards the end of week twenty-four, I had begun to feel lethargic. My appetite had decreased, and I had developed a cough, as well as severe hip pain. I continued to exercise every second day, but found that if I ran my usual five kilometres, I had to lay down breathless for a few hours afterwards, to recover. I changed my diet, and started to substitute food for a lot of fruit and vegetable juices and soy-based protein smoothies. I struggled to provide my body with optimum nutrients, whilst I slowly poured a stream of chemicals into it, my daily dose of kryptonite. Weight started to fall from my body. Those stubborn kilos I thought I would never lose were being shed quite rapidly. My weekends had become infected by the virus as much as my body. The TV dominated my days off and created a virtual world that would encapsulate me. It would exaggerate and provide a contrast to the world I was stuck in. Week twenty-four crept thoughtfully into my existence. It brought a new sense of anxiety and apprehension. The mandatory tests had been requested, and were now completed. This was it. I would have my answer. Would I be cured, or would I be left to fend for myself on the desolate savannah? It was a pale grey world as I looked out towards the skyline. Nondescript pine trees zipped past as we drove towards my answers. Dull luminous clouds hid the natural beauty and obscured the horizon from view but it didn't change the fact that I had reached a critical point in the journey.

We approached the now very familiar surroundings of the specialist's office and took up our usually place next to the water fountain. Even the glints of the suns rays piercing through the low hanging cloud cover could not alleviate my feelings. Well defined shadows danced through the panes of glass and still a level of foreboding hung over me. I felt like a ticking time bomb. Raw emotions ascended to the surface and my desperation was evident for the whole world to see.

Living with this virus felt like the sun setting over the feeding grounds on the plains in an African desert. As the cloud cover increased and the darkness descended it allowed the lowly scavenger's time to slither around and destroy me cell by cell. Night is a great camouflage for the hunters, but not so for the hunted. I felt like I was the hunted. I knew if I didn't clear this virus, I would be enthusiastically stalked and prepared for the final kill.

From the depths of my thoughts a voice rang in my ears calling my name. The specialist greeted us both at the door. He grabbed my partner's hand, shook it, leant forward and kissed me on the cheek, then ushered us into his very familiar office. Before he had a chance to sit in his chair, I asked him if I was able to continue on treatment.

He turned to peer at me over the rims of his spectacles. Over the past six months, I had grown to really like and trust this man, he was honest, open and upfront. We had many debates and discussions about testing procedures, disease progression and upcoming new treatments. The latest theories were always a hot topic between us.

He didn't always agree with where my research took me, especially when I discussed O-zone therapy in the USA. We debated to and fro about this subject me for him against. He listened intently to my latest findings, then composedly and solemnly informed me that people were dying from blood poisoning, to which I had no response.

He also didn't agree with my faith in natural therapies, often commenting to my partner about it 'being a waste of money'. I believed there was a place for all types of medicine, and complementary medicine had in my mind been proven time and time again, even when conventional medicine had failed.

It was my life and I had to choose what I thought was best for me. It was up to me to navigate through the mine field of predators out there in the world. This lioness was not about to change her mind on her choice to utilise the skills of the natural therapist in combination with the current course of chemotherapy.

He sat down and faced me, crossed his arms over his chest and informed me quite matter of factly that I had not been able to clear the virus. A silence reigned over us whilst I digested the information. I knew what this meant. I would have to go off treatment. I had no other options. He could do nothing further for me except monitor my liver progression and hopefully catch a potential cancer before it was inoperable.

I felt frozen, anesthetized. The ancient virus race from which HCV had sprung had won this battle. It was very adept at surviving in this kind of savage environment; it had proven it time and time again. A pitch black night descended upon me. Its bitter coldness seeped deep into my bones. I was back at square one, the wind gone, completely removed from my sails. I was speechless. That hidden, compressed hope was now squashed, replace by devastation.

I thought I had tamed the beast within me, discarded it, but it slowly made its presence known to me as it invaded me, like an uninvited cancer. Fear slipped down my spine and wrapped its cold long fingers around the vertebrae of my hunched over spine. My mind froze with astonishment and my thoughts refused to thaw. I hadn't cleared the virus. I was still infected.

Slowly feelings returned as my mind slowly unfroze. Thoughts and emotions spread subtly but thoroughly throughout my body, saturating my being in hopelessness, like a gathering of feeding sharks around a weakened bleeding fish. Like me the fish had valiantly fought, but would eventually lose the battle. I would leave here, once again defeated, the glory to be offered to someone else. A revelation I didn't want to hear.

My mind shut down. I was unable to process any more of the soundless words that fell from his lips. My resolve had been weakened. My eyes faded, and the floor became my primary focus. I thought I was prepared for those words, but I wasn't. I thought I had equipped myself for this day, but in reality, I hadn't. Anguish hits some harder than others, and I was literally shattered.

As I sat in his office, I realised that I secretly anticipated I would beat it. I had come to truly believe in the lie I told others. I believed I had a fighting chance. All my acting and bravado was an actual audition for the real deal, a part I didn't receive, but secretly believed I would. I recounted every day. I knew I had adhered to the treatment regime stringently, not missing one day. I ruminated over questions I dared not ask. What could have gone wrong? What did I do wrong? What would happen now? That answer paralysed me.

I couldn't move or speak. I sat motionless, like a petrified statue. I felt a pressure on my hand, as it was totally engulfed. I felt like I was becoming mentally unstable. A big burden weighed heavy on me, and it defeated me. A panic stricken voice spoke beside me, rousing me from my oppression, "what happens now?"

I knew monitoring was my only option. I would be required to have an ultrasound every six months and more blood tests to assess cancer markers—alpha feta protein tests. This was hardly the reassurance John desired. He wanted more conviction, more certainty, but it was not offered, as it wasn't the truth.

I was like a loose cannon. My mind triggered explosive muscle responses, and negative thought processes blasted over my synapses. I needed to refocus and get some perspective. I needed to stop and draw a deep breath. Relax my body. Control my emotions. I needed to pull myself together. I drew a big, deep breath, and pure cool air filled my lungs. My heart pumped its fleeting calming effects around my body. It briefly soothed me and brought clarity back to my mind. My concentration centred back on the doctor. I witnessed the sympathy and sincerity; it was spoken in his tone and written on the lines on his face. His focused eyes gripped me compelling me to listen as he explained the last twenty four weeks had not been done in vain. The benefits of treatment included a decrease in viral load, and this fact alone provided my liver time to heal.

The words bounced around me but failed to actually connect with me. Inside me all the words began to smudge as my inner tears fell and melded with the dark ink written on the paper of my soul. The remaining words held a story of failure. A soft voice murmured words telling me this was my entire fault. They spoke of how I had failed, once again. The horizon that once held such promise and beauty was now empty and distant.

I heard a distant voice as it inquired about the new

treatments—the protease inhibitors; at the time of finalising this twenty four weeks of my treatment regime these treatments were still in the final stages of trials so would not be available for another two or three years. This didn't stop my husband and the specialist from debating the success rates.

I recalled that first day of treatment and just how far I had come since then. The injections although still not liked were a part of my life, the little pink tablets had become like my daily vitamins. These vitamins however didn't build the body up but instead caused havoc depleting the body of its natural immune responses replacing it with a chemical solution.

I have no idea just how long I sat there oblivious to the world around me. I was brought back to reality by a hand nudging me and a voice inquiring if I was alright. The look of concern in John's eyes which wrapped around mine scared me. I slowly nodded in agreement. Once again the conversation rang around me like loud, tolling church bells, a constant rambling sound, in which nothing was discernible. My ears were closed but my inner voice could still be heard loud and clear.

Finally the hour glass tipped and our time was up. Unanswered questions, like a bright red lipstick, lingered on my lips. I would never ask any of them, I wasn't ready for the answers. I did however ask one question, a question that had a burning desire to be released. I discharged it and waited for it to return to me answered, was I going to make another five years. The answer ricocheted off the walls and came straight back at me "numerous studies demonstrated that people who go on HCV treatment live longer and also have lower incidences of liver cancer, so, most likely yes, but there were no guarantees in life".

I walked into the afternoon numb and vague.

Chapter 33

Entombed

The drive home was long and silent, the air heavy with words unspoken. The outside view I saw through the window offered a small sense of solace as it swiftly sped past me in a blur of shapes and colour. I could think of nothing profound or reassuring to say. I was inarticulate, words adrift in the turbulent sea of my thoughts. During the silent drive, what I did see in the windows was harrowing motion pictures depicting my impending death and the destruction of the family unit.

I refused to meet John's periodic gaze, which regularly probed me for answers I couldn't provide. The dark passengers voice grew stronger and insanity crept closer, its long fingers reached out and touched my mind, clenching it and imbedding plans to leave the family, to run away, and die somewhere on my own.

I didn't think I could possibly coexist with a virus for the rest of my life. I felt accursed, hemmed up on all sides, nothing working in my favour but everything working against me. I felt irredeemably contaminated on every level. I found myself again, asking God WHY? This punishment was rather extreme, I thought.

A lifetime of torment the price for a small window of time misspent. My heart condemned me on every level. I remembered something my brother once told me about allowing your own heart to condemn you. He said "our self-worth and our self-confidence diminishes if we allow self-condemnation to occur. He further said "when we miss the mark we have to realize that we are forgiven, a long time ago a man paid a high price for us and that deserves a bit of our servitude". "Holy living is something we do so we don't get condemned". I have to say sitting in that silent car I didn't feel very holy or much forgiven.

What I did feel was the urge to run away. I didn't know how I would be able to share intimate relations with my family? How could I make love to my husband? My life would never be the same. I would never be the same. I felt unclean, dirty, rotting away from the inside out. I asked myself if it was all worth it?

No, I didn't think so.

As the silence deepened so did my thoughts. It made me feel curiously detached. I planned my diversion, my getaway. I made up my mind not to put my family in any more risk. I would leave and allow them the opportunity to live a normal, happy life; hopefully a gratifying life, without the constant threat of infection from what lurked inside me. I wanted them to move on, without me. As painful as I knew it would be, I also rationalised that this option was the best for everyone.

Over the next few days I started to sabotage my relationship with John. It was quite easy to do and it didn't take long for our relationship to spiral downwards. I found myself trapped in one of those moments where I felt pathetic and inconsequential. I had this uncanny knack of pushing people away by some form of long distance telepathy. I didn't even have to speak and everyone knew not to engage with me.

I found myself living in the land of the lost. My self-imposed isolation just made me want to curl up under a warm blanket and cry. My self-induced self-pity was stupid because I knew out in the real world I had friends I should be calling on in this hour of need, but pride got in the way instead. Often I would pick up the receiver but my voice would choke before I could speak. What I became over those few days was a severely injured lioness, flanked by millions of tiny predators, waiting whilst my will to live ebbed away each day.

I had nowhere to go in every sense of the word, my life was on hold.

I wanted the solid ground beneath me to open up and swallow me, and it did. I was buried whilst still living. A coffin of conviction imprisoned me. It held me deep in the ground. I felt completely submerged; the protective garments I once wore were now discarded on the surface. I lay entombed within myself, and allowed the darkness to totally seize the worthy and enjoyable portions of my life and place dark shadows over them.

The bad dreams started to come back, dreams filled with fear. They brought insomnia with them. It was too hard to fight them so I quit trying to sleep. What I did instead was start a nocturnal walking program, one that would be with me throughout the long dark moments ahead. That first night I slowly walked around the three kilometres. It was an unlit block so I had to carefully place my feet as the moon's slight glow was my only guiding light. The safe neighbourhood in which I lived had no street lights to illuminate a path. As the cool air bit my cheeks and rustled my hair I contemplated my situation and calculated a very loose plan of attack.

That next morning after I awoke from a few fitful hours of slumber I believed a hand was being openly extended to me. It was like a small light flickered far above me, through the grey clouds over head. My local GP called to see how I was and I went to see him. I sat in his office and cried as I offloaded my perception of the situation I was in. He listened intently. His caring nature just made me cry even more, his words of acceptance and encouragement were beyond imagining. I remember he gently patted me on the hand and turned to his droning computer. As his two dominate fingers jabbed and poked at the keyboard, he explained he would order more tests, and then together we could make some real decisions. I was stunned. I didn't think there were any other options available to me. As his words boomeranged around in my mind I felt the unbearable weight of the ground above me shift slightly. I had not considered anything other than what I was told by the specialist.

My GP ordered the tests online then told me they should only take a few days as the blood was already on hand. Wow! I walked out of his office with a slight glimmer of hope radiating from me. And, once again I found myself waiting for test results.

Reflecting back, I can see I missed the whole point to this part of the journey. I believe a lesson was to be learnt but of course I didn't learn it at that time. I had been given an opening to seek support to learn to trust and rely on others, but I failed. My suspicious nature prevented me from giving others the opportunity to 'have my back'. I was so fixated on doing it my way, thinking I had the best solutions and only I had the best options.

Writing this now I feel so arrogant, so stupid, it wasn't like I did everything perfectly, because I didn't. I made more mistakes than most people. I guess the difference was that I kept getting up, if nothing else I was persistent. What I realised was I let go of everything positive I had learned and slipped back into the true nature of myself. My childhood closed off, my way or the highway nature reigned and my father's aptly named 'von grupen fuher' persona rose again. It triumphed over all the hard work I had done over the years. How stupid of me.

By shutting myself off from any sort of support system I had no defence perimeter to defend me. I was left alone with my dark thoughts which often crept in and invaded me from every angle. I had over the years fought many battles with this negativity. I thought I had perfected most defence moves, and for a long time I had held my ground. We had skirmished and won positions only to fight again and lose them. The problem was the situation had changed and my motives were all personal and selfish and they were hopeless against the negativity that had become so intimate with every part of me. What I did forget was just how important it was to have your personal army around you. I had pushed all my soldiers away and I alone stood on the battlefield facing a colossal opponent.

Unfortunately it wasn't until much later that I would realise I was not on a solo mission, countless others were involved whether I liked it or not. I also came to understand I was not a nomadic single commander. I lived like I was, but, I was not. I lived amongst peers who required alliances and partnership more than a commanding presence or a dictator like I was.

In my mind I justified my attitudes, perceptions and behaviour with a lot of internal self-talk, I didn't want to burden others with the responsibility of looking after me if and when I became ill. I also wanted to prevent them from experiencing shame and guilt because I perceived they were afraid of becoming infected. These were all *my* thoughts because I never asked anyone how they felt about the situation.

I knew if one of them became infected at my hand, it would cause a lot of internal pain and personal echoes of damnation would linger to this day and beyond.

Chapter 34

Darkness prevails

It was the middle of spring, a slight coolness hung in the air and the night still lingered in the background tinged with ragged streamers of cloud. The 4am high pitched alarm droned from the wooden bed side table and woke both John and I. John sluggishly rolled out of bed to get himself ready for his work day ahead, me I was on a day off and had nothing planned for the upcoming day. I am not one of those people who have the wonderful capacity to roll over and go back to sleep, this is not part of my nature. Conveniently for me as soon as I wake up, my mind becomes fully alert and ready to go. This day was no different.

As soon as my blue eyes engaged with the world so did my mind and I was flooded with the internal cinema. Now I love movies I have to say it one of my favourite past times but when the movies are constantly filled with horror, disgust and despair they wear a bit thin. I saw fast forwarded clips displaying death, funerals, family, suffering, isolation and regret. I didn't need to see anymore pictures certainly not movie length epics because self-loathing and condemnation had already taken up permanent residence, so if that was the goal then they need not have bothered. I already had squatters in my life and believe me my constant roommates never let me forget where we were at.

I slipped out of bed, believing that a change of scenery would stop my self-imposed harassment and change my internal state. I snuggled deep into the soft lounge chair, and waited for the sun to lighten my world. Hours passed as I pondered and meditated on my circumstances. I saw the bars of morning sunlight as it cut across the rich reds and blues of the large cotton tablecloth spread out on the six seater wooden dining table. As I sat in that comfortable arm chair and the sky lightened around me, overwhelming desires to pack up, run and give in, detonated around me like strategically planted bombs. I tried to rationalise what had happened to me, how I could be in this situation. How did I get here and where could I go from here, was there even an option.

Daylight trickled into the room, and I moved into the dining room. I found myself alone in the quietness of a familiar, yet unchanging, motionless house as my son made his own way to school. As the minutes ticked by, the rays of sunlight shone brilliantly through the pane of glass of the long open window and cast a well-defined shadow on the table. Theses silhouettes danced and flaunted themselves on the large wooden table, where I sat. The warmth of the day touched me. Its long fingers caressed and warmed the skin on my face. It conveyed a soft soothing, calming presence.

On the outside the ambience was peaceful and serene.

Nevertheless, my thoughts were bleak and sinister. I found my internal eyes were much sharper and clearer in the shadowy world, where they regularly dwelt during these early months. My dark thoughts often turned ominously to the end. But on this particular day insanity crept even closer. Its fingers caressed my thoughts. I saw hallucinations of my life alone, waiting to die, isolated from everyone. Movies length screenings of my family frolicking and playing in another world played on the screen as I sat watching them enjoy a happy life without me. Musical sounds reached my ears. Lyrics of soulful tunes told me to do the right thing. Poetic and meaningful words stated I needed to be taken permanently out of the equation.

Another movie streamed this time I watched myself alone living a life in Cairns. As the music played I heard a distinct message. This time the words weren't whispered or sung with empathy, the essence had changed. The message was clear and sung with heavy undertones. Should I stay or should I go. If I stayed no one would have closure, but, my death would provide just that. The words of my childhood music idol Alice Cooper's song swirled in my head

Welcome to my nightmare, I think you're gonna like it, I think you're gonna feel you belong . . . . Welcome to my breakdown. I hope I didn't scare you . . . .

I realised my death would bring a quick closure and enable them to move on a lot easier than knowing I was out there somewhere.

An unedited funeral played out before me. One I had visually created and planned in great detail. I knew I could easily implement it. I made a decision. I would no longer make promises to anyone, because I knew I wouldn't keep any of them. I had nothing to lose as I thought my life was already over.

On the table lay a large notepad and a black pen. They waited for my instructions. My steady hand automatically commenced writing. Unwavering clear words filled the paper with an uncontrolled compulsion. My own funeral service was created in well-defined detail with flawless instructions. The curtain was now drawn on my life. My demons had won. I had relinquished my life, and here it lay in black and white.

I was surprised how little time this task took, how easy it was. The final feature film I had produced consumed me for hours. It was a perfect example of how effortlessly I could consider ending it all. No food or drink passed my lips as the final preparations were made.

The wrench of the three o'clock school pick up broke my self-absorbed trance. It forced me to resurface from my six hour obsession. I was overcome with a horrific realisation. I had spent all day visualising and playing out my own death. How macabre! Welcome to my breakdown alright, it scared me to think I had taken a six hour vacation from reality and just like the words of the song I had felt right at home.

It was then I knew something was very wrong with me. I had

spiralled down like a corkscrew imbedding itself into the cork, twisting deeper into the darkness. It was not just the absence of light but the absence of hope that held me in these thoughts for such a long time. I was held captive for six hours and during that time a piece of me died. My heart was wounded by loss and failure and my mind was held by a fear of seeing the suffering of my family, people whom I love but was powerless to save.

Generally in my darkest moments, my kids were my guiding light, but their bulbs had blown, and the lighthouse that once guided me was empty, devoid of any radiance. Darkness now prevailed where their light had once been.

I always thought that if you played a role long enough, the role would somehow become real. However my performance as a laisser-faire, happy go lucky human being, was not the role I chose I had chosen the death march instead.

My son, now at home, settled comfortably into his natural routine. I decided to go for a long walk to finalise the details of my plan. I wanted it all to end. For me, the deal was done, written on a notepad which sat on the table. Everything was clear and settled in my heart and I was ready and willing to hand my life over. I was ready to take that nocturnal vacation and visit the place where we sweat, laugh and scream and feel right at home like Alice Copper sung to me.

As I walked a fleeting thought crossed my mind which made me to wonder what could bring me to this place. Was this depression? How could I be fine last week, and feel so different today? I was actually contemplating the end of my life. What was wrong with me? I held a strong belief that suicide was wrong. As for going to hell well I didn't even cross my mind when I wrote that funeral plan. But it was a thought that was thrown at me as my feet pounded the bitumen. Its presence actually frightened me.

This was the first time in my life I had contemplated taken this path. I now have an understanding of why people want to commit suicide! They want to end the pain that they are in, the emotional or physical pain that seems to be never ending. Suicide is not always a call for attention it's a call for HELP! I think that was what I was doing; my problem was I had isolated myself so much that if I attempted it, I would have done it, simply because no one would have known. I questioned if God loved me surely He would send someone to help me.

The words of another of my brother's songs hit me in the face like the mud pies we threw at each other as children.

Now faith is a substance By faith all things are possible But without faith to please Him is impossible It's the evidence of things not seen See all you gotta do, is have a little faith There aint nothing he cant do My God will see you through

Have faith, what did that really mean. I pondered this statement. Was it even possible that this situation would be turned around. I was afraid to hope.

I believe at that point in time I was in a lot of emotional pain and I wasn't thinking clearly. Emotional pain had caused me to lose my clear perspective on life. Something completely out of character for me.

Suicide and its link to Hell, I am not so sure about. Granted suicide is a said to be a sin, but by all accounts no sin is too great for God to forgive. I had to believe God was bigger than that. I wouldn't condemn my child to a life in his room for doing something wrong or immoral I would in fact try and help him to correct his behaviour. So wouldn't God do the same? We are all sinners, Not one of us is perfect. Although I used to think I was, but I soon came to realise I was far from it. LOL.

One of the questions I ask myself was whether or not the treatment I had just finished could radically change the way I thought? I recalled one of the side effects was depression. But, what I was feeling was so intense, so real, so powerful and so consuming. Was that depression? I didn't know. I wondered if I would succumb to the internal demons that overshadowed my convictions and my principles. Would I be strong enough to resist the temptation, or would I take the easy option, which was continually flaunted in my face throughout that fateful day?

Walking, like running, always released my mind from its prison cell, and today my stave of execution was granted. The further I walked, the more I became liberated from the overpowering, crushing reflections that had held me captive all day. My vision cleared. A new icon rallied under the spotlight, **anger**. Early in the day all I wanted to do was to crawl into the pit, cover myself with the thick mud, then pull the pit in after myself amercing myself in it. But this walk had changed my perspective, my delusions no longer controlled my movements or thoughts they lingered in the back drop but they were replaced by a new purpose. I had new focus, anger. A new cause rolled in and settled over me. I vowed to survive this day. I would not 'top myself'not today. I would try and get through this, hopefully remaining sane enough to wake up the next day and beat this ride.

I started to yell and scream at God. Words I will not repeat here. I was angry, furious with Him, for allowing this to happen.

Visions of starving, emaciated children who suffered throughout the world immediately flooded my awareness. Fleetingly, I felt guilty for my thoughts, but I was so self-consumed, I easily ignored these mental pictures. I needed help, and I needed someone to help me, otherwise it was over for me. Rivulets of tears streaked my windblown face, as I loudly and furiously yelled into the void. I can't do this anymore! Just take me! Take me now!

Through my ranting and my anger, I felt tranquillity fall. A quite peaceful calm covered me. I stood in the eye of a cyclone, whilst debris floated around me. Words and phrases both spoken and unspoken encircled me, trapped in the raging winds. A name dropped with the torrent of rain. An omen. She was a woman I had not had contact with for many years. I wondered if she was still around.

I momentarily ceased walking, stunned. Did that really just happen, or did I imagine it? Did I hear it correctly? I think someone actually spoke to me. Was that God, instructing me? Yes, I think it could have been.

As I started to walk again I felt such emotional pain. I believe I was at the lowest point in my life right in that moment. I was literally in an emotional gutter, a place I would have been physically if I hadn't changed my life many years ago. This was my last dance, God was the final name on my personal dance card. Would He dance with me this late in the game. If He wouldn't help me then I was doomed. I would twirl through the final stages of my life alone and without hope.

My father had always said that God claims his children in the final hour. This was my final hour and I was acutely aware of it. However every step homeward brought me a little more strength and a little more courage. A new attitude formed. It rose slowly from the ashes of the decaying world around me just like the attitudes of those strong Japanese people who gallantly rose and overcome their devastated lives after the worst bombing in history, the fire bombings back in 1945 that killed millions of people.

My house came into view, and as I looked at it, it beckoned me. It reached out for me and invited me to stay. As I looked at it, I felt encouraged. My history was mingled with the paint on its walls and the bricks that held it in place. I stood for a few moments, the wind flitting around my face and stared at its familiarity. It spoke to me, its mind reached mine and told me to rise up and be the woman I was supposed to be. I needed to be strong. This journey had an end date, giving up was not an option.

Standing there as the yellow sky turned orange I realised I wasn't prepared to throw my life away. But, if I was to keep living, I would need to start to really fight for my place here on this earth. I had allowed my enemies to get a foothold in my life. As I crossed the threshold of my home I knew a battle of self-control and determination would need to be waged.

I made a promise as much to my home as to myself, I would never allow the pit to pull me in so deep that I ever considered killing myself again, no matter how bad things got.

I had been given a name 'Betty'. A saviour, a friend, a helper, someone to overcome this dark time in the hour glass. Finally, I felt someone was listening to me. I felt heard, and now I understood there could be another way. It didn't have to end like I had previously planned and written.

Chapter 35

A lifeline is offered

"Continuous effort—not strength or intelligence— is the key to unlocking our potential."

-Winston Churchill

Betty was a kind, gentle, God-fearing woman. We had shared a surrogate mother-daughter relationship in another time. A strong bond of mentoring, love, trust and acceptance had once joined us but was long gone as my current path had separated us. Oddly, as I searched the telephone directory, I found her number straight away, it jumped out at me from the pages, like it was there waiting for me all this time.

As the day began to turn a deep purple and the dwindling light turned red I called her. There was no pause our lines connected and so did our lives. Her buoyant cheerful voice filled the air ways and tears filled my eyes. I didn't realize just how much I needed someone, I needed my mother and here she was a true gift laid out for me. It was like I had just seen her yesterday.

Her question shocked me. I was unaware that she was knew of

my situation. She wanted to know what had taken me so long to call her. She told me she had been waiting for me to make contact with her for quite some time. She told me God had prepared her, but she was not to call me as I had to initiate this part of my healing. I had to swallow my pride and ask for help. However during this time she was preparing herself to assist me for the battle ahead.

My heart lifted, why didn't I think to ring her sooner? As the darkness slowly deepened around me the heavy yoke that shrouded my life, for the previous six months, slowly lifted with the rising of the old yellow moon and the battle to regain a foothold in my life began. The dark, depressing previous hours faded, replaced by a new optimistic time. A path reincarnated from yesteryear. I experienced a new feeling of excitement and elation. I knew I needed her now, more than ever.

I still felt scared, reluctant to go on, but her encouraging words echoed loudly in my ear. I could overcome this, but I needed to trust God. Together Betty and I focused on constructing a new road. A road I could understand and walk upon. She told me, overall success was my final destination, but really it was the journey that truly mattered. The goal was to reach the end, however, I needed the ability to look back and appreciate all of the bumps and potholes, as well as, knowing I did the best I could.

I put the phone down. Fear no longer drove me. Hope was resurrected, and it sat firmly in the driver's seat, taking full control. Over the following weeks, she helped me to uncover the truth. The truth that I really did have something to live for: my family and my friends. She made me realise that my life had meaning to so many others. It didn't matter what had happened, because everything has a beginning and an end. The journey is the part that teaches us life's lessons and everything in life is worth partaking of. It doesn't matter how crappy things look from the outside, something good always rises from it.

A marathon was about to begin, a long slow run that hopefully would go on for the next forty odd years. My endurance would be tested and it would be a battle all the way to the finish line. I would run the race of my life. Hopefully, my supporters would celebrate my milestones with me and congratulate me on my successes. She helped me find a new sense of purpose and made me identify that the only real legacy I had was not what others thought of me, but what God thinks. Betty gave me all this insight with just a few conversations.

I wondered why I had kept myself in the darkness for so long. Why did I think I could do this journey alone? I obviously couldn't. Look what had come to pass from my previous decisions. I was depressed, composing funeral plans! What a mess I had made of my life! I had pushed John and the rest of the family away. I sensed I needed to refocus on rebuilding my relationships, and over the next few weeks that was exactly what I did. I made them like the gears in my new vehicle. They became my priority.

Another ray of sunshine had been sent my way when I reconnected with her. The whole situation was more than I understood. It was a great mystery, but it provided immeasurable love to me in my darkest hour. Excitement and joy filled me every time I drove to meet her, all my doubts and fears replaced by acceptance and love. She would rush out to greet me before I had even locked the car. She would grab and hug me tightly like I was her long lost child.

I felt warm, loved, yearned for. She made me feel like no mountain was too big for me to climb. Only a loving mother could soothe, console and reassure injured children, and this was exactly how she made me feel. We spoke for hours as we discussed all my options and read the Bible together. We prayed and she helped me to recreate my faith into a more liveable and understandable fashion. It was awesome. I felt renewed. I became a new woman. I no longer felt defeated. I replaced the old wounded lioness with a more resilient and tough one. I became a lioness that could stalk and hunt her own prey. I was no longer the hunted, but instead I had become the hunter.

Every time I left her presence, my emotional and physical batteries were topped up, overflowing even. Her words and support made me feel worthy to be on this path. Why me? I still didn't know, but I realised it no longer mattered. What mattered was what I would do with the lessons learnt from this situation. She taught me to step out in faith and she gave me instructions on what I would need to do to win this battle and blame had no part in this. Forgiveness, tolerance and acceptance were where she led me. I had a lot of growing up to do. I thought I was mature but in reality

I was still a child in so many areas of my life and I needed to grow. They say pride comes before a fall. Well I fell a long way off my pedestal, and let's just say pride didn't dominate my life much after this. Pain brings growth. I had a lot of it those first twenty four weeks but little did I know that a lot more was to follow.

Unfortunately, our paths were separated when she got very ill and I couldn't see her for a while. It didn't matter, because together we had chartered a new course for me. She had provided me with the tools I needed to move forward. This was my journey, my lessons to learn, and only I could walk this path of discovery. She had equipped me and given me the strength to go on, and I would be eternally grateful to her for loving me in spite of everything.

I was thankful I had reached out to her, even if it was for a short time. She was just what I needed. She taught me to use my past experiences to correct my mistakes and to seek the future with a sense of purpose and vision, but also to cherish the moment in which I lived in, and that's exactly what I did.

Thanks Betty I love you

Chapter 36

Finding a will to fight

"What is the difference between an obstacle and an opportunity? Our attitude toward it. Every opportunity has a difficulty, and every difficulty has an opportunity."

-J. Sidlow Baxter

Shortly after dancing a few salsas with the devil, then reuniting with Betty, I took the first positive steps in accepting and reconnecting with the life I had been given. Coming through this period of darkness renewed my determination to be more proactive. My first affirmative action step was to get the results of the last test and review them thoroughly. Then I would follow this up with a more informed decision. In the back of my mind I knew there were alternative options, ones I had researched and looked at thoroughly during the course of this trial. They included o-zone therapy, a health farm for liver regeneration, or a push to continue treatment. I would decide after my meeting with my local friendly Egyptian GP.

I found myself again sitting in his familiar reception area

waiting. I heard my name called and I took the first step into empowerment and taking back my life. I held my breath and pushed his door open wide enough to enable me full access. I stepped inside and plonked myself down in one of the two chairs beside his large messy paper laden desk. I had to fight an internal urge to tidy everything up, but I knew he would have a system only he appreciated and understood, so I fought my urge and sat quietly instead. From my position at the end of his small narrow table I saw a framed photograph of a smiling woman who I presumed to be his wife, was placed on the adjacent floor to ceiling well-endowed book case. One whole area was a wall of books, paper, pharmaceutical paraphernalia and handouts. I sat forward in my chair so I could have a better view of the screen, but I could only see a very small vertical slice of the humming computer monitor. I realised I was blatantly and obviously searching the screen for something that was not there.

A flashing little icon on the bottom of his screen jumped to life and the screen filled with numbers ad columns of data, my results lay hidden in there somewhere. He turned the screen to face me and we methodically reviewed the results. We discussed the findings, and I asked for his interpretation. He turned towards me, his smile lit up his whole face as he optimistically informed me that the treatment had definitely worked. The tests showed I had a dramatic drop in my viral load. My count was under 500 copies per unit of blood, down from well over 1.5 million copies. I knew the specialists hands were tied as he had to work under the stringent governmental guidelines. This prevented him from offering me a government sponsored position, but I knew I would continue and attempt to pay for it myself if need be. However firstly I would fight for my place to continue with the current treatment regime.

My spirits lifted as I drove home. I had a strategy and had taken the first steps to re-enter the arena. I went straight home and emailed the specialist. I asked, well, let's be real here I demanded, to be put back on treatment. I followed this up with a telephone conversation the next day, and I was back on treatment within a few short days. I calculated I had missed no more than ten days of treatment. During those ten days I had mentally prepared myself to diligently face another twenty-four weeks of the chemical regime. I didn't care about the side effects. I decided not to worry about something I couldn't control. I vowed just to take it as it came and deal with the negative side effects as they fell upon me. I was more determined than ever to complete this regime with rigid discipline.

The days passed in a string of days and nights. Life has a certain forward momentum and nothing gets in its way including chemical induced illnesses. Small treatment imposed knots formed on the rope which held John and me together. They were insignificant hindrances to our path, small strains on our relationship, but not enough of a problem to cause either of us any major concern. Optimism and hope was our anchor and we held fast to it.

The first six months of treatment had bound us strongly and securely together and the last six would be no different.

I embraced the last twenty four weeks with more enthusiasm, I knew what to expect, I was not afraid and John was ever present at my side. The tireless demonstration of his love was never ending. I would often come home from work to the lovely smell of lavender, lemon myrtle and bergamot all poured into the awaiting hot aromatherapy bath. At least once a week, he would prepare the massage table with plush towels and a soft pillow and as I arrived home he would funnel me straight into the room for a lingering pampering session. Most days I was met at the door with a nice refreshing fresh vegetable juice. I know some of you will think yuk but I needed the nutrients. Both John and I were aware that as the summer turned into autumn my desire for food was no longer present. I didn't realise just how much food provided me with comfort, it wasn't just the sensation of chewing it was the flavours and smells I missed. The enjoyment of chewing a juicy steak or sucking a piece of dark chocolate or savouring a steamy cup of coffee vanished. With these desire well and truly gone my body shed its stubborn kilos.

As a carer John deserved to win an award, he was fantastic. Even though I had this ongoing support I still found this last portion of treatment to be a lot tougher to endure than the previous section. It also came with more severe side effects. The battle for me was not to throw in the towel especially when I became quite weak and physically ill. Even before I got up in the morning I had to mentally prepare and motivate myself to continually keep taking those little pink pills which caused such nausea. I knew I couldn't give in, simply because I needed a clearance from this virus. I wanted it more than the air I breathed and the food I ate.

Mentally it was important for me to retain even the smallest portion of my life. This meant continuing to work in the prison and pretend I was ok to everyone outside my immediate circle. And this was exactly what I did I continue to work throughout the whole journey. However, it was a daily battle to maintain the façade I had created around me. I fought ongoing nausea, headaches and body aches and often when I was managing prisoners I would throw up and my partner for the day would become quite concerned. None the less I had a way of offhandedly explaining it away . . . . a big night out covers most situations . . . . this always made people believe me, no matter how bad I looked.

Night shifts were the worst. Our designated duties rotated throughout the night but mostly we walked the whole prison every two hours counting and watching prisoners as they slept peacefully in their beds. For me sleep had become an ancient concept and working these night shifts added to my lethargy and erratic moods. My body forgot what a prolonged rest felt like, yet it earnestly craved the replenishment it offered. John once again jumped to my aid. His selfless acts of kindness were astonishing. He took on some of my night shifts until I could speak to HR and go on permanent day shift roster which I did around week thirty. So John not only worked his full complement of shifts but took on some of mine as well. He was amazing.

His dedication to 'us' amazed me. I knew I had never been

that committed. Before I found myself in this situation I always considered my role as his wife to be something that I had previously considered a temporary assignment, but now I viewed it as eternal and vitally important. It was realistically the role of my lifetime. I came to realise my marriage was a precious gift; one I had taken for granted all those years. This journey taught me the importance of my relationship by opening my eyes to the real world I lived in. I was essentially unplugged from the matrix and living in what they referred to as the 'real world'. Betty had reminded me to cherish every moment, and that was what I planned to do.

This last round of treatment was spent tackling and reducing the effects of the treatment. At times, I needed to decrease my ribavirn dose, due to ongoing nausea, fatigue and anaemia. I found my weekends offered some relief from the tension of the three twelve-hour shifts I worked. However my weekends had been fully infected by the virus as well as my body, we both shared the chemical cloud. The great thing about the weekends was that I didn't have to wear the cheerful workplace mask—a mask which I discarded every time I walked in my front door. It was a necessary pretence when I was out and about but I was glad to be rid of it on my days off.

I felt like an old worn out ragged face washer used one too many times to clean away the dirt on someone's body. I didn't think I would ever be pain free or warm and comfortable ever again. All I really wanted to do was sleep away the rest of my time on treatment, but feeling this awful was a vast improvement to living with a virus inside me. My days off were spent in a ritualistic format, sprawled out on the lounge, encased in a temporary haven of blankets, watching movie after movie. From the soft lounge chair which had a permanent impression of my body 's outline etched into the soft spongy cushions, my eyes could drift around the rooms interior and take stock of the furniture and enabled me to feel a sense of security.

Time passed slowly at first then gathered momentum. It seemed to get faster towards the end of my treatment, once I hit half way through the second half the clocks hand swung around to focus on the end date. May loomed in front of me. A couple of interesting things occurred towards the end of treatment, the first was I was offered a position in the prison in Education which was permanent day shift Monday to Friday. With this change of employment status came more money, flexibility and exposure to the staff at the hepatitis council and other non-government agencies. One of which would later offer me a job. But I am getting ahead of myself again. Also I had a new manager and she was caring, compassionate and absolutely fabulous. This new position was a far cry from the confinement of prisoner management and for a while I flourished.

As the last few weeks of treatment approached I found it quite hard to juggle the new job, meeting the specialist and maintaining my facade. However I was able to get around this by telling my new manger of my chemo regime, not about my diagnosis. I found she was understanding and offered time off to finalise my treatment. The great thing about being in education was the access to a phone. I was able to talk to John and my friends more regularly and this offered me a little lifeline to manage the final hours. I shared hours of conversation with my nurse friend. We talked about treatment and life after treatment as well as the options if I didn't clear. This was a concept I had real trouble accepting. I refused to allow myself to grow mentally weak, however adverse the circumstances. I would not let my own mind lure me to throw in the towel, just because the fight was getting tougher, especially as my undaunted opponent stood steadfast.

I vowed not to let my guard down because I knew HCV was an insidious little virus that at the height of the battle could turn peacefully away lulling me into a false sense of security. This lull could just be a time for the virus to regroup and get ready for the next assault. I understood its soul intent was to kill me. I knew it would not relent and neither could I. Evil never relents. I simply had to defeat it, not just conquer it but totally destroy it. The cocktail of ribavirn and interferon would hopefully have completed this task for me, purifying my body and ridding my blood of HCV forever. However I was also aware if one seed remained it had the potential to germinate and bloom and my body would be re-infected with a virus with resistance to the treatment tools already used.

As the time drew to a formal close John and I envisaged something indescribable.

We saw a life without hepatitis C.

Chapter 37

Thor's hammer strikes a mighty blow

Life can only be understood backwards, but it must be lived forwards.
—Soren Kierkegaard

My final injection and my last day of tablets surfaced. That final day generated great delight in me. Pure satisfaction. I could say I had run the gauntlet and finished the race. I had completed it to the best of my ability. The question was, would I now be eligible for the prize? The cup of life was something I greatly desired.

My coach held the results in his hand. The final outcome would be pronounced in a few short hours.

I found I couldn't pace around the house waiting for my afternoon appointment so I sauntered up the street. I wished I had brought a light jumper with me as the morning held a slight brisk tone to it. I also forgot my sunglasses which was not good as my eyes had become quite sensitive to the sunlight. I came to a small quaint coffee shop nestled between the larger shops. It advertised freshly baked pastries. I hadn't tasted one of these in well over six months and my stomach churned just at the thought of the remembered sweet flavours. I thought why not. I ordered a coffee, a soy cappuccino. I also hadn't had one of these in nearly a year. The order arrived and I savoured the aroma as well as the sweet flavours, they were delicious however I was unable to finish either of them, my shrunken stomach unable to process the added burden these two items placed on it.

I returned home. It was time to leave. I stood on the front porch, the house open and creaking in the mid-day sun as it steadily beat upon the tin roof. I met John on the brick stairs with my paperwork in hand ready for the trip. Silence prevailed as we followed a small blue car as it rolled out of our street, another learner driver practicing in the safe environment our estate offered. I had trouble stilling my minds so I focused on the cars harmonic rhythm as we drove the long hour to see my specialist.

We finally arrived and somehow we jumped the queue, numerous curious faces peered at us above their glossy magazines as we were ushered into his rooms. I sat uncomfortably in his office. It was time to stand on the podium and receive my trophy. Would I walk away a winner, or a loser? In seconds, I would know. I tried to think positively, in tune with my inner desires, but the present reality was a sensation of physical discomfort. Would I experience a moment of ecstasy or affliction?

There was a sudden quietness in the midst of the turmoil. All eyes watched me closely as the findings were publicised. He finally spoke. The words I dreaded fell from his lips. The facts were all presented and I knew they were connected somehow. They meant something, just not to me in that moment, their meaning no clearer to me than a book written in Braille. I heard the words I had failed, 'not been successful'. The words rung in my ears but my blind eyes tried to discern the message I couldn't see, not yet anyway.

The jewelled crown I once thought would be mine still sat on the table, it would never be placed upon my head, for I had failed. My efforts had been in vain. I was the loser, defeated.

A state of physical discomfort and anguish poured over me, it drenched me in a painful sorrow, which surged like the tide. A freezing wind blew within me; it's cold bite pierced every inch of me. A loneliness without comparison descended upon me, consuming me. I felt like I was driving on an isolated highway, towards an abandoned crossroad, in the middle of Antarctica. All my hopes, dreams and inspirations were forever lost, swept away in the merciless winds. How could I move forward now? What did this mean? How would this affect me? How would this affect my relationship?

I looked at John. Sorrow didn't merely pool in his melancholy eyes but radiated from them. When I met his sad stare I felt my heart sink. Disappointment and disbelief sat on his shoulders and they slumped under their weight. Underneath another emotion flourished it was closer to a deep torture rather than physical sorrow it was a look of tragic loss.

As I searched his face I wondered what he would think of me now. We both had believed I would be healed. I sat in that frigid yet friendly environment still infected, back at square one. It resembled my very first day in this surgery. I sat in the same chair talking to the same man with the same prognosis—infected. Unbelievable. I did all that for nothing. I felt like crap for twenty four weeks, aches and pains insomnia, nausea and vomiting, headaches for what.

On the up side I lost twelve kilos and was looking good for it. My relationship had blossomed. But what would happen with this situation after this day. How would we both react to this news? I could not answer because I didn't know how I was going to respond to the situation.

Everything I believed and wanted was stolen from me that day. I just stood in the arena and allowed Thor's hammer to slam down upon me, yet again. The first time I was unaware but this time I was a willing party. I thought it crushed me last time, but this time it broke all my armour, it massacred every single dream with its characteristic blow and it left me battered and bleeding in the ring with two spectators watching.

This outcome rocked my world, but I refused to allow myself to sink into the quicksand which threatened to swallow my whole, twenty four weeks before. Betty had helped me regain my bearings, I was naïve back then. I made a promise to her not to revisit that period again and I wouldn't. Things had changed in my life during the last treatment period. I had grown in knowledge and understanding. My new position had exposed me to outside support agencies coming into the prison to assist prisoners. Their presence in my life exposed me to a very different world, one where acceptance and compassion was practiced. Over the next six months I worked closely with them as the prison liaison person. I learnt so much by sitting in the health education session and listening intently as they offered advice.

Internally I still battled with the defeat I had experienced and to keep the sorrow from overwhelming me I tried to remain focused on the beauty of the world. During all my nocturnal exercise routines I came to realise that beauty surrounds each of us on every side we just have to look for it. The world we all share is full of variety from the brilliant colours of dawn to the glorious diamond skies at night, the mighty strength of the tiniest ant to the tranquillity of the tallest giraffe. Each of us has a purpose, sometimes the journey is rough and sometimes it is smooth. I had hit a rough patch but I would not bow this time in submission to the persistent, internal threats to overpower and bury me. I was stronger, more in control now, and I would not surrender my life. Not whilst there was still a fight left in me.

Meeting these organisations taught me vicariously that I would find myself again, and I would re-challenge my co-host another time and in another way. What I needed at that point in time was moment to go away and lick my wounds so I could regroup.

For now, my race was run, completed. But like the saying goes ‘it is not over to the fat lady sings’ and this fat lady was not singing not yet.

Chapter 38

Two paths, two destinies

There was a period of time between seeing my specialist and finding myself which was like the dark ages before the renaissance and lasted for nearly a year. Looking back, there must have been at least a few sunny days during that bleak 2005. But I can't recall too many. All I can remember are old crumpled images trying to find their way into the tormented crevices of my mind, in spite of the many positive affirmations I tried to read or apply in my life. The pictures of that time are no longer glossy but are dull and dim.

The bad dreams flourished and filled me with more than fear this time they filled me with dread. My nightly walking program was still in effect but was now a sombre walk that began around midnight and sometimes didn't finish until the day tried to break through the night shade. During this dark time, I placed my feelings in a solid, sealed casket and buried them deep within myself, not allowing any of them to resurface. My vault was full of undeveloped negatives, labelled apprehension, dismay and trepidation. They were all processed, waiting to be placed in my internal album for deep storage.

I became a living symbol of a life full of guilt. I was emotionally dead like a corpse. I was broken. The race had been too intense, too long, and my endurance was spent. This time, instead of creating funeral plans I chose to escape into an illusion, a fabrication of my real life. I also took on a state wide management position with one of the non-government organisations that supported the prisoners. This position enabled me to really escape. I left my old life behind and travelled the country side visiting prisons and promoting blood borne virus management. I chose to be away more than I was home and the effects of this choice would not be truly felt until much later but the ramifications would be devastating.

I entered this new role like a cyclone. I was hungry for more HCV knowledge and exposure to the services that supported people living with these viruses so I could eventually fight my war and feel more empowered. I became a disruptive wind, which brought major disturbances and stormy weather, but I really kicked some mighty goals. I threw myself into work, as it was a familiar concept, and I allowed it to consume me for quite some time. Conquering the summit didn't make me feel any better about myself, but work was the ultimate distraction from my internal convictions. For two years, I focused my heart and soul into a job that offered nothing in return, and I threw away what was truly important to me. My family and friends, as well as everything I had built, was now gone and I was alone, and I didn't really like how it felt.

I reached the top of my chosen profession. But, I did it like a destructive force and left many ruins in my wake. John was one of them. The built-up stress and the accumulated strain of not clearing the virus caused a shift in my inner core, and my life became like an earthquake waiting to happen. Strings of menacing clouds sailed in from the east and loomed at my back whilst most of the sky remained clear and blue. The sun lay well short of the horizon and as I shaded my eyes I could see John slipping amid the shadows and blending with the trees as he commenced his own personal quest. He had dutifully waited for me but my absence had been long and hard. After waiting and comprehending my absence was permanent he turned from our family and walked away. I watched as he became surrounded by the large pine trees and melded into the background, he never once looked back at me. His choice was made.

When I finally noticed his persistent absence my life began to slip back into disorder and nature reset itself. Leaving me alone in the quietness that surrounded me.

My way of coping was to drag out the mental photo gallery and reminisce. For quite some time I lived these memories, rather than actually being present in the real world. For me it was a way of holding onto the things I loved, without letting them go, but at the same time, not actually engaging with any of them. I told myself that withdrawing from my life in this fashion was not really running away, as I was still physically present. I feared being constantly present in my marriage, especially whilst there was more reason to fear than to hope in a future. I didn't think I would be able to handle rejection on top of everything else that was present in my life.

John initially chose to escape by any means at his disposal. He chose to work more and more and with his increased absence our house took on a creepy haunted vibe. Alcohol and misrepresentation were his preferred choices after working. Unable to adequately withdraw into himself, he chose to disguise himself with lies and falsehoods, which provided him with a few quiet moments of comfort. His medication of choice, alcohol, became his anaesthetic to help him endure the operation of life. His drinking had always been hard to take, bearable but the indifference and his resentment that came with it all had become impossible to live with.

During our dark ages—a term used to emphasise cultural and economic deterioration, in our case it signified our family deterioration but not our economic down turn as this was by far the most prosperous period in our relationship—we both struggled to climb the mountain that grew between us. We climbed it but not as one team, as single mountaineers.

I made the climb up the southern face of the ridge. Its rocky jagged surface shielded me from the prevailing winds. But as I struggled over the lip of the last bare rocky plateau the full force of the polar winds struck me and the chill made the temperature around me plummet. Through my tinted snow goggles I could see where I actually stood. To the right was nothing, to the left was also nothingness, below me was a rocky valley and above me a pale heartless ball rolled along the horizon filling the world with a greyish tinge.

As I walked around the tiny plateau my sharp eyes could see John alone on another ledge far in the distance. Memories of things past returned to me. The two of us laughing, sharing a joke, crying together when things were sad, relying and trusting each other when life was tough. The dreams I remembered were of John and I enjoying a sun-drenched moment holding hands as we walked the streets of Hobart, of running along the beaches of the sunshine coast, the white sand under our feet, the sun setting in the distance as a yellow orb rose and of holding each other in the warmth and comfort that only we could share. As I looked at him from my vantage point these images tormented me.

My Renaissance period occurred on top of that mountain. It can be described as an age of curiosity, individualism, exploration and adventure. All of which I experienced during this time. It was a time of self-reflection, awareness, self-examination and discovery. This period of time is described also as the rebirth of human creativity and it certainly offered me a reawakening.

I came to realise even though we had climbed different faces of the same mountain, the terrain was steeper than either of us expected. Our previous love and devotion for each other became less abundant as time moved forward. The climate of our relationship became harsher and harsher, and it was physically too tough to endure for both of us.

The problem was, we had lost any ability to reason logically. We couldn't see anything beyond the steep ascent. We had both decided to continue the climb, but chose routes that suited our own individual needs. Neither of us considered the other in anything we did, in effect we opted for vastly different paths. I had hiked to the summit at a cracking pace, alone. I had faced and conquered large walls of frozen ice. Meanwhile, John sought refuge from the onslaught by deflecting the avalanches I sent cascading down from my rapid climb.

I left him alone on that ledge, whilst I pursued a career and a life that didn't include him. I reached the summit with no one at my side. As I looked back I could no longer see any visible representation of my old self or my former life. The man who had stuck by me all those years, who had fought with me to conquer this disease, the man who had pledged his undying love and support for me, was now just a speck on the plain below and his back was turned towards me. I had reached the top, but for what purpose? I realised, if there was no one to share it with, it was pointless.

I would be lying to you if I told you it was awful standing in that place. It was absolutely beautiful as I stood on the summit. I knew I had a choice I could have stayed there if I had really wanted to. The view was spectacular, I could see in every direction. However when I really studied the stunning surroundings I experienced a tragic sense of loss. I knew if I chose to stay there I would always be alone trapped in my own world in my own grief.

As I looked down I saw shreds of mist as it hovered protecting the lower slopes. A small break in the low lying cloud enabled me to visually connect with John as he stood alone on his own rocky ledge.

The air around me was chilly and biting with life. It brought awareness to the choices I had made and enabled me to understand what I had truly done. With that realisation came truth and for the first time I noticed my feet were actually bleeding. The deep colour against the stark beauty of the surroundings made me wondered just how it was that I had not noticed I could get in such a condition. What had I done to my life? The more troubling question was why. I knew I had tried to balance the wildly diverse aspects of my world as a project manager, a student, a wife, a mother and a person doing treatment. But with my feet in such a condition I realised I had lost a major battle. I had only begun to be aware of the injuries I sustained under such harsh conditions. As I looked at John beneath me I grasped just how unsuccessful I had been and I wondered about the extent of his injuries.

As always I had thrown myself into the challenge of learning about HCV, enthusiastically thinking as I broke the first rock face with my hammer and my crampons bit into the icy surface of Mt Everest those I loved would somehow follow. But they didn't. I left them a long time ago back at base camp struggling to put on the cold weather mountain gear needed to follow my footsteps. They had tried, each of them unable to put there harnesses on without me, but by the time they were ready I was already a speck against the stark white snow covered face.

This journey had also provided me with some benefits as well. It had made me a strong, resourceful, independent woman, but in essence my life was still really bleak. I had been offered a great life with John, and for a short time we had lived it, basking in the glory of our love, and once again I had sabotaged it and thrown it away. My grief and fear, as well as, my perception that he could never accept me overruled sound logic. Yes, I had HCV, but as I looked down at him I realised he loved me. He had demonstrated that time and time again, but still I doubted it. As time passed I came to understand how stupid I had been. I realised that the mess my life was in was a direct consequence of my actions, beliefs, perceptions and behaviours.

I knew I had to go home. I also wanted to go home. Returning to my family was a duty I could not deny, especially if I wanted peace in my life. I missed them in my world. The question was how I could achieve it, and how I could do it successfully.

I didn't move for a few months. I needed time to contemplate my next move and strategically tried to plan the home. I sat on that frozen wintry ledge, surrounded by the wind whispering words of encouragement. In March 2008, on my final six week trip away to Townsville, I decided to take action. I was mentally and physically ready to do something. I wanted to fight again and I was well equipped to do so.

This time I had two battles to win, one for my health and the other for my relationship. I had been defeated before, but I had more knowledge now. I was stronger, more resilient, and a lot more was at stake. This time, to win, I would mentally have to confront the dark parts of myself, and work towards *completely* banishing them with reason and self-forgiveness. I knew if I could willingly face my demons, I had the possibility of overcoming their persistent hold over me. By doing this, I hoped I could restore all that I had allowed to be stolen from me.

During those long inactive yet reflective months, the living ice beneath me buckled and moved and breathed life back into me. I was restored, renewed, ***re-born***.

On one of those final weeks of my self imposed mountain sabbatical, the day temporarily became a pleasant autumn afternoon. The ragged curtain of mist briefly cleared and I saw a glimpse of the world below in crystal clarity. Unfortunately the clouds returned quickly but through the snow haze I saw a clear vision of the path I needed to take. I also noticed someone had left me a life line, a way home. A plane waited on the ice below ready to funnel me to a home where I would need to dance another round with the devil to regain what was rightfully mine. But this wouldn't be a dance to forget it would be more like a horrid violent skirmish as we both wrestled for what we wanted. I could not afford to lose this round.

Home was where I needed to be and the urge to go home grew stronger daily. That realisation punched me hard in the solar plexus, severely winding me. As I drew in shallow quick breathes the freezing air unearthed the fact I had once had it all and had consciously thrown it all away. I discovered my heart longed to be with and belonged only with my family, a family I had helped to create. I had finally uncovered the truth. I knew my sole purpose.

Previously I had stood on this precipice searching the white and blue patchy skies, evaluating my options from a selfish point of view. I tried not to dwell on my life, my family or myself but just how to achieve the latest outcome. Over the years since my diagnosis I thought I had become quite good at heading off the storm of emotions and the thoughts they brought with them. I had learnt how to identify the signs and the overwhelming feelings of hollowness and disappointment before they could take hold of me. In effect I had learnt to suppress them more than conquer them.

However as I stood on that icy surface, during those final weeks before my descent, I allowed all those feelings to fully hit me, to saturate me and assault my senses. I consciously removed my warm jacket, spread my arms and lifted my face to the heavens and allowed the cold crispness to bite my skin as it swirled around me, licking my cheeks and leaving a streak of ice in its wake. I wanted to feel them all. I had locked myself up not allowing myself to feel anything and as I stood there I just wanted to simply feel everything.

I felt tentacles of pain as it crept along my collarbone and up my neck as the uncovered skin turned pink. It was amazing to actually feel these sensations again. Feelings flooded and filled the barren numbness, the emotionless deadness my life had become. The deep throbbing agony forced me to comprehend I could no longer live my life as a detached or unresponsive spectator. I stood there and allowed my life to freeze and thaw and it was flooded with emotions and feelings.

Days passed and the feelings of urgency escalated. I needed to return home immediately, time was running out, I knew it. I had mapped my route down the mountain, it would take time but I needed to return in a well-adjusted positive frame of mind, I needed to be in a completely changed state. To do this I needed to readjust all my mental and physical equipment. I needed to check the anchors and the lines so I would not fall during the long descent. My previous climbing route consisted of permanently anchored bolts fitted with hangers, a chain and rings but these were lost as the time progressed. I took one last deep breath of the pure air, relishing the view and started the journey down the icy face. The thick blue nylon cord laced through my carabineers would be my only support until I reached the ground and walked back to the vacant base camp.

I didn't come down that mountain as quick as you would think. It took me another good three months to mentally reach base camp. The last two hundred metres were the toughest because I could see where I needed to go but I just couldn't rush, otherwise I could make a mistake and that would be costly. Climbing down required a lot of time and dedication which included allowing my faith feed line to break my falls. During the final and steepest part of the descent I uncovered and overcame my personal insecurities. As I touched ground at base camp my spirits were high, my resolution was as solid as the ground beneath my feet. I was ready to rebuild the desolate neglected world I had created. From this vantage point it resembled the Japanese countryside after the fire bombings; it was desolate, barren and confronting.

However my conviction was stronger than ever. There would be no more running. I vowed to challenge my opponent face to face. I would stand in the HCV treatment ring again, this time until the very end with a lot more dedication. No matter how hard I got punched or beaten, I knew I would stand firm in this principle. And I would also reignite my relationship. I would return us to where we stood three years ago.

I had once been blinded and infatuated with the lure of power and success, but now, the lenses in my new glasses forced me to see the real picture. I sensed the potential my marriage had, and during my long descent I relived the gift we shared all those months ago. The gift we both threw away, after our defeat.

I disrobed unstrapping my harness and releasing my feet from the snares they had been in. What I did notice upon my return and my feet were unencumbered was the children had weathered the storms and waited, but John was long gone as I suspected he would be, He was nowhere to be seen from this position. This did not deter me. I had a new mission and I would fulfil it.

So, I gathered the children and together we flew home.

Chapter 39

Preparing for battle

As I returned to my empty home devoid of emotion, a dark fog of anger rose in me. It was as if the marrow in my bones hardened and spread throughout my body making me tremble. This anger became a red mist that followed me everywhere bringing a wrath with it and a thirst for justice. I knew I could not allow these negative emotions to take hold as I had work to do. First things first I wanted another shot at treatment and once that was in place I would fight for my marriage. I would fight for what was rightfully mine.

Climbing my Everest as devastating and lonely as it had been it had armed me with knowledge and the latest research about the disease I carried within me. The other advantage I had was that I had gained skills and experience from my previous treatment journey. I had learnt that I was what they called a 'slow responder'. Slow responders need more time, eighteen months of treatment offered a higher cure rate and that was what I was after. I was angry that the specialist had not informed me of this this first time and that it had taken my close to two years to uncover this fact. I funnelled my anger into righteous indignation; I was so close last time. If only I knew what I knew now, back then . . . .

Anyway in June 2008 I stood my ground and fought a hard verbal fight backed by evidence and research as well as a friend who believed in me. She was someone who I worked very closely with on the prison blood borne virus project and we had forged a hard standing friendship. I must say I won because my persistence paid off and I was offered a place back with my well known ally, my previous, friendly gastroenterologist on the Sunshine Coast. I was scheduled to start in November which provided me with enough time to leverage my life to support the long eighteen months ahead.

I believe when we face challenges in life that are far beyond our own power, it is an opportunity to build on our faith as well as our inner strength and courage. I couldn't control the cards I was dealt. What I could control was my attitude. I found as I spent numerous long lonely nights in the many Queensland motel rooms alone, it enabled me to learn how to master change rather than allowing it to master me. Change is hard and sometimes very uncomfortable but it is inevitable for all of us. The big lesson I learnt was my attitudes and perceptions brought about my reactions. I identified my attitude could make the situations I was in tougher or it could make them easier. I liked the easier option. What I found was I was happier when life was easier.

All those months spent alone on the summit of that mountain watching John walk off into the distance taught me that my attitude was more important than anything. It was a lot more important than appearances, money, knowledge, or skill. Attitudes break people. They destroy families. My attitude and misguided beliefs had done just that. A remarkable choice is presented to us each day. What sort of attitude will we embrace? Will it be one of compassion and forgiveness, or one of criticism or blame? I no longer took on the latter because I witnessed first-hand the destruction they could cause. I understood I was the only one in control of my attitude. No one else had that authority. I came to understand just what a difference a positive attitude could make. I had read about it in and partially adopted some of the principles earlier in this journey but I had forgotten their meaning. As I opened my heart and mind to them again and actually started living the values and philosophies my whole life changed.

With this new found positive attitude I made some strategic decisions including quitting my job and securing an executive position with a company called Queensland Injectors Health Network (QuIHN). It was a company that assisted drug addicts by providing support, welfare, education, health care and counselling. This particular company was well known for supporting staff and I thought that if need be I could disclose my situation to the management team and reduce my work load. The up side to working for QuIHN was the general manager was a counsellor and the other senior managers were compassionate in nature, one actually was on the board of the Hepatitis Council and the other was a practicing psychologist. For me it was more than a strategic move, it was one of the best things I could have done at the time.

In early August I started work with them giving myself three months to establish my skill and knowledge within the organisation, before I commenced treatment. This proved to be a very sound decision as I really did need that settling-in period.

I walked into a mediation nightmare and was exposed to the plight that drug users face each day, in effect I was swimming in a pool full of fish and the sharks hovered. It was great, I loved the work and the management team was fabulous to work with. Over time I created a strong healthy team of health promotion workers who were passionate about their work and cared for the people they supported.

Ultimately I was happy with my decision and I was well placed to start my treatment journey.

Chapter 40

An empty harbour

November rolled around and I started treatment again, still no one knew of my plight. It would continue for eighteen long months through till April 2010, a daunting prospect. It would be a relentless and arduous task for anyone to bear, but I was ready. I had prepared as much as I could. I had a new supportive job. I had access to counselling services if I needed them and I had enrolled in uni to finish my Masters, as a backup to keep my mind active if I had to give up work. Physically I had lost weight and was in better shape and health to combat the effects of the treatment. I don't think I could have been more prepared than I was at that particular moment.

A major problem still lurked in the background, but I knew I could only fight one fight at a time and treatment was the one I needed to do first before I tried to rebuild something I had intentionally destroyed. I thought if I could just reach out to him slowly then maybe we would have a chance. As I came down the mountain preparing myself for this exact moment I knew I would do the treatment journey alone. John was long gone emotionally. I also knew this would be a radically different therapy regime.

My marriage was in ruins. We were a union in name only. Our bond and ongoing friendship helped us to create an illusion that we offered to the outside world. There would be no support for me, not like last time as John was mentally removed from the situation, caught up in his own career and his own life.

I would not let this prevent me from doing what I considered to be the most important thing of this time. So, I set sail alone but much better equipped and well-organised this time, ready for the extensive eighteen-month voyage. Its cargo complete with prescribed amounts of harmful chemicals, as well as supporting naturopathic aids. I plotted my solitary course on the vast ocean where I knew loneliness would reside and surround me.

When I stood on that mountain a few months earlier I perceived what solitude was, I had felt it to some extent up on the cold icy summit. What I wasn't ready for was just how far it would extend into my life. I guess this is what John felt when I mentally left our relationship and started my climb away from him shortly after my last treatment failure. Here I sat fully present in the relationship for the first time in years and I found it extremely hard to rest and wait for something that may not ever return.

As I travelled the highway of treatment, I walked amongst bustling streets crammed with people, but never felt a part of any of them. I think this was mostly my fault as I lived my life as two separate people and maybe on an unconscious level other people become somewhat aware that I was not really real. I discerned a crowd does not always offer company as I was continually surrounded by unsuspecting people but I did not feel part of the brotherhood. Treatment made it quite clear to me that we are all primates who move in the same jungle. Our communication processes are sometimes just undecipherable sounds that no one cares to try and understand. This became a real fact to me as I tried and tried to reach John to no avail, there were moments of connection but there were often lost in the clutter of the noisy world we lived in. Loneliness is hard to bear when you are a social creature, and I missed the company and affection that was once mine a long time ago.

Work provided me with the social contact that I so desperately cried out for. Every morning my ritual began with opening the blinds and allowing the light to filter in and light the room. Shadows gathered in the corners of the room but I would always be confident that I was alone. I would stand at the large window and gaze out at the pool and mentally prepare myself for the day. I would shower and commence the tablet regime, pink chemicals followed by a handful of herbs and vitamins. This would be followed by a long drive to work, then the pretence of wellness and the ongoing attempt to not show any signs of illness. My façade never wavered and I got very good at maintaining it.

I always kept my plight to myself. I learnt to live inside myself, in a safe place, where I could renew my own springs of life-giving water by reading the Bible and praying.

My husband was physically present, but no longer mentally by my side. He offered minimal assistance by giving me my weekly injections and basic support. His life had changed radically, something I would be unaware of for quite some time. He was trapped in the past unable to remember the pleasures our life together once held or even the love he felt for me during the first bout of treatment. All of that was lost in the aftermath of the devastating news given to us a few years past.

I wouldn't find out to after my treatment had finished that he was caught in his own pit of despair delving more and more with the internet and the on line chat rooms. This pulled him further and further into his own form of depression and as the deceptions grew so did his level of depression. He was caught up living a false life on websites that would never offer him more than untruth and invention. As well as this, his new career in the mining sector challenged him and demanded long hours. His rotational roster consisted of seven days on and two or three off which prevented him from engaging with me on any level. What it did offer him was free and easy internet access.

By May 2009 treatment was really starting to impact me on every level. Living on acreage was the perfect retreat. It became a protective realm around me. It was large enough to offer space and distance from the outside world. As treatment progressed I felt only barely capable of handling my job let alone the constraints and the problems the outside world offered. So distance was my best option and this meant separating my self from my friends as well. I really geared up my mental telepathy and pushed them all away.

You might not understand this but for me people require a lot of attention, time and resources and I just didn't have the energy to nurture anyone. At that particular time I was doing everything I could to survive the ride with as much energy as I could muster up. Sometimes people are hard work and I didn't have the vitality or momentum to maintain any of them.

This also affected John and I because I simply didn't have any energy to sink into maintaining the little we had left. The times he reached out to me I couldn't muster the strength to reciprocate. All I could hope for was that the bonds of time, our twenty-four years of history would anchor us together in the same port. Most days, both of us returned to the same marina.

Chapter 41

Destructive forces at work

Six months into my treatment program, the ground realigned itself with earth shattering force. It not only moved, it pounded both our lives from all sides. I was temporarily working in Cairns when I received a message that my sister-in-law had been taken to hospital with a suspected liver problem. She was, at that time, just having tests. No thorough diagnosis had been given, so I maintained my schedule and returned home the following day. Upon my homecoming, I contacted my brother-in-law for an update.

He was genuinely distressed and troubled by her now pronounced condition. A harsh reality had struck him fully in the face. His words barely escaped his lips before his weeping began. She had been diagnosed with liver cancer, and her mortality advanced very quickly. So quickly, in fact, that treatment was not an option. She had been placed in a clinical hospital room, waiting only for death to take her. The words were unexpected, and they pierced my heart. I had only seen her a few weeks ago in the shopping centre where we had a brief chat about life. She looked happy and healthy. I never suspected or guessed she was terminally ill.

I drove straight to the hospital with my unpacked bags still in the car. I hadn't eaten anything all morning and the little pink pills threatened my empty stomach which screamed for attention. Fatigue overwhelmed me, as it had been a crazy, hectic few days in Cairns. We had launched a new program and I had visited numerous local services. My body ached all over, the toll of the treatment regime. I knew I couldn't focus on my problems. I needed to see my sister-in-law. I quickly walked down the well-lit hall and stopped at the nurses' station to inquire which room she was in.

As I neared the door to her room, I was struck by a smell, a sickly sweet, overpowering odour, which permeated the air all around me. It assaulted my lungs and brought the nausea I had fought all day to the surface. When I looked in, I noticed she was sitting on her designated cot, dressed in street clothing. The white, heavily starched bed linen rustled beneath her fragile weight as she twisted to greet me. Her single room was clean and sterile. A window offered a view of a tiny well-manicured garden, which was unseen from where her bed was positioned. Stark white walls devoid of any emotion surrounded her.

I knew I had to change her room, modify it, make it homier, more alive and inviting. Its current bareness depressed me, and I didn't have to spend the rest of my time on earth in it. I knew that I had some large, laminated pictures of Norfolk Island, Vanuatu and

Hawaii, as well as other beautiful landscapes at home, *somewhere*, remnants of my massage days. I used to place them under the massage table for people to look at as I pummelled the muscles of their backs, a profession I gave away at the same time as my personal training business. I vowed to find them and strategically place them around her to offer a better picture than the current one. I was also determined to buy some flowering plants to create a more pleasant environment, one that smelt nice and was visually pleasing and uplifting.

Her husband affectionately stroked her arm, whilst they shared a special moment. Her laughter filled the air and made me smile. I stood at the end of the bed and mentally captured every picture. My mind catalogued the scene. The comparison between the once vibrant beautiful woman I knew and the one I saw now was vastly different. She wore a disease-ravaged body, with yellow skin and piercing eyes that glowed like 'Mystiques' from the X-Men movies. Liquid cysts rose and fell with her every breath, but she still managed to smile and her eyes softened as they connected with me.

I kissed her and asked how she was going. We talked and I tried to process the landscape before me. The outlook was not optimistic and both of us knew the end was near. I spent the rest of her conscious time pretending to be a hospital jester. I wanted laughter and fun to surround her as she experienced her final days. I helped her recall wonderful and happy moments in her life, and brought some cheerfulness into this depressing situation.

I visited her every day until her death, eight days later. I decorated her room with flowers, plants and pictures of places she had been, and dreamed of going. We talked about travelling, building dreams, both knowing they would never come to fruition. I continued this until her mind surrendered to the void between life and death, a place where speech to the living was no longer heard. It was a place where her body was unyielding and trapped in an internal war. Caught in a fight she would inevitably lose.

I watched her suffer daily, as she battled to live. I saw a reflection of my own potential death. If I did not clear this virus this time, what would be my options? Would I end up like her, dying in pain, in an isolated, unhomely, sterile room? This was liver cancer. A cancer that stalked me. I watched it as it slowly stole a life right in front of me. I already had cirrhosis. Liver cancer was the next progression. Would this happen to me if I didn't clear this virus? Would I die like this? This thought horrified me. It literally freaked me out!

Even though the cavern between us deepened with every breath she laboriously took, I maintained my vigilance. My one-sided conversations were filled with words of love and the gift of God's grace. The nurses encouraged me to continue to talk to her, informing me that the hearing sense is the last sense to go. This restored my confidence in my belief that she could understand what I said.

During this time, I struggled internally with my own fears. However, it also made me realise just how much I had to live for, and just how much I actually wanted to live. As I watched this unfold before me I learnt to be comfortable with who I was and accept who I was not. Ephesians 2 verse10:12-18 talks about being Gods workmanship built for a purpose. We all have limitations in our lives and its about accepting these. Watching this beautiful soul die in this fashion showed me that each of us are full of Gods grace if we can put our pride aside and be humble enough to accept it. She had it etched into every aspect of her face

Time passes even when it seems it shouldn't. As the hands moved around the clock, for me they moved in mysterious charges and comatose stillness's.

The thick treatment fog that blurred my days was sometimes confusing. Up until this point this didn't really bother me as loosing track of time was the best I could ask out of my chemically laden life. But sitting in the hospital changed all that. It made me appreciate my situation and made me more aware of all the things I still wanted to do. I didn't want any of it taken from me by this disease or a stolen by an insidious little cancer that crept silently up on me.

As I sat there I learnt the power of language, my words have meaning and could make people smile. This also made me realise I could change my life by changing the words I spoke. There were no words that could save the girl before me but there were words that could save me and John. I could edify and build her up but it would not overcome the evilness that was taking her away from us. But I could edify and encourage John as her legacy to us, I could add value to his life and spread some joy, a joy she would never witness. I would also start visualising health and vitality as well as happiness and life instead of living life like it was baptised in prune juice.

"We are God's workmanship, created to do good works which has been prepared in advance." Ephesians 2:10

Chapter 42

Winds blow from every side

A few weeks before my sister-in-law's verdict, my brother-in-law was also diagnosed with aggressive prostate cancer. Before I left for my program launch in Cairns I had the opportunity to assist him by accompanying him to the specialist appointment. My aim was to ask the hard questions, ones that his emotions would prevent him from asking. My hope was he would be able to make a more informed decision with all the facts. My science studies enabled me to aid and offer support to him in comprehending the minefield of information that he was given. As I left for Cairns he made his choice and scheduled his surgery for the day I returned. As fate would have it these events fell on exactly the same day. I don't know what the odds of that would be but I am guessing it would be low.

I remember feeling torn between the two siblings. I knew it was impossible to support both of them simultaneously, so I decided to sit beside the one I knew for sure was terminal. She also lived in the same city as me, and I would maintain vigilance by phone for the other one.

I was lucky my working conditions were flexible enough to enable me to work from the hospital room. Those nights I went home to an empty house. Sometimes I slept most times I couldn't. This one particular night I remember going for one of those long jaunts I was very familiar with. However this night I felt inspired and hungry, so I ran home to fire up the computer and made myself a vegemite sandwich. I had forgotten the strong salty taste and relished it as it sat and sizzled on my tongue, it felt good.

The house was silent as John was away working his normal long twelve hour night shift in the city. I switched on the radio and classic rock filled the air and my foot automatically started tapping to the strong steady beat. That night I created a brand new program, my brain more alive than it had been for some time. The words and phrases rolled forth with ease, my fingers tapped the keyboard until the sun peaked through the wooden slats. A masterpiece created by a chemically laden mind and a sleep deprived body. I fell into bed as dawns light reached out and caressed me.

During this traumatic time, as Johns sister battled in a hospital he mentally and physically returned to our marriage. He chose to fully reengage in our life, and out life was full of love again. Life without your best friend is like living on a deserted island.

Two siblings fought simultaneously together, both faced fatal illnesses. One would go on for the next eighteen months, and battle fearlessly for his life, plagued by complications from his surgery. He required more hospital stays, more surgery, rehabilitation and counselling to regain his life. The other would lose her battle and go on to a better place.

Our short re-engagement enabled us to multiply the good in our lives, and divide up the unpleasantness. We fleetingly shared the pain and the sorrow of the moment, but unfortunately, it didn't last.

The final hours approached. Preparations had been made, family members were called, and still she grasped life with all her strength. She held on. She battled and seized every moment.
Every breath was laboured as her heart and lungs struggled to feed a dying body. The doctors and nurse were impressed by her strength, but I wondered why she would wage such a war. I was told she was most likely waiting for someone. Besides her husband, only my children had engaged with her during this, her final crusade.

Her mother and sister lived one and a half hours away on the Gold Coast, and unfortunately, both chose to stay by the brother's side, even though they were aware she was terminally ill. Like a medic on a battlefield conducting triage, the choice was where to spend one's time. Who do you devote time and energy to? The doomed or the injured? In this case, both appeared doomed. John's brother was in intensive care with the real possibility of dying any day as well. He was divorced and had no partner. John's sister was married, and her partner was beside her. How does a mother choose between two dying children? I hoped I would never have to make such a decision.

Like many families, the years, and a series of incidents, had caused rifts in their cohesion as a family unit. Memories are long and I found this family nursed the bitter ones more than the happy ones. Miscommunications, unresolved issues which stemmed from childhood and adolescence choices and behaviours, as well as personality clashes and expectations not met, caused reactions of anger, fear and retaliation, this family did not need or want any of those feelings to surface at this time. John had naturally known some reasons for their dysfupnctionality, but was unable to fix his own situation, let alone anyone else's.

I, personally, couldn't understand why her mother did not visit. A coherent answer eluded me. What unknown tragedies and afflictions had affected this family, that none would come now, and see this family member? What rifts could cause such reactions and decisions? I only knew of my own devastating childhood and adolescence. John's explanations of his family dysfunctions were never fully explained or uncovered.

Even as I tried to understand and process these things, a fire burned within me, a fury I could not stop. It burnt fiercely, and I found it hard to quench. I knew I needed to douse their flames as it was not the time for inappropriate behaviour on my part.

I was tired from my extended stays and trying to work within the hospital setting. I needed a break. I rang her mother and pleaded with her to come, to be with her daughter. I explained the situation and informed her of what the doctors had rationalized, about why she would not let go, even though she was in immense pain. Relief swept over me, tears filled my eyes, as she finally agreed to come.

I was physically exhausted, unsure how much longer I could maintain this level of effectiveness. My treatment and hospital regime and my lack of sleep and limited nutrition, as well as trying to maintain my management position and complete the last two modules of my Masters, were all taking their toll.

The phone call over, and with reinforcements set to arrive shortly, I started to uncontrollably weep. My sobs echoed down the long empty corridor, breaking the silence. My grief and tension was able to be truly released, freed from its oppression.

I counted down the hours to my liberation. My bedridden companion's continuous laboured breathing provided a constant steady rhythm, as my fingers hit the keyboard of my laptop, and my mind created a new program for work. The smell of her pungent sweat surrounded me, and her infrequent small whimpers and sighs, periodically distracted me. My mobile buzzed in my pocket, notifying me of the family's arrival. I was thankful, grateful, that they had come. I hoped this woman who lay on the bed, dying, could now finally find peace.

However, I was shocked to find only her sister had come. My mother-in-law failed to appear. This left a dark shadow in a space only a mother's presence could fill. My heart sank. I was confounded and shocked by her absence, her choice a complete mystery to me.

I called her, and again I pleaded for her to come. A mother's plea, from a mother to another mother. I held my mobile to her daughter's ear, with the hope she would at least be able to hear and comprehend her mother's words of endearment as they passed to her dying child. I begged again, and finally she accepted. She said she would arrive that night. I had won a battle. A battle that should never have been fought. It was no victory for me. The triumphant moment was solely for a beautiful, unconscious girl.

The family was fully reunited, bar one; a brother who fought in an ICU for his own life, elsewhere. I left them to make peace. I had said my final goodbye. A glorious, yet sorrowful point in time, and I went home and slept a fit, full sleep, my conflict over. I knew I had done the best I could. I had done everything possible to make her last journey as good as it could be, under the circumstances.

She died, willingly relinquishing her spirit in my husband's presence early the next morning.

Chapter 43

Destructive paths destroy lives

We were all temporarily trapped in our sadness. John suffered more than I did, but both our grieving changed us in unimaginable ways. My husband withdrew more and more into himself. He decided to choose a voluntary madness of inebriation and the devious forces it brought with it. Later he would explain he was unable to cope with the plight of his two siblings as well as a wife fighting the battle for her life and undergoing a lengthy treatment regime. All of this led him to wander alone into another alternative dimension, like something out of The Talisman by Stephen King, a story of a boy who remained the same, but had the opportunity to run away into a parallel universe.

John sought happiness and joy to replace the doom and gloom of the real world. The evidence of his life with me displaced and left way behind. There were no footprints, no broken branches the path he had trodden was icy cold. I walked and walked trying to find him and then I got lost in the waves of pain that lapped at me again. Unknown to me at the time, John started to live a dual existence; one where he was the family man, and the other where he was the player on the internet, where he could pretend to be something unreal, a fictional character that in reality he was not.

Me, I became more obsessed and addicted to my work. I devoted every waking hour to it, forfeiting everything else. I withdrew from everyone, my friends and family included. I hid my grief within myself, behind a rebuilt wall of my castle. One of my friends never gave up on me. She repeatedly tried to reach out to me, and she often quoted, "Laurie, you know people are lonely because they build walls instead of bridges."

I knew she was right, but I just didn't have the strength to combat my grief as well as try to survive the ride of treatment and work, and to nurture my family and friends. It just wasn't in me right at that moment. So I left the nurturing part out, for now. She was rather philosophical, as she would tell me I couldn't change the direction of the wind, but what I could adjust was my sails to accommodate it. I understood the message she was referring to; my standpoint. But I really didn't think I had the energy to sustain any sort of relationship with anyone. I found just living hard enough.

Time made no sense to me as I tried to re-find something that was so lost. It was like standing in a maze surrounded by large over grown hedges, leaves and branches sticking out and poking at you. There simply appeared to be no way out. As I silently stood amongst the greenery the months passed like days. For me time had frozen. The house was always empty devoid of human life. I walked around it like the resident ghost, muttering to myself. The nights were always so dark and so lonely. I can remember thinking surely the streamers of moonlight could filter down through the clouds and find me where I stood surely there is some semblance of light in all this darkness.

John worked constantly. We hardly saw each other. As the months punched on so did I. I took on more work making myself too busy to care. At times after my nightly walks I would work creating new health programs or new activities. I was highly productive in that area just not so lucky on the home front.

The other factor I think that drove a wedge between John and I was my fear of what I had seen. I was afraid of a disease that threatened my life and had stolen the life of John's sister. I knew I needed to take care of myself with or without John beside me. I had just witnessed how fast liver cancer could strike, and kill you. I watched its burning fingers eat away at a life that had much more to offer to this world and I didn't want that happening to me. The whole scenario terrified me and some part of my brain associated John with that so in effect I ran away again mentally.

During those many nights alone, I learnt to reflect on the things affecting my life. One of which was this treatment journey and the vast difference between the two bouts. My initial forty-eight week regime was wholly supported by a loving husband, who regularly massaged my aching body, ran aromatherapy baths for me, cooked and made juices for me, stroked my body, and tried to take the pain away. He even covered some of my shifts at work when I was too tired or sick to attend. This bout was a lonely, unsupported and demanding seventy-two week journey. A gruelling battle I alone endured.

One night close to the forty eight week mark, I had an experience where I really needed someone to help me, but of course I was alone. As I stood at the enormous window on the street side of our house I could see a thorough darkness washed by a yellow glow as the moon slowly rose in the east. In the distance I heard a car as it raced up the street outside our front gate. A menacing roll of thunder filled the sky and a flash of lightening lit the yard. Bullet like rain battered the tin roof. My head spun and my eyes blurred, I tried to make my way up the hallway but I was barely able to see through the murky darkness. In the bathroom I grabbed a face washer and swabbed my face and neck before I fell to the ground too weak to remain standing. As I lay on the cold tile floor I was struck with a revelation. I felt as though everything that had happened and was still happening had been designed to get me to this precise moment in time. At that moment as I lay unable to move on that hard floor I knew my life was exactly where it needed to be.

I lay there for a time laughing with the cat meowing beside me. I might have been in the right place for a certain reason but knowing this fact didn't make the journey any easier. I couldn't change where I was at or what had happened but I could change the way I interacted with the future. I could change my world and how I affected it. I needed to move forward in the most positive way I could and right at that point in time for me that meant keeping my mind in a good place.

I needed support so I felt it was time to tell the GM of QuIHN about my treatment program. It was one of the most positive things I did as he was understanding, caring and often offered his counselling services to me which I took. I simply replaced the rejection and loss I felt at home with work and the support networks I had there. I placed them in the void that had once been filled with gaiety and laughter. Work became my safe haven, where I felt accepted, needed and appreciated. A place where I could positively engage from.

I think one of the hardest parts of this situation was I had to attend all my appointments unaccompanied. John didn't seem to care, the kids were too busy and I had isolated myself from my friends, my family were too far away so I had no one to regularly talk to about how I was going with it all. What a difference five years and an illness can make to a marriage!

I sensed a perpetual cycle was set in motion when I didn't clear the virus the first time. We were both so disappointed and devastated by the news that we never talked about it. We never made any plans to positively move forward or discussed what we were going to do. We simply didn't talk. The strain damaged our relationship and caused a rift to grow between us, what we should have done in hindsight was seek some counselling some support to assist us with our emotions and the sense of loss that overwhelmed both of us. We could have even visited the hepatitis council again. We both needed help, but we did neither of these things.

Our love was far from gone. It was just lost in the chasm that had formed between us. John often did things to remind me of that, little pockets of love left on the pillow or weekends away rekindling our spirits but they were always followed by the drone of the treadmill as it took us away on another journey. We both knew we needed each other like the desert needs the rain, but neither of us sought the oasis that would have saved us.

The funny thing was we both signed up for the same eighteen-month marathon. We both entered and ran the race side by side however the road between us had become divided and a barrier separated us especially as we neared the forty km mark. The end was in sight but neither of us discussed the potential outcome. We sought the same goal, but our iPods were tuned to different channels, the music and lyrics drowned out the reality of how we could have done this journey more efficiently, together.

As we neared the final bend the barrier between us had grown in size and width, I could no longer consider jumping over to join him. I felt a deep loss in my heart. To keep me focussed on my goal of reuniting us, I would replay internal movies of our lives in much happier circumstances. I would allow then and encourage them to flow easily and create lasting visual pictures I could hold onto. They always brought a smile to my lips, but a tear to my eye. They made me question, what had gone wrong? What had really happened to us?

On one of those regular lonely nightly walks I was able to discern how and why I had pushed him away. Fear was the most dominate emotion in my life it drove most of my actions. I was scared of him, scared he would hurt me, scared of the fact I could die. In affect I was scared of life. I realised life is for living not hiding from. I needed to embrace all aspects of it bad and good. And, for the first time, I really looked and saw through his behaviour. I saw the needs of his heart and I realised I had never met any of these needs. My independence, self-reliance, my hardened heart and inflexible nature had caused the first fissures to form in our relationship a long time ago. Treatment had just closed them up, sealing us inside. What did I expect? A person can only take so much rejection. As I turned the corner and saw my home beckoning I realised just how I had contributed to the void that lay between us. I just had to figure out what to do about it and how to build a bridge.

Chapter 44

My bronze crown

In October 2009, eleven months after I started my second regime of treatment, I kicked my first goal. I had won a major battle. A bronze crown now lay upon my head. My tests informed me the treatment was working. I had cleared the virus! The virus was undetectable in my blood. I was not yet able to stand on the podium and receive my gold crown, but I was one step closer to this cherished accolade. I could see it, taste it, feel it upon my skin, and I vowed to receive it.

This news lifted my spirits. I was like an eagle that soared above the clouds. It was excellent news, incomparable. However, being genotype 1a1b and a slow responder, I still faced another six months of the bombardment of chemicals. However, nothing would stand in my way of the glory that would be mine. Pegasys bombs could merrily explode within me, for my mental defence had been reinforced and reinstated.

A new optimism inspired my faith, defeated my hopelessness, rid me of my internal despair and it dared me to believe that I may live a normal, long life; one not overshadowed by HCV. Up until this point I was convinced I had no definite certainty in my life, no guarantees or assurances, no dependability. Nothing was constant or solid. Could I possibly still be here in another five, ten years? Did I dare to dream again, make plans for a noteworthy future?

Were all my prayers finally answered? Had God listened to me? It appeared unquestionable, crystal-clear. Could I now start to rebuild my shattered world? My Father would often tell me, "Laurie, God can take the bits and pieces of your un-reached goals, and put them back together again. He takes the shattered fragments of your life and restores them to wholeness."

He also told me God can take the fragments of what I once believed, and make them as new and fresh as the dawning sun. Was that a possibility? Could He restore my health? *My relationship?* Was that possible? Often I would discuss topics like this with him and at times, I would ask Dad why he thought this was happening. His answer was simple, "we are all still at school. *God's school.* Sometimes the lessons are tough, really tough as you are witnessing but we are here on earth to learn and teach others. Graduation only really occurs when we die." Uni, lessons and learning I understood all that, what he said had substance, ti held meaning.

My journey had already taught me so much about life, and about myself. How much more was there? I knew I had not used the previous lessons I had learnt wisely. I had gone back to a lot of my old familiar behaviours, backsliding in to the pit and sabotaging all the relationships around me. I pushed people away and reconstructed my castle walls. I also played with the skills of the chameleon. Maybe the lesson for me was it was time to be honest and allow people to see the real me. Maybe, just maybe, it was time to become the real Laurie, the person I was afraid of revealing to the world.

My life changing news arrived a week before my father had a serious heart attack. I rushed to his side to assist as he was taken to a remote hospital, and then airlifted to Prince Charles Hospital for triple bypass surgery.

I have to say 2009 was the worst year imaginable. John and I aptly named 2009 "the year of the hospital." The year had started with his sister's death, and then his brother's numerous bouts of surgery, which at times required lengthy stays in hospital, and now, my dad. Three events. One ended in tragedy and two battled on and of course I hung in the background.

My father fought arduously for his life. His recovery was long and problematic. The surgery a success, but his body and mind struggled under the torrent of medications and the confinement that hospital entails. His belief that pharmaceutical drugs were poison made it hard for the medical staff to positively address all his needs. His extended stay also induced a depressed state in him.

I would sit everyday with the man I had come to adore, and attempt to revitalize and renew his failing spirits. Many a night we would discuss our treatments, our health and our future plans. We daydreamed of spending time in Cairns together, taking holidays and building many more memories. I placed inspirational posters around him, surrounding him with messages of love and hope. I also plastered his room with vibrant pictures of Cairns and a place called Paranella Park, in the hope of creating a liveable dream within him. Paranella Park was a place I had previously visited, and I promised to take him there when he was well enough to travel. I watched as he slowly created a mental picture of this, and a smile rose to his lips for the first time in nearly a month.

His low point came one night when I was with him. He had simply had enough of the tubes, the medications and the loss of dignity. The time in hospital, for him, unbearable. He could see no light at the end of the tunnel. His future had become a vision that was blurry in the distance. I sat on the cold, tiled floor beside him. I held his hand and spoke of a time many months ago, when I was so desperate, so disgusted in myself that I was ready to finish my life.

We shared a moment and we cried together. We both knew just how close each of us had truly come to giving up. As I drove away from the hospital towards home, I realised just how vulnerable we all are, and just how precious life actually is.

Not long after this, he was released from hospital. He had triumphed over his adversity. His skirmish with the initial throes of death was finally over. However, he would engage in a battle to survive, struggling with an enemy for another eight months.

Six months later, as I was nearing the end of my treatment, I went to Cairns for work and dad came for a holiday, and we did visit Paranella Park.

Chapter 45

Footprints in the sand

Days fell into a steady rhythm. A consistent pattern emerged around me. Treatment a ceaseless hum constantly in the background of every situation, nausea a continual reminder of the phase I was in. I had now lost eighteen kilograms. My hormones played havoc with my moods and bodily functions. I found it hard to function outside of work. I was more aggressive, physically exhausted from months of broken sleep and I had absolutely no social life.

My energy levels were so low, I needed to rest frequently. I had become quite breathless, and my body, especially my hips, ached constantly with a deep penetrating throb which hindered my movements. My beloved exercise regime had become non-existent. However every so often I would still participate in a very slow nocturnal walking program.

Sleep persistently eluded me, yet I was so tired, both physically and mentally weary. Pain burned deep within my muscles. Its fingers persistently stabbed me. For hours I would alternate between lying still and violent thrashing trapping myself in the sheets. Acid blazed up the long tube of my oesophagus, bringing a smouldering agony. It prevented me from lying down for any length of time. Most nights, in the darkest hours, I would get up and work, eager for some form of relief. Hours later, totally exhausted and still in pain, I would fall back into bed and try to gain some strength to face the challenges of the new day.

My life became very ritualistic work, home, medication, lounge and TV. Some days were much harder than others. On those particular days I would "fly under the radar" so to speak, so nobody would notice how ill I was. Then, I would come home to an empty house, an empty bed and I would watch a little mind-numbing television. Each morning as the sun roused me from my bed or from the computer I would prepare my disguise. I never missed a day's work, the thought of being alone at home didn't appeal to me at all and work was a much better distraction. The drive to work offered me just enough time to cover my decaying essence with a stoic, manageable smile.

John and I were not always estranged. At times, when our rosters aligned, we would share unique, loving moments. However, our relationship was nowhere near as intimate as it had been. It was strangely guarded. I felt John had pulled away and was caught, trapped in a cave with no easily found exit. I felt he held himself back from me, but at the same time I was too sick to comprehend what was happening. My focus was just getting through treatment.

We had become cohabitants that enjoyed a deep, mutual friendship. What I really missed was the companionship. My heart knew where it belonged. It didn't understand the restriction of treatment. It just knew it was painfully chained up, confined. To lose someone you love alters your life forever. No one can fill their place in your life. Their particular energy is unique, irreplaceable, and it leaves a gap that never closes. I guess it is like losing a child, another child never replaces the one lost. Their essence is always around you.

Some people are transients in life; they touch us then quickly move on. Others stay and leave footprints in the sands of your soul, which change us forever. John had left a mark on me; one I would never be able to erase. A mark I didn't want to erase. When I said my vows to him in 1988, I realised meant them.

I don't believe love ever dies a natural death. It dies simply because it is not nurtured or replenished. It dies, slowly affected by betrayals, blindness, significant illnesses, wounds that penetrate deeply and the weariness of life. I knew we were close to losing everything. I felt it deep within me. However, I believed and stood firm to the convictions that we could have a great future together. Now that I had the first taste of a future without HCV, I was not going to live it without the man who had fought for our relationship so courageously just a few years before.

In the midst of everything that was happening around me I somehow felt a kind of gathering clarity even though treatment fogged my brain. I felt a sense of awakening, a beginning to understand it all. Current events had conspired to make me imagine how my life with John could be, but previous events flashed from the past, they flickered and filled the open crevices in my mind. I began to feel part of a larger design, a blueprint underpinned by love and conviction. I had only seen the outline before but now I saw a draft of the diversity and range my life could hold including my faith, my family, John, my work, my friends and joy. Everything started to appear less threatening, colours became more vivid, words became crisper, sharper, possibilities flashed and were flaunted before me on large neon signs. People of meaning with unforgettable faces floated around me and I was encased in a dome of love. John lingered in the back drop waiting for me to extend a hand. The draft was vivid and contrasting but I believed it was mine for the taking if I was bold enough to take it.

In the back of my mind I wondered if John and I could repair our relationship, whether or not we could forgive each other for the sheer selfishness of our choices, for loading our schedules and complicating our lives which drove us apart. We had travelled so far, been through so much, twenty four years is a long time.

The last two years had seen us attending different universities learning individualised lessons, as well as meeting and working with different people who influenced us differently. My teachers were more from a counselling background that supported, guided and nurtured my self-development, whereas his were from the school of hard knocks, promoting and encouraging poor choices. I was encouraged to positively reach the treatment summit, to not give up as it was well within my reach. I was also encouraged to stand strong and fight for the life I wanted.

Laurie Smyth

Whilst I was at *my* university, I attended in-depth painting lessons. I know that sounds funny, but, that's the best way to describe it to you the reader. To paint, you need to really learn to see more clearly. Seeing is more than just looking at something. It is discerning the deeper essence of what's presented before you, assessing every part individually and comprehending beyond what's *obviously* seen.

People are not the same, we may be similar in features, we might share the same colour or religion but none of us are identical. The deeper meaning of the human spirit and soul needs to be uncovered. People need to be explored, peeled back layer by layer and then you can really appreciate the true canvas painted before you. Underneath our external layers we all still crave and need the same things love and acceptance.

People are more than the colours and textures they present on the surface. Inside them exists unique qualities, hidden talents and wonderful histories. I learnt to see John in this manner. I saw the hurts, the pain, the rejection and the barriers he had constructed to protect himself. I saw his vulnerabilities. His particular canvas was tainted with dark colours and broad sweeping strokes but as I looked at it, it revealed to me his true meaning and I loved him even more. I learnt to see past what was being presented to me on the surface and started to explore the layers underneath, the bright colours and the depth and clarity of the tiny lines that made up those broad strokes. His canvas was just like yours and mine, unique and gorgeous by design.

I ask you as we move towards the final stages of my story, will I fade in your memory like so many other fictional characters that you have read about in other stories, will my canvas fade, or will I linger for a short moment, a heartbeat, maybe. Have I planted a seed deep in your life that just may sprout one day when someone comes to water it? I hope so. What happens to me now that my story is reaching its climax, will I go on and live out my days like any other human being on this mighty planet, or will my story etch itself onto the canvas of your soul?

Will a piece of my canvas, my history, meld with your canvas, your future? Quite a large piece of me and my life now lies in your memory; the question is what will you do with it?

Chapter 46

A fearful moment

I awoke on this one particular day to a world that was different slightly altered in a subtle yet unmistakable way. The air was warmer enriched somehow, the colour of the purple bedroom wall and doona covering the now made bed much brighter. The red eyes of the electric clock glowed 5:37. I had always been intuitive, sharper at noticing things; I guess you could say I was more aware. I think what happens is people get so accustomed to things, to new situations or to people that they no longer enjoy or appreciate them. Treatment had certainly dulled my sense but I had a sense of something pending that day, something evil lurked in the shadows on this fateful day.

It was late December 2009 and John administered my interferon injection as per every other week, the only difference was it was Saturday instead of Friday. As he was placing the syringe in the now very full disposal bin he was stabbed in the thumb by an upended needle, causing a deep puncture wound, which bled profusely.

We were both stunned. I immediately told him to make it

bleed, squeezing it repeatedly, whilst holding it under cold water, allowing the blood to flow freely. My mind quickly processed the odds of exposure and the risk to him from infection. We didn't know how long the needle had been there. I had been virus free for a couple of months so, his risks were small, but there was still a risk. I didn't really want to think about it.

I silently questioned just how long the needle would have been in there. Was it fresh? I knew the virus weakened and died within 72 hours, it also didn't like sunlight, preferring a dark, humid environment. Even though I weighed all these facts up, I was still anxious that I may have infected him. I drew on the strength of knowing without a doubt that I was no longer infected and this offered a distinctive advantage, but there was still an element of doubt in my mind.

We bandaged the wound, and later in the day I rang my work colleague, a male counsellor who could talk to John about his risk factors. I could not suppress the feelings of hopelessness and dread, and I allowed them to flow freely through me. Anxious, uneasy tears comforted me that night, and fear and worry troubled me during the days that followed, whilst I waited for the results to come in. I would not totally succumb to the voices this time. They could have their moment, but that would be all I would allow.

John's outside wound healed, but his heart hardened, as he waited for his pending test results.

We certainly didn't need any more mayhem or chaos in our lives but it always seemed to find us. I didn't think I could handle any more turmoil but there I was right in the thick of it again. All I really wanted was peace, tranquillity and space to restore order in all this disorder.

I read somewhere that a person can live forty days without food, but only three days without water. However, if we have no hope, we can't live at all, not one second. I couldn't believe that this journey was all for nothing, that I would lose everything as I entered the final phase. I had lived my whole life full of fear. Fear of rejection, not being worthy, not smart enough, and all that had changed. After all that I had been through I knew without a doubt that I had worth, I knew I was significant and most of all

I knew I had a purpose. I also knew God had a purpose and plan for my life. I was still at uni learning the skills I needed to get me through to the final stage but graduation from this course wasn't too far away.

I had learnt so much but there was still a lot I needed to learn. I was for the first time embracing a teachable spirit and I discovered I loved learning. I was not always the best student and like my days at school, I was rebellious and wagged classes. The problem was there wasn't any running away or avoiding lessons at this particular school because my lecturer was omnipresent.

Running away was another hurdle I needed to circumnavigate. However I had the best teacher. He never once gave up on me. He picked me up and dusted me off when I fell into the miry clay and showed me the things I had only once dreamed of were tangible. He gave me courage to believe I would not be beaten by a needle stick injury or the guilt that surrounded it. And I stood on what I was told.

I don't believe circumstances happen by chance. Every little occurrence holds a deeper meaning. Our eyes are sometimes clouded by our perceptions but they do eventually clear and reveal something extraordinary. These internal beliefs can prevent us from seeing things clearly, but if we seek further and expand our perspective, maybe even look outside the box, so to speak, eventually, all is revealed. I didn't understand what was happening in my life, but I believed it would be revealed to me when I was ready and could understand and deal with it.

I was offered another gift one week after this misadventure. John's first HCV test returned negative.

This event and how I dealt with it made me appreciate what a magnificent gift we are all born with. Our brain helps us accomplish everything. Its reach is unfathomable. If we can become our own counsellors and change how we internally speak to ourselves I believe we can change our lives. This is exactly what I did, my self talk helped my get through this period of waiting without mentally beating myself up. Yes I had moments but I refused to give them a lot of air play. I believed and spoke positive words out into the universe that he would not be infected and consequently his second and third tests also came back negative.

Challenges like this, I believe, are sent as an opportunity not only to learn but to learn the art of giving more than others expect. My positive attitude impacted on Johns behaviour. I found when I gave to others when I was depleted of all my resources it changed me inside. It made me feel good about myself and I witnessed the rewards far outstrips the cost. I found this with John the more I gave the more I received. I believed in him, in us, during a time when he didn't. But only a few short years before, he was in exactly the same position as where I now stood.

I was powerless and insignificant to change the world around John and I. all I knew was that I needed to put it out there. I believed God could fix things, all things. I trusted that He would and I believe He did.

Anthony Robbins states in Awakening the Giant Within

'nothing is more crippling to a person's ability to take action than learned helplessness: it is the primary obstacle that prevents us from changing our lives or taking action to help other people change theirs'.

I could not just sit around after everything John had done previously to fight for us and not take some action to bring it all back. Both of us had 'learned helplessness' but this didn't mean I had to accept it or believe it was relevant to me in this situation, because I simply wouldn't accept that. I had to at least try and restore our relationship. If it was over it was over I would accept that. But I would give it my last and best shot first before I conceded. I would never succumb to the principle of learned helplessness especially when God dwelt in my camp. With Him beside me I knew all things were possible.

My life had become more and more like a building project. And as my treatment regime drew its final breathe I noticed the outline of the bridge I designed was there. The bridge didn't go up overnight, but by using due diligence, it was created, and I knew my efforts today would help create tomorrow's results.

I had changed dramatically during this bout of treatment. I believed for the better. I had learnt compassion, empathy and the true meaning of life—people, family. I just needed to get Johns attention, get him to notice. But first I needed to finish the bridge then I would make him see me.

Chapter 47

Flowers in full bloom

I got out of bed wrapped only in a light sarong and looked through the large open bedroom window, it was April and I entered the arena for the final victory lap, my last self-administered injection, and my last five tablets were taken. A tremendous fact occurred to me. In some sense the world I knew for the last eighteen months had died around me and in a few short days when treatment had left my body and be done, finished, I would have to reengage with an identical world, similar but different to the one I had lived in for all those months. It would be more vivid, more colourful, sharper, crisper and painless but I would be welcomed back into the real world, once again unplugged from the 'matrix'. As I stood at that window I knew the door on treatment would forever be closed.

I had completed the marathon, I had made it. The battle completed, eighteen long months broken into bite size pieces of seventy two blocks of days and hours. I looked back at it with pride. It was the hardest, toughest experience I had ever faced, and I had conquered and completed it. It lay behind me.

It was a great sense of relief and happiness to know that my world had passed under the chemical shadow where I had lingered for seventy two very long weeks. I had passed out from under its silhouette and gloom unscathed. And on that April autumn day I felt the full sunlight as it came through the window and touched my face. I felt unshackled, released from my bondage. The fight was finally over.

I had adhered to the highest dose of ribavirn all the way through, not changing and not missing a single day. This was something that differentiated this treatment from the last bout. Even though this was a hard task, the science had proven that higher doses of ribavirin enhanced clearance rates, and I wanted to be set free. I had made my mind up to continue on the highest dose, regardless of any symptoms. I was lucky that my blood stabilized at week forty-eight, which enabled me to physically continue on this harsh regime. I was anaemic, tired and rundown, but none of that mattered as the warmth caressed my skin. I had chosen to continue this harsh regime because I knew the benefits far outweighed the costs.

I moved to the shower and allowed the water to run over my warm thin bruised and shattered body knowing tomorrow the healing would begin and sleep would follow. Laughter filled the air, birds chirped around me, nothing would prevent my enjoying this pure moment of joy.

Everywhere I went that day and the following week exhilaration radiated out of me with the force of an atomic bomb, and it surrounded everyone and everything I came in contact with. People commented on my happiness and it became infectious. Even Johns laughter touched our home.

Once I re-found laughter, I knew I could survive any painful situation that may come my way in the future. With humour, I learnt I could soften some of the catastrophic strikes that life also delivered. Life is about change. We can't stop it, just as we can't stop the earth from spinning, we just have to embrace it, hold onto what we have and enjoy the moment just like a roller coaster ride.

For me, a healthy attitude, as well as the ability to forgive and not hold onto things is how I brought joy and contentment back into my life. I have heard a statement that many people die at twenty-five, but are not buried till they are seventy. I didn't want to live my life like that.

Before this journey, I believe that statement may have just been about me.

I can honestly say, I am glad I went through all of what I have told you about. I might not have said that five years ago but I can certainly and truthfully say it now. I am grateful for my life. I am grateful for the people that surround me. I am grateful that I am loved, and I am grateful that I have been given a second chance. Mostly I am grateful that I am not the same person I was five years ago.

Thankyou God

Chapter 48

The crown is finally mine to keep

"In this world, there is no clarity. There is only love and action."
—Mother Teresa

Remember back in October, I had cleared the virus well it was now late April. I was due for the first of three PCR tests that you are required to have when treatment id finished. My Octobers result encouraged me. I knew it was six months ago so I reasoned I had a good chance, but it was hard to keep doubt from seeping in again and of course the dark passenger had a word or two to say about everything. However I allowed him his time and then moved him on. The power and strength he once had over me was left on that icy cold summit when I gave the voices full reign to torment me. As I thawed and learnt to feel again on my own, I bundled it up and left it amongst the ice covered rocks.

As the snow fell upon my face I came to realise I had isolated myself because I had been hurt by people. But, I had achieved nothing by being so bitter and so resentful. I know a lot of people today are also angry and hurt, like I was. Most of us justify these feelings and get stuck in one moment in time for so long we forget what got us there in the first place. We harbour such resentment and un-forgiveness allowing it to reign in our hearts and quietly destroy each of us. I realised I couldn't enjoy my life if I was full of these things. On that mountain I learnt that I could polish up my outward act but what I needed to do was change my heart. There is a saying 'the truth will set us free' I believed I was freed that day on that mountain. I was freed from the bondage of the dark passenger and I was offered a new beginning. I learnt it was never too late to start life over again. I began my own inner journey with personal forgiveness. The other lesson I learnt was that forgiving others enabled forgiveness to be given to me, and I needed my fair share of it.

Even though the mountain had taught me so much, I was at times still fearful. The wait for the new round of test results brought on a time of fear. An overwhelming feeling of failure surrounded each grain of sand as it poured through my hour glass. On the surface, I was optimistic, but underneath I walked in a pure nightmare. In the distance I heard whispered questions from the ice covered distant mountain. Where would my life take me if I didn't clear virus this time round? What options would lay before me? The questions rolled around in my brain but remained silent on my lips. Would I come out with nothing or something at the end of these eighteen months of torment? Would the cost be outweighed by the prize? I hoped so.

The wait was arduous and when the time was ready I went to

see my Egyptian GP to get the results alone. John's ongoing coldness and unresponsiveness struck a blow to my heart, wounding it deeply. However this was my moment and I vowed not to let his indifference cause bitterness to rise within me again. I would protect my heart and believe the best. I simply could not mentally afford to revisit that path. I didn't really want to either.

The waiting room was, as always, overcrowded and busy, filled with anxious people seeking solace in trashy magazines and the gossip they held. My nervousness prevented me from focusing on anything but the door that hid my results. As I sat amongst the noise and confusion, I promised myself to move forward no matter what the conclusion today. My determination was to stand steadfast, not succumbing to the afflictions and despair of the past. I would completely strip myself of my old habits, behaviours, attitudes and beliefs, and replace them with the new person I had become. Today would symbolize a brand new beginning. Either way, I would start again, despite what was said today.

The door opened and there he stood, his Egyptian welcoming gaze fell on my anxious, dismayed face. His smile broadened and lit up his entire face. His hands at once ushered me into his congested office. I sat once again at the end of his long cluttered table with the same urge to tidy it up as always. This time we faced each other and together we searched the computer screen seeking my results.

He knew exactly why I was there, and he wasted no time providing me with my answer. He turned, his face animated, beaming. He congratulated me. Telling me I had finally done it. I jumped up, unable to contain my excitement, embracing him and thanking him.

What a joyous moment that was! My heart pounded like a galloping race horse. Elation filled me. I felt like dancing not with the devil this time but on top of him. Pure pleasure emanated from my friendly GP as he accompanied me to the door, steering me into the waiting room. I glowed as I walked to the counter, my cheeks blushing like a school girls. He visually followed, smiling.

I had never felt so happy. I didn't know who to share the news with, so I just started ringing everyone who knew.

That day changed the structures of my whole internal world. Creeping rose bushes brought forth budding beautiful flowers and made their home around my life. Their smell exotic and wonderful. The carefree life I had lived so long ago in Madang resurfaced. The same feelings I experienced up there, all those years ago, rose up within me. I saw my future open up with every new bloom. I laughed as I drove away from his surgery not just any sort of laugh but a good deep belly laugh until tears rolled down my face.

I would not allow life to be stolen from me again. Not now, not ever.

I made a declaration that I would not look back, guaranteeing only to focus on a bright, positive future. My oath: to do whatever it took to rebuild my life. All my life I had been a pretender. It was time for me to stop acting and to step into the spot light. I was ready to really audition for the role of my life. I would never again be that wounded lioness, as I would become a strong and capable, caring woman and I would have life.

I had made a choice to be happy and optimistic. My hope was a fire I chose to stoke daily. I learnt that I could not access joy or happiness in tangible things; I had to access it from inside myself. I knew I had previously surrounded myself with stuff that would never make me happy, and I slowly started to remove them, learning to draw on my own internal strengths.

More meaningful interactions with my husband, and others, resulted from this decision, and I stored these positive small milestones on my internal mantel piece. They were like magnets which intensified my efforts to succeed.

I had never felt more happy or content in my whole entire life. I held a constructive, optimistic future in the palm of my hand, and I planned to ride this wave all the way to the beach, again and again. I traded my mountain climbing gear in which helped my climb Mt Everest for the biggest surfboard I could find and set off for the beautiful coastline of Mooloolaba. I hoped I would never fall off my surf board and scrape myself as much as did when I took on my climbing career.

My second and third test came back negative. I had been given a second chance. I was no longer emancipated, held to ransom by a disease. I was free, released from my self-imposed imprisonment.

Life opened up before me. I stood on a new rock face. I stared at an expanse of water stretched out as far as my eye could see. I saw the rippling, swelling waves that demanded changes and I allowed them to flow over me.

The world was more intense, richer, and more colourful, now the sky had lightened. I knew and believed that in this moment nothing was impossible. The isolated ledge where John still stood was still a sheer drop, but the dive was now achievable and I was not afraid of heights. Diving from this position was no longer unmanageable; I would just have to go and get him and somehow teach him how to dive.

I saw all the potential and the promises that lay at my feet. The life which I now embraced carried hope, unbound expectations, enlightenment and prospects.

However, in the not so distant future the horizon was gathering its army and another dark cloud loomed ominously, its destructive force and lightning strike would soon hit me and I would find myself tackling the devil again, engaged in another dance that threatened to destroy all I had achieved.

I would hold steadfast to a promise.

A promise from God. The best was yet to come.

Laurie Smyth

Take care I wish you every success in your life as you walk upon your chosen path. May God bless you in all that you do in your life.

You can visit us at www.newlifepersectives.com.au or email me laurie@newlifeperspectives.com.au